Psychology of Nutrition

Psychology of Nutrition

D.A. Booth

Taylor & Francis
Publishers since 1798

UK   Taylor & Francis Ltd, 4 John St., London WC1N 2ET
USA   Taylor & Francis Inc., 1900 Frost Road, Suite 101, Bristol, PA 19007

First published 1994

A Catalogue Record for this book is available from the British Library

ISBN 0 7484 0158 X
ISBN 0 7484 0159 8 pbk

Library of Congress Cataloging-in-Publication Data are available on request

Cover design by Amanda Barragry

Typeset in 10/12pt Garamond
by Graphicraft Typesetters Ltd., Hong Kong

Printed in Great Britain by Burgess Science Press, Basingstoke on paper which has a specified pH value on final paper manufacture of not less than 7.5 and is therefore 'acid free'.

Contents

Preface

Professor Booth has been one of the world's leading research investigators and theoreticians in appetite, ingestive behaviour and preferences for foodstuffs for over 30 years. He has published 6 books and more than 200 scientific papers on this and related topics. He has also made a major contribution to the methodology of measuring the dimensions which make up our perceptions of the taste, texture, aroma and colour of the food and drink we consume.

This book is about food and what we do with it. Food includes all the sorts of things we eat, ranging from a banquet or a liqueur chocolate to a hamburger or an apple, also the drinks we have with food or by themselves, whether it is water, juice, soda, or a dose of the demon alcohol. David Booth's book deals with any material that any of us puts into our mouth and swallows.

Behaviour towards foods and drinks takes up a major part of human life. This is true even for the most affluent citizen of a contemporary, highly industrialised country (the societies with which this book will be primarily concerned), where food is available in such abundance that no personal effort is required to obtain it, and other people can be paid to prepare and serve it. Yet the richest and most well-fed people still spend much of their time on food, not only eating and drinking, but talking and thinking about food and drink as well.

This book tackles questions about what goes on in eaters' and drinkers' minds about the foods and beverages they are consuming; about the effects on their bodies; and about the cultural meaning of meals and other eating occasions. The exposition is centred round a cognitive psychological theory, based on evidence for a learned integration of dietary, bodily and social information.

A psychologist can relate the principles invoked in this book to other areas of psychology. The thinking conveyed here can also readily be carried through to a more technical level of psychological research. To assist this, Professor Booth has, where possible, referred to the conceptually related psychological literature on other topics.

Nevertheless, psychological concepts are introduced only as needed and, so far as possible, from bases in commonsense language and everyday experience. A non-psychologist should, therefore, be able to follow the main scientific content of what is being said about behaviour and the mental processes organising people's acts and reactions. Links are frequently provided to relevant natural sciences of nutrition and food and to social sciences such as anthropology, which specialists in those areas can use to relate the book to their main expertise.

There are only very few behaviours which need to be repeated so frequently, as eating and drinking, and to be so perfectly judged in order to sustain life, and there are very few other behaviours which are so immediately at the interface of biology and social psychology. In summarizing his three decades of research and theory building, Professor Booth has produced a book that places the psychology of nutrition among the central elements of behaviour which psychologists need to incorporate in any fully satisfactory understanding of human motivation.

Raymond Cochrane
Birmingham

Acknowledgments

This book could never have been written without the colleagues and students who have had the curiosity and patience to make me explain my ideas so that they could understand and use them. I have been able to get some of them acknowledgment as co-authors on published research reports and reviews, but quite a few undergraduates will, I hope, receive credit one day in print for what they contributed in taking on projects and practicals with me.

    I am also most grateful to Ray Cochrane and to the Publisher for the invitation to make this first attempt at putting my main academic interest into monograph form and for their encouragement to complete the writing without undue delay.

David Booth
Edgbaston

Chapter 1

Food and Drink

The basic elements of a cognitive theory of food and drink are presented in this chapter.

What is Food and Drink?

Food, in one sense, is any material that an individual seriously regards as edible. Drink similarly might be defined as any fluid that is considered by some people to be potable.

That 'psychological' definition of food and drink is used in this book. This however is not to deny the scientific legitimacy – and the commonsense too – of the established definition of food as bodily sustenance. Neither is it to discount in any way the social and indeed moral issues about what really should count as food and hence as a real need for food.

The conventional scientific concept of food is restricted to its biological function. Food is material that can be shown to be nutritious. That is, its ingestion is necessary for survival, for good health and for growth of the young. Nutrients are those chemical compounds in foods that in some instances are essential to health and even to life for a given species. Other nutrients help to sustain the normal functioning of tissues but the particular compound is dispensable and other compounds can serve the functions instead.

Insufficiency of nutrients in the foods and drinks in the amounts that people can obtain is one of the major ethical challenges and political problems that the world currently faces. Yet even where the technology exists to produce more food, there often remain great ecological, economic and cultural difficulties just in emergency feeding of the hungry, let alone enabling famine-stricken groups to produce and trade enough to feed themselves. So a purely biological concept of need for food is amply sufficient to make heavy demands on our social and personal understanding of humanity.

Nevertheless, the most nutritious material hardly counts as food if nobody will eat it. As the saying goes, one person's meat is another person's poison. Even the starving are reputed to have refused foodstuffs that had never been in their diet.

Moreover, some of what richer peoples regard as food is nutritionally imbalanced or even inadequate. We certainly do not need to eat all the items of food that we do in order to survive or to be healthy. So a strictly biological definition of food would not be realistic to human behaviour, nor probably for other species.

Further to the point, hunger and thirst are personal states of wanting to eat and drink materials perceived as foods and beverages. However, these appetites are not limited to the necessities of physical existence. It is a truism in applied nutrition that people do not eat nutrients; they eat foods. This means that they don't usually think of what they are eating in terms of the nutrients in it. The point of a psychological and social definition of food and ingestive appetite is that a substantial part of consumption has nothing to do with nutritiousness, even indirectly or unconsciously. Some of the causation of the ingestive behaviour is unconnected with nutrients. It may even be anti-nutritious. That is, some of the effects of eating may be unhealthy and the eater is aware of the possibility. So the purely biological definition of food and drink and of hunger or thirst must be wrong. Anti-nutritious ingestion only proves the point, though. Eating and drinking not motivated by physical needs can be neutral with respect to health. Indeed, the main point of recognizing food as perceived ingestibles and not just nutrient mixtures is to correct the intellectual and political error of treating the motivation to eat and drink as relating only to benefits to the body or its detriment.

The German language draws a distinction between Lebensmittel (the stuff of life, normally translated food) and Genussmittel (literally, pleasure material, meaning a luxury, including a food item that is a treat). One might argue whether sugar or alcohol was Lebensmittel or Genussmittel but this is in danger of confusing biology with moralizing. Both these substances are sources of energy, which we all certainly need in substantial minimum quantities. They constitute a part of the diets of many people who are eating entirely healthily. Foods and drinks containing sugar or alcohol are among the objects of ordinary appetite; they include both staples and luxuries. In such contexts, sugar and alcohol can contribute a great deal to the pleasures of eating and drinking. Yet neither substance is nutritionally necessary. Also, of course, certain uses of sugar or of alcohol can be unhealthy or unsafe and a risk to others as well. Yet an essential nutrient too can be poisonous, when consumed in excess.

Thus, we should go further in 'psychologizing' the definition of food. Even the biological concept of food cannot be reduced to a chemical definition, as a mixture of nutrients. Whether a substance is nutritive or not is in part an inherently behavioural matter. It sometimes depends not only on what is eaten but also on how much is eaten when and in what circumstances.

These are some reasons for broadening the definition of food to materials that are perceived and treated as foods and drinks by individuals. This approach could apply to members of other species whose behaviour is complex enough to justify the ascription of such perception. Also, in the human case at least, this definition is social because much of the content of individual perception depends on the culture within which the person operates. Finally, this psychosocial construct of food and hunger does not exclude the biological concept; rather it encompasses it. After all, eaters and drinkers often believe that their bodies need the calories, the water and sometimes other constituents of what they are consuming – and generally speaking those beliefs are broadly correct. So the psychological definition as a matter of sociological fact partly presupposes lay concepts of nutritional function and thereby approximates to the biological definition.

How Does the Mind Work in Eating and Drinking?

The theoretical position underpinning the cognitive approach of this book is that hunger and thirst are motives driven by recognition of similarity (like indeed any learned motivation). The basic theory is that an individual's disposition to eat or drink in a sufficiently familiar situation is inversely proportional to the distance of that situation from the most appetizing version of those circumstances for that person (or animal). The same theory applies to positive emotions towards the foods and drinks that are available there and then or even merely thought of or pictured. Also, an active inhibition of eating or drinking and negative emotions will be as strong as the situation is close to a learned sating or averting of appetite for food or drink.

This is a quantitative theory of the cognitive processes of hunger and thirst that in fact applies to all learned behaviour and experience (Booth, 1994). Such linear control by similarity to norm has always been presupposed in a qualitative form by experimental and social psychologists and in statistical form by psychometricians (Glymour *et al.*, 1987). Mathematical psychologists have recently been clarifying this common foundation to the diverse streams of psychological research (e.g. Ashby and Perrin, 1988; Macmillan and Creelman, 1991). However, the simplest conceivable ways of measuring this mental causation within an individual's behaviour have been developed over the last decade for the appetite for food (Booth, Thompson and Shahedian, 1983).

Another way of summarizing this cognitive approach to eating and drinking is to say that the desire to consume an item depends on recognizing how close it is to the ideal that the individual has acquired for those circumstances. When the social situation and bodily state recur where the consumption of an item having certain salient perceptible characteristics has been most reinforcing, the individual finds that item maximally attractive and entirely appropriate to consume.

This is not to deny the possibility of unlearned processes affecting behaviour and experience; it is simply to point out that they have to be treated as special cases which are least likely to be relevant with familiar foods in common sorts of situation. The obvious examples are infants before experience of eating accumulates and children or adults faced with cuisines or eating contexts that are, in important respects, unlike anything they have experienced before. These cases are rare and it has been a mistake to model theories of eating and drinking (or any other psychology) on people's or animals' responses to strange situations that are experimentally convenient to impose, such as drinks of plain sweet solutions or lots of food to eat within an hour or so of having filled up.

Thus the explanation of actions and feelings towards food and drink depends on the mental dynamics of recognizing appropriate situations for eating and drinking.

Psychology of Food Recognition

Food, whatever the definition, therefore provides major challenges and opportunities for psychology. Solutions to the fundamental and practical scientific problems about foods and drinks depend on finding out how we recognize such materials to be eaten and drunk and so can decide whether or not to select them.

As with so many of our everyday abilities, knowing that an item is a food and whether we like it or not comes so naturally and easily that it may be hard to see this recognition as an achievement requiring scientific explanation. Ask a creative cook, though, or a developer of new food products. They are likely to be all too aware of the practical consequences of designing foods and not understanding how people recognize what they want. Consider for yourself all that is involved in buying a supply of food for a day or more, choosing a meal from a service counter or a restaurant menu, or making up your mind how good the souffle or sponge-cake is that you have just cooked.

The Task of Recognition

An item of food or drink, like any other object, is perceived as an integral combination of features set at particular levels. That's quite a mouthful (in more senses than one). Nevertheless, it is a succinct summary of the apparent nature of the problem that we face in gaining a scientific understanding of how we perceive foods. Let's take this formulation in bite-sized chunks.

Some features are categorical or all-or-none. They can only be present or absent, like the stone in a plum or the brand name on a can of cola. Nevertheless, even a categorical feature is present at one of two levels: 100 or 0 per cent.

Many aspects of foods and drinks are graded in level, though. The feature may be there in larger or smaller quantity or size, such as cheese in a egg souffle and jam or some other filling in a sponge-cake.

In some cases, a graded (quantitative) feature can be absent or undetectable and the material is still perceived as being a food. A souffle without cheese is still a souffle and sponge-cake without jam is still sponge. In that sense, the distinction between graded and categorical features is not absolute.

Nevertheless, a cheese souffle must have some degree of cheesey flavour to it. A jam sponge is not a jam sponge without some jam. Yet the thickness of the jam layer(s) can be minimal or generous. In either case, it is still recognizably a jam sponge.

Yet could not the jam be so thin that it is not just unacceptable as a jam sponge but not even really a jam sponge at all? At the other extreme, could not one have so much jam and so little cake that it would no longer be a slice of jam sponge but a serving of jam, decorated with a sliver of sponge as a hat on top and kept off the plate by another sliver underneath, and not normally edible by itself? This switch between really sponge and really jam is a little like the reversal between the figure and the background shown by some ambiguous black-and-white diagrams. Figure-ground reversals are a subjectively dramatic illustration of a second major point about recognition processes, namely its holistic character.

A recognizable item is also perceived as a whole: it is an *integral* combination of features. The air bubbles in the souffle do not just sit alongside the softness and stickiness of the solid matrix, the cheesey aroma and taste, the almost white colour and the less pale yellow and harder egg at the surface. They are all inseparable parts of the one entity. Whether or not the whole is in some sense more (or less) than the parts, the recognizable item is certainly different from a collection of independent parts. The features interact or are combined in some fashion which is subtler

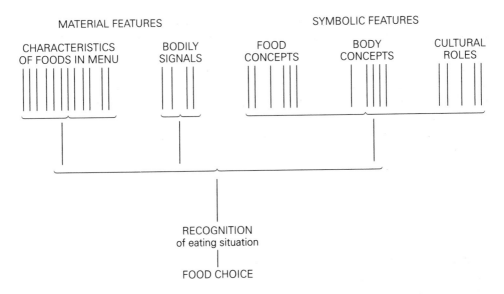

Figure 1.1 Combining perceptible features into recognition of a whole item.

than simply piling them up randomly in a heap or adding them together in a long line.

This conception of the processes of recognition can be represented in a diagram (Figure 1.1). Each vertical line in the upper part of the diagram represents the possibility of perceiving the level of a distinct feature of the item in a particular context. A person in the act of eating or selecting a food item may not be under the influence of all the possible perceptual processes at that moment, but that person and others on some occasions may be influenced by each such feature that is perceptible.

The bracketing lines below, pointing down to the act that shows correct or incorrect recognition, represent the processes of combining whatever feature levels are perceived into an integral percept of the item as a whole. The rules of combination may or may not preserve the features in an obvious form. If they do not and the integral result bears no readily evident relationship to the elements, the whole will be psychologically quite different from a collection of its apparent parts.

Note also that a feature may itself be an integral of simpler features. In other words, Figure 1.1 can be nested. It represents one level of analysis and synthesis in a hierarchical system.

For example, the price on a food item may be perceived as a sign of high quality as well as a sign of expense to the purchaser's budget. 'Low in fat' may be taken to imply good for the heart and good for the waistline (and the two health benefits perceived in different proportions by men and women). The strength of a cup of coffee may reflect sugar and cream contents as well as levels of coffee solids. Such resolutions of a candidate feature into a combination of features might get rid of fuzziness in our scientific account of perception of price, the low-fat label or coffee strength. The fuzziness arose from hitherto poor identification of the more basic features underlying the higher-level construct. Perhaps the rule by which these sub-features are integrated into the named feature of the food item does not preserve those sub-features in a way that is obvious to the investigator or the food-perceiver. The feature emerges as a whole without obvious elements.

Despite these points, this approach may seem to be begging fundamental questions about the holism of perception and indeed the existence of such distinguishable features. What is being suggested, however, is that we try an approach to the mental organization within behaviour that is the same as the way in which any other sort of phenomenon has been approached in modern science. Indeed, the broad principles of the psychology of recognition described above seem inescapable for any systematic quantitative investigation of functioning entities of any sort.

We attempt to explain the workings of the whole solar system, lithium nucleus, liver cell or national economy in terms of theoretically distinct causal processes that interact in a theoretically synthesized overall performance. We can go wrong in theoretical analysis and theoretical synthesis. So the initially obvious candidates for perceptual features may become fuzzier as we examine the behavioural evidence more closely. The rules of integration that we first hypothesize do not put any features together in a way that accounts for recognition very well. Nevertheless, in either case, we can look for more precisely defined features and more successful integration rules. If we discover some that explain existing data better and stand up well under further investigation, our understanding of the phenomena is improving.

Conscious and Preconscious Processes

An impression that there is no scientific problem about food recognition mechanisms may arise because so often it seems that we just recognize an item without consciously working out what it is. We immediately reach for the choice that we want among the array of items. The right name for the fruit or vegetable just pops into mind, without thinking through a list or a semantic tree or any sort of mental filing cabinet of which we are aware. In other words, much of the mental processing in recognizing a food never comes to attention.

This is true of many of our abilities to name common objects. Moreover, in the process of recognizing a relative or a famous person, let alone a bicycle or a knife, some of the mentation can never become available even to the most careful self-monitoring of one's thoughts and actions. Indeed, the perceptual processes of recognition of facial identity are so deep below consciousness that as yet cognitive psychologists have made almost no progress in characterizing what aspects of a face actually are used and how the mind puts them together, despite the obviousness of facial features and of variations in them and some successes at improving photofit techniques and describing the overall structure of face-recognition mechanisms.

Many who accept that recognition mechanisms are a scientific problem do not see it as a matter for psychology, however. They assume that only brain scientists can find out how we recognize objects in ways of which we are unaware. The assumption is that psychology is concerned only with conscious processes and perhaps also (or instead) with 'behaviour' in the sense of movements of the body and the physical events that the movements produce (such as the disappearance of food down the throat).

On this view, what people say is not anything that they perform with greater or less success. Rather, words are a window through which the hearer (or reader) can see directly and with certainty into the contents of the utterer's consciousness, at least if the speaker (or writer) is instructed in the maintenance of certain disciplines of 'introspection'.

This view was strong in psychology itself for half a century or more after its emergence as an experimental discipline 150 years ago. Many remnants of that subjective approach persist in psychology to this day, especially in areas out of touch with the cognitive experimental tradition of the British 'Cambridge School' of Bartlett, Craik and Broadbent. Outside psychology, this misconception of the mind is particularly strong in medical circles but it is prevalent among thoughtful people generally. It is of a piece with the dualistic view of a human being (and perhaps members of some other species) as a biological machine which we can observe which is inhabited by a ghostly mind (Ryle, 1949) on which we can only introspect (Lyons, 1988).

The view of mind as only consciousness fails to treat a person's (or an animal's) observable behaviour, in deeds or words, as the performance of transformations on patterns coming from the environment into patterns going out into the environment. The transformations achieved by a person's reactions to, or actions on, situations (including symbolic communications) can be diagnosed from the relationships between the observable stimulus patterns and the observable response patterns – the rule that person seems to be following indicated by the evidence to hand (Wittgenstein, 1953). Notice that such diagnosis depends only on analysis of what the individual is observably achieving, whether or not words are part of the evidence of the pattern-transformation that is going on in that person. Also note that the issue does not necessarily arise as to whether a mental process that is necessary to explain the behaviour is conscious or not. The role of this or that particular content of our undoubted general awareness in the performance of, say, a recognition task is a further question and much more complicated than even most psychologists have assumed until recently (Marcel, 1983; Reingold and Merikle, 1988).

So the basic approach needed to advance our understanding of the psychological mechanisms in eating and drinking is to seek the variations in the food or the context that have strong and specific effects. From such evidence, we should be able to work out what stimulus patterns (i.e. feature combinations) from a food item are transformed in what way to produce its correct recognition, whether by naming, by quantitative judgments of quality or by choice or rejection in the shop or at the table.

There is nothing in this specification that requires the person to be aware of the mental transformation processes. Nonetheless, it might well help the design of a rapid or precise diagnosis if the assessor can express in words some of the transformations that account for the observed performance, especially if the investigator has no idea how the trick might be done. Yet elaborate descriptions could be misleading as a guide to the processes involved in the immediate, unreflective act of recognition.

Of course, we are usually well able to describe several, maybe many, properties of an item of food or drink, both in its presence and from memory. Tasting experts and food scientists have developed rich vocabularies of description. Sensory evaluators can train assessment panels to use the descriptors in consistent ways by giving them standard examples. Nevertheless, with the partial exceptions of colour hues, simple shapes and a few taste compounds, the exact pattern of stimulation that evokes a particular descriptive term remains to be determined in any case – the smell of strawberries, the crumbliness of a cheese, the taste of a tomato, the visual appearance of coffee with cream, and so on.

Even aside from those problems, very little evidence has yet been gathered on the issue whether someone actually is using a particular describable property in recognizing a food item to select or reject in a given context. Furthermore, experimental analysis of mental transformations has hardly begun to tackle the issue of how these features are fitted together in the mind to create the whole perception of the particular food, or even which of the describable properties are used and whether others as yet undescribed (or inadequately described) are needed.

Instead, a practical discipline called sensory analysis has been developed. Descriptive vocabulary is used to collect ratings of foods and those numbers are converted statistically into patterns that are interpreted in terms of food composition on the one hand or on the other hand, with even greater difficulty, in terms of consumer preferences (see Chapter 5).

Beyond Description Maps to Recognition Mechanisms

The describable properties of foods can be immediately sensed characteristics of the material, such as for marzipan, light yellow in colour, almond-smelling, pastey soft, grainy in feel within the mouth and sweet-tasting. The properties can be the attributes that we know the food to have by feeling after-effects of eating it or by seeing or hearing information about it. For marzipan, these attributes might include how filling it is, what it does to the teeth, the waistline or the heart, how much it costs or how appropriate it is under the icing on a child's birthday cake.

We perceive all of these qualities, whether inherent or attached to the food item, by stimulation of the senses. 'Sensory' analysts, however, work closely with the production and processing end of the food business and so have traditionally concerned themselves exclusively with the first category of properties of the food materials themselves, as perceived by the external senses and in the mouth. Sensory evaluators use descriptions of the inherent features of food to obtain numerical scores reflecting the strength or amount of the feature and perhaps its physicochemical basis in the food's constitution. Thus, a set of intensity ratings of yellowness, softness, sweetness, etc. from a panel of assessors is called a sensory profile or quantitative descriptive analysis of the item. This technique of scoring the strengths of described features in sample items has been used from the beginning of experimental psychology, in the subdiscipline known as psychophysics.

What is Being Recognized?

It is commonly assumed by psychophysicists and sensory analysts that they are measuring processes at receptors and in the first neural relays into the brain. Even the traditional introspectionist interpretation of psychophysical investigation, that the scores measure the strengths of sensations, conventionally regards the subjective magnitude as generated in the sensory pathway. However, descriptions of inherent characteristics known to stimulate specific sensory receptors must involve further processing, neurally and mentally, in order to be correctly described and precisely quantitated. Indeed, it is mere assumption that inherent characteristics are processed differently from conceptual attributes sensed through labels and more obviously dependent on memory of past uses. Even the intensity rating of yellowness or sweetness depends on memory of similar items and uses of that vocabulary and quite likely on culture-specific experiences to boot. Indeed, graininess and almondiness ratings could well require more complex mentation (albeit preconscious) than recognition of the filling power or price of a food item.

The neural level and the cognitive depth of processing of a description or a strength judgment are empirical issues. They cannot be resolved by fiat, by verbal argument or by the mathematical modelling of patterns of uses of words. Some physical manipulation or measurement on the senses or even within the nervous system is necessary to get any evidence as to the neural level that is crucial. For example, if a taste rating combines information from the left and right sides of the tongue, it must have been processed after the nerves from each side come together in the brain, whereas a task that can be done from stimulation on one side alone might be processed closer to the receptors (Kroeze, 1990). Diagnosis of the cognitive level requires careful experimental design with multiple stimuli and multiple responses, illustrated below.

Statisticians in psychology and in the food industry have built maps of sets of foodstuffs. These spaces of one, two, three or more dimensions, with foods scattered through them, are calculated from assessors' ratings of the strengths of described features of samples of the foods. Maps can be made too without descriptions, out of rated or sorted degrees of difference and similarity among the food samples. Spaces can be calculated for responses to isolated features as well – smells alone, just tastes, the sight of colours, etc. However, these non-descriptive tasks must be carried out by mental analysis of features and their combination into decisions between responses. So the same empirical issues arise about which physicochemical aspects of the food and its context are being used and how they and their conceptual interpretation are put together into action.

These methods of patterning responses are not designed to work out how the sensed features of the test items are perceived and interact in making the observed decisions. They take the ratings or the sortings at their face value. Also, they combine them or their variabilities in a single way which is determined by statistical convenience, not by the scientific criteria of testing theory as to how the assessors are transforming incoming information into the verbal response or action on the food. Statistical maps are usually just adding ratings or variances in ratings or performing some similar mathematical operation for which a computer program exists. This may be nothing like the way the mind works on the information coming in from the senses, using memory retrieved from past experiences. Diagnosing those perceptual workings is a theoretical and methodological challenge, not just a matter for arranging data into discussable shapes.

Hence, in order to move beyond statistical patterning of descriptive data towards scientific analysis of recognition mechanisms, an essential step is to relate the ratings to measured properties of the food items. That move from analysis only of response effects to the analysis of stimulus-response or cause–effect relationships is not enough by itself though. Statistical mapping of chemical and physical measures in with the ratings has been developed but that begs the scientific questions. A mechanistic theory of how the person might be generating descriptive ratings from the measured physicochemical properties is also necessary. Otherwise, the choice of calculation of psychophysical input–output relationships remains a matter merely of statistical and logistic convenience. Only the testing against data of hypotheses on candidate causes and effects can yield growth in scientific understanding.

Psychophysics has consisted traditionally of relating a single physical variation and measure to one descriptive rating, typically in isolation from recognizable objects. Such designs not only risk irrelevance to normal perception, they are logically incapable of identifying the mental mechanisms that mediate the control of the ratings that is exerted by the physical variation in the environment. Characterization of the transformation processes requires designs that have uncorrelated variations in two or more physical features and achieve some uncorrelated ratings as well. The simplest form of this design is the quantitative version of the logic of double dissociation: cause X goes only with effect A and cause Y goes only with effect B in the same set of data. Multiple descriptions (profiles) of a set of mixtures of features have to meet these conditions before they can tell us anything about candidate mechanisms of perceptual performance.

Recognition Equations

The last main requirement for building a theory of cognitive mechanisms is that a distinct quantitative account can be given of the observed data on performance in the task. We know we are coming to grips with how things work when we find that repeated sets of observations of the same phenomenon fit one theoretical equation better than they fit other candidate formulae. By that criterion, neither academic psychology nor food research has approached recognition experiments scientifically to date.

Traditional psychophysics has been plagued with arguments over the form of the equation relating the chosen physical measure to the ratings, the psychophysical function. No exact equation has been established for all single features or even (I would say) conclusively for any one feature. On the argument above, this is a consequence of using merely one-dimensional designs, since they are mechanistically uninterpretable. Even when a form of equation has been found which creates an approximate straight-line relationship ($R = mP + c$) between some measure of the physical levels (P) and the descriptive ratings or a transformation of them (R), the slope (m) and the intercept (c) vary widely between experiments on the same feature and descriptor. Physicists would not claim to understand the first thing about motion or light if their data fitted Newton's equation $F = ma$ or Einstein's $E = mc^2$ so badly.

Without any cognitive theory of multi-feature descriptive analysis to apply, psychophysicists in food research were reduced to fitting an arbitrary set of equations to each new set of data (Moskowitz, 1983). Any reasonably smooth shape of curve relating a physical measure to a descriptive rating across a set of food samples can be fitted roughly by a polynomial regression equation with enough terms in it, i.e.

$$R = k + aP + bP^2 + cP^3 + \cdots + e$$

where e is error, the variance in the data unaccounted for by this equation of a curve. If another physical feature is also having effects on a rating, then its measurements (Q) can be included in the regression, as an independent predictor (rQ, sQ^2, etc.) or in some combination with the other feature, e.g. wPQ. Note, however, that the introduction of each predictive term is begging major mechanistic issues. Is the measurement of the feature a good measure of that aspect of the feature that is actually influencing that rating? Is the effect really linear, quadratic, cubic, or whatever term is statistically highly predictive or is this merely an empty statistical fix on that particular data set? (The proportionality constants or slopes, a, b, r, s, etc., and the intercept constant, k, will be stable across data sets if the regression equation has any theoretical meaning.) Do effects of feature Q really add to effects of feature P, as P and Q are measured? (Evidence for this would be not only aP and rQ being the main predictors but also a, r and k being constant across replicate sets of data.) Or do P's and Q's effects multiply (wPQ being the only good predictor and w and k staying stable)? Unless the pattern of predictors and the best fitting values of the constant remain quite similar across data from different experiments on the same products and market, the regression equation contains no theoretically interpretable information and furthermore could be an unreliable basis for practical decisions.

Recognition Without Description

The final step in a scientific approach to recognition mechanisms is to test hypotheses on performance data that do not include descriptions of the inherent or attributed features that might be involved. Description can be very helpful in building up realistic preliminary hypotheses on which to design such studies. Even some qualitative descriptions by a few individuals can be an important check on the investigator's intuitions from personal experience. Nevertheless, the process of describing a food, even in one's own words, may alter the way in which it would otherwise be perceived. So, in order to examine how one food item compares overall with another sample or with a familiar or preferred version in the context where a decision is made without descriptive analysis, we must characterize the mental mechanisms used from the overall response.

To do this, we have to measure the material and symbolic features of the test foods that are hypothesized to contribute to overall recognition in a particular context. Those physicochemical measurements and cultural categories (words, pictures, etc.) have to be converted into estimates of the strength of the patterns of stimulation or meaning that are hypothesized to be perceived in the features.

Then observations must be made of behaviour showing recognition. The quickest way to collect data is by ratings of the tendency to behave in the way that is of interest. Of course, for practical purposes at least, such ratings may have to be validated on actual behaviour. These recognition ratings could include how high in quality or how appropriate the test sample is for the use under investigation. The responses certainly should include some behaviourally definite criterion, such as whether that item would be chosen or not, or the judged chance that it would be chosen in the circumstances of the test.

Finally, the equation hypothetically representing the mental processes by which the physical patterns influence the observed recognition response should be tested on the data. The goodness of fit of this equation should be compared with the fit of the most plausible alternative equations to the same data. Also, the conclusion from this comparison of degrees of fit of alternative hypotheses should be tested by carrying out the same comparisons on additional data.

Increasingly, food-product developers are relating overall quality or preference responses to physical measures, although usually to the unconverted measurements that are easily made on available laboratory instruments. Descriptive ratings are sometimes also included in the analysis, as predictors of the physicochemical measurements and/or as supplements to them, to predict quality better. Powerful statistical procedures of very general application are now available to analyse the data, such as forms of multiple regression again, repeated cycles of mismatch-reducing calculations (e.g. Simplex optimization) or developments of conjoint analysis or multidimensional scaling. As explained above, a data-fitting calculation may not be a plausible model of how the mind actually works. The techniques are so good at finding order in the data that they tend to come up with conclusions that do not generalize across different sets of data well enough to distinguish between hypothetical cognitive mechanisms.

Hence, understanding is likely to advance faster and practical efficiency to improve if we analyse data by using quantitative psychological theory of how recognition is done. Such theory leads to more precise and realistic conclusions, because it constrains the design of the test samples and situations and specifies how to convert both the physical and chemical measurements and the no less influential symbolic categories into measures of the perceived features. Moreover, fewer data are needed because irrelevancies are excluded and the model is more exact.

Furthermore, this approach can operate at the level where the mental processing actually is occurring, in the individual mind, rather than several steps removed in a presumed and only indirectly testable cultural consensus (see Chapter 4, p. 84). Indeed, where perception tends to be personal in the ideal levels of features and in how features interact, it is much more productive to collect and analyse out the data individual by individual and only then to compare individuals' characteristics or to aggregate their predicted responses to specified situations. Also, to reach conclusions about how people are doing a task, considerably fewer assessors are needed than in the usual procedure of applying nonspecific statistical models to grouped data.

Such a personalized multi-dimensional psychophysics can be approached quite effectively for practical purposes without specific models, by the use of multiple conjoint or 'trade-off' analyses (e.g. Sawtooth utility values). Nevertheless, the building of exact mechanistic theories of particular recognition tasks provides practitioners with the prospect of more precise, economical and generalizable optimizations. Such operational theory can be constructed only from investigations that are founded on a theory of psychological measurement and realistic hypotheses as to the cognitive processes involved.

Building Food Recognition Theory

As we have seen, the basic theory of recognition mechanisms has to be that patterns are extracted from the array of incoming information and combined to produce the act or name that performs overall recognition of the food items. Such transformations of information from the senses and memory are no less required to produce the ratings and sortings that the experimenter demands. That is, the numbers that the assessor produces need cognitive explanation in terms of the incoming patterns of information, just as much as the overall recognition of the food does.

Thus fundamental advances in the psychology of food can come from successful characterization of the cognitive mechanisms by which assessors produce sensory ratings or attitude scores as well as food choices and intakes in the laboratory or in life. As generally in applied science, effective investigation of real-life (field research), which has to operate under severe constraints, is possible only on the basis of well-developed mechanistic theory that has been developed from highly controlled experiments that model life sufficiently realistically.

Indeed, fundamental issues also can only be addressed effectively after we have explained both model situations and some of the few available real situations. How does a person's awareness of the bases for his or her choices vary among people and with type of situation? When does description or sorting precede recognition and when does it follow? Even when description precedes recognition, is it actually part of the recognition process or does it operate more or less separately in parallel? The task of descriptive rating is often much more difficult than an overall judgment such as how much one likes an item. One may suspect therefore that some analytical processes are quite unlike the mechanisms used to come to a correct overall conclusion about the identity of a food.

How we recognize foods and drinks is thus a problem for psychology, the science whose job it is to identify and measure the mental processes by which we achieve such performances.

The Psychology of Object Recognition

Cognitive psychologists have indeed been doing a lot of work on object recognition in recent years. Yet they have not used foods in their research. Neither has research into food taken on board the advances in cognitive psychology. One reason for this is the importance of the senses of touch, taste and smell in recognition and appreciation of food. Sight and hearing are so important in human behaviour, and vision research has been making such exciting advances in recent decades, that a great deal of this research has been on the fundamentals of visual recognition, with the remainder on auditory recognition (mainly speech).

Nevertheless, some general principles of pattern recognition have recently emerged. As pointed out earlier, this issue is relevant to all quantitative mechanistic sciences. Oddly enough, psychologists for over a century have had the theory and much of the methodology for highly effective diagnosis of the causal processes going on within a well performing system. However, this method has only been put into full effect very recently, and so far almost exclusively on food recognition in the mouth. Studies of the role of tastes, textures, odours and colours over the last decade or so have yielded some basic methods for measuring the elemental mental processes that translate patterns on the receptors into a recognition of a foodstuff and discrimination of differences between test samples and the real thing.

Indeed, food must be one of the best areas in which to develop ways of diagnosing the mental processes in object recognition. Foods and drinks are well suited to variations from the real thing that make the test sample seem different from normal without being too different. A food or drink item can readily be either large or small as a whole or stronger or weaker than usual overall. Alternatively, test food can be regarded as poorer in quality than the real thing because the size or character of some feature is abnormal. One must hope that the psychology of food can move rapidly now into the mainstream of cognitive psychology, widening it beyond memory, language and the sense of sight.

Measuring Performance

To get to the mechanisms of recognition we must abandon the longstanding assumption that assigning numbers or positions on a line anchored on one or more levels of a feature described by a sensation or emotion word is measuring or directly scaling a subjective quantity referred to by that description. An appropriate way to rate test objects would be to position them on a dimension between a point representing recognition of the standard object and an equally objective point such as a different object or the more subjective anchor of something that is not at all like the standard. What is necessary in addition, however, is to ascertain the performance of the ratings at discriminating between objective features of the test objects. Whatever controlled or measured feature accounts most precisely for the ratings is the one that is being processed in recognizing the standard level of that feature in the context of those test objects.

This is simply a case of the general scientific strategy of identifying causes by the power of their influence on the effect to be explained. In the case of rating performance, the physical pattern that is most effective at changing the scores produced is the one which the assessor is using to carry out that task of rating. Psychology has in fact been ahead of engineering, physiology, economics and other sciences concerned to characterize causal processes within systems and measure their strengths, although even the psychologists have not generally seen it that way. This basic principle for measuring mental processes in fact goes back well over a century; it was proposed by the nineteenth century psychophysicist G.E. Fechner, albeit in subjectivist language (in terms of introspection on sensations). Fechner speculated that we perceive the strengths of sensations by the same processes as those by which we perceive differences between sensations. However, the methods that psychologists developed for measuring perceptual differences did not necessarily depend on the inspection of the contents of private consciousness, such as how similar or different two stimuli were. Some methods simply collected data showing whether the assessor could perceive a difference or not.

More precisely, perceptual difference measurement was based on how reliably a difference was detected when real differences were larger and smaller. Each of two feature levels being compared could produce one of a range of signals. The ranges could overlap when the actual difference was small enough. Then the signal from the lower level of the feature could on occasion be as large as or even larger than the signal from the higher level. If the range of signals arises from a simple random process then the probabilities of different signal strengths will be distributed in a normal (Gaussian) curve (Thurstone, 1927a; Tanner and Swets, 1954). We can therefore calculate the reliability of discriminative performance from the overlap of the observed response variabilities between an actual difference.

Weber noticed that, when the smallest distinguishable differences were considered in the usual physical units (e.g. concentrations of substance, energy of radiation), the physical differences that were equal in perceptual difference (by the criteria that amount to equal discriminativeness in objective performance) were roughly in constant ratio to the physical level of the two different levels being discriminated, at least in the moderate range of levels (above the lowest easily recognizable levels and below levels approaching receptor saturation). Hence, if Fechner's principle is right, the perceived strength of a stimulus will increase in proportion to equal ratios of the appropriate physical difference. In other words, rated stimulus strengths should form a straight line against the logarithm of the physical stimulus units. This theoretical semilogarithmic psychophysical plot has been called Fechner's Law or the Fechner–Weber function.

This semilog function should not be regarded as an empirical law of perception, however. Rather, it is a special case of a very high-level theoretical assumption, at the basis of a universal methodological principle for investigating causal processes in effectively functioning systems, like the principle of uniformity in cosmology. The assumption is that equal differences in the cause will produce equal differences in the effect, at least in the normal range of operation of that causal mechanism. This principle of causal linearity is the basis for extracting scientific laws, i.e. exact equations for causal functions, by testing simple and general hypotheses on successive sets of quantitative data. The signal discrimination principle could be shown to be wrong, just as the principle of uniformity might conceivably be refutable, but that could only be by the principle ceasing to be useful at improving concrete theory in the way it has so far been (and that could hardly happen except in the sense that the principle is found to be an approximation to some more general principle covering its past successes as well as dealing with its new failures).

In other words, it is arguable quite generally that the output levels from a well-functioning system should be in proportion to levels of input. In the case of physical signals, that is the material impact of an object on the senses, the levels of that input are likely not to be differences but ratios of stimulation energy, i.e. scaled in logarithms of the appropriate physical units. This is because of the realities both of adapted systems and of the environments within which they have to function. From the point of view of the system's ability to perform well despite very large variations in the environment (as in light or sound energy, for example), then a system having a limited range of response strengths had better respond less sensitively at high levels of stimulation than at low levels: if equal differences in input provoked equal differences in output, the system would have to have either a high zero response or a low maximum response or both. At the same time, from the point of view of the information available from the environment, small differences in weak input are more likely to be meaningful than small differences in strong input (Norwich, 1990).

Those arguments do not exclude the possibility that the sensitivity tuning or adaptation might be less or more extreme than in ratio – between linear and logarithmic or beyond logarithmic. However, it is clear that a considerable variety of mental processes in response to physical stimulation do work in constant ratio over a fair range. For differences in stimulation that make just discriminable difference in response, this ratio is named after the early experimental psychologist Weber, because he pointed out that it was fairly constant over the middle range of a particular stimulus for a wide variety of stimuli; since ratios accumulate as logarithms, Fechner's semilog function is straight when the Weber ratio is constant. Since this occurs in so many cases where our physical measurements are close to what is stimulating the receptors, there is evidence for a presumption for ratios. From that, it follows that deviations from constancy in Weber's ratio should be examined to determine whether the actual physical pattern of stimulation is correctly represented by the physical measure. For example, in the case of tastants, does competition for receptors change at low concentrations and do associations between solute molecules or their hydrations change in highly concentrated tastant solutions? Also, if some data deviate from a semilog function in the region of Weber ratio constancy, we should consider other evidence for stimulus or response biases and its relevance to our test conditions.

On this approach, one cannot consider transforming the response measure because that is what has to be explained by a stimulus pattern. Taking logarithms of the response is a particularly degenerate (theoretically uninformative) move, because most monotonic curves are made into nearly straight lines by the resulting power function.

This interpretation of semilog psychophysical functions has the corollary that it is a misunderstanding to regard the semilog form of equation as an empirical law of quantitative judgment, to which Stevens' power law is a rival. Thurstone (1927a) pointed out that we can always force out the semilog function when Weber's ratio is constant. This is similar to a normal-variance step taken by some item-response theorists in questionnaire psychometrics, that Thurstone (1927b) also anticipated in his scaling techniques and was picked up by signal detection theory, as cited above.

The final step in this approach is more novel. This is to regard constancy of the Weber ratio as evidence that the physical measurement being used is of the phenomenon that is actually being perceived in the pattern of stimulation on the receptors. This move also reconciles ecological (Gibson, 1979), neurophysical (Beidler, 1962) and computational (Marr, 1982) approaches to perception.

This final point should be stated more generally, because it is fundamental to the diagnosis of causal processes. An hypothesis as to a mechanism is confirmed by obtaining not just the form but also the parameter values of an exact equation that fits the data better than rival forms of equation having comparable simplicity, e.g. also linear and containing the same number of variables. The best equation does not in the first instance have to be accurate at extreme values of the variables, especially if those extremes seldom occur during the system's operation and so can be left for later investigation. The exact values of the parameters and indeed the exact nature of the variables can be unclear when the equation is first established. In the early days of measuring Newton's gravitional constant, it varied by 30–50 per cent either way depending on how one did the experiment. Newton's laws of motion are not so much contradicted by Einstein's relativistic equations as shown to become poor approximations at speeds approaching that of light.

For research into object recognition mechanisms, the integration equation and the psychophysical functions for the contributing elements should be an exact linear function for a given situation for a given person over the familiar range of variations in that situation. However, at unusual extremes, the learned patterns may become less usable and the system will be pushed back onto operating according to the characteristics of its physical structure, showing for example receptor saturation effects at high levels of stimulation (Beidler, 1962) or square-root rather than logarithmic performance near detection threshold (Laming, 1986).

This discussion has been largely in terms of the perception of physical objects and materials. Nevertheless, the implications are entirely general for all cognitive analysis. The main difference is the scaling of stimulus features: verbal and other symbolic influences on recognition are likely to act in equal differences, not equal ratios. This is because the range from conceptual maximum to absence of such a feature puts no strains on the physical apparatus of the senses. It is also consistent with the fact that all sorts of verbal response are linear against equal-ratio (logarithmic) scales of a physical stimulus: hence a verbal response should serve as an equal-difference (linear) stimulus for other verbal responses.

Requirements for Recognizing a Food

To sum up, then, what distinguishes one object, like a food item, from another is the particular combination of features it displays. The item not only has a set of attributes. These attributes also usually have particular levels or strengths, or at least a limited range of attribute levels is normal. In the case of foods (and other sorts of item that we choose from amongst variants), an eater's personal preference for a type of food can be distinguished from less preferred versions in the same way: maximum preference is a response to recognizing a combination of some of that food's perceived attributes set within particular ranges. What count as features and which or how many are essential is an empirical question for each type of object and the exemplars that have to be recognized. The system could be hierarchical and symmetrical, with objects at one level becoming features at a higher level and vice versa, down to patterns of energy falling on receptors and up to the naming of whole situations in which people find themselves, like having a birthday party meal.

The requirements on recognizing a food are therefore to perceive that enough distinguishing features are sufficiently close to the features and levels appropriate to that food in the context in which it is being considered. This is a task of multi-dimensional discrimination. How close the food item is to being recognized will depend on how features are put together to produce a near-realistic concept.

Two ways of constructing the perception of an object from its features and their levels have been considered in recent literature. One is to add the distances of features levels from the proper level. The effect might be qualitatively similar if the distances were multiplied or averaged, insofar as that amounts also to addition but with distances rescaled. Addition would be sensible for qualitatively similar features, such as two sorts of sweetener or the number of biscuits in a packet. This sort of model has often been applied to disparate features but in a loose and indeterminate manner. Multiple regression and other statistical techniques reweight feature values to make addition predictive for a particular set of data. This is not evidence of how the mind actually does work unless the same weightings recur in different data sets from the same recognition task. Factorial analyses of variance in raw ratings have also been used in algebraic models of disparate dimensions of motivation and in Anderson's (1981) functional measurement. When actual concentrations of sugars are used, the most precise predictions yet published are only that sweetness is somewhere intermediate between the sweetnesses of each of a pair of sugars alone (de Graaf and Frijters, 1988).

Problems arise for those approaches from subjectivist assumptions and weak scaling principles. When discriminative performance units are used to measure the distances of perceptually identical but physically different features from a standard level, their unweighted addition is highly predictive of differences between test

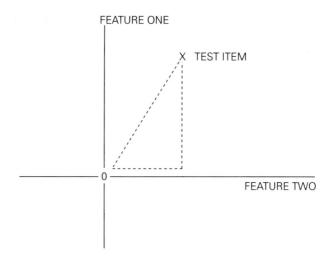

Figure 1.2 Distance between a test object and the standard (at the origin of the graph) differing in size of two features.

stimuli and standard. The sweetnesses of two sugars add exactly when discrimination distances are used, as do the sournesses of two acids (Freeman and Booth, 1994a).

In contrast, disparate features should be orthogonal, rather than colinear. That is, they operate in independent directions (at right angles) and so their distances from standard should combine in a multi-dimensional space. The net distance between the test object and standard object for two features is the length of the hypotenuse that is formed from a right-angled triangle having sides equal to the distance of each feature from standard (Figure 1.2).

Hence when sweetness and sourness combine into the appropriate taste for an orange-flavoured drink, the sugar and acid distances from the levels giving an orangey taste are squared and added and the square root taken to give the distance of that test mixture from the most realistic mixture for orange (as distinct from lemon or apple, say).

The features do not have to be simple. Creaminess is a combination of viscosity and the evenness of and distance between fat globules. Yet it can be combined with sweetness, bitterness, colour and temperature into a cup of instant coffee. The features do not have to be physical: they can be conceptual, such as price and healthfulness. Physical and conceptual features combine, such as the sweetness and the described calorie content of a sweetener. Sweetener level and sweetener calorie level combine in Euclidean space into preference for the orange drink (Freeman and Booth, 1994b) and for the coffee drink (Booth and Blair, 1988).

These principles of perception are not limited to food items, meals and other objects or situational aspects readily attributed to them, such as economic cost or bodily after-effect. They can be extended to recognition of the whole situation and its appropriateness for eating a type of food or menu. This includes the state of the body and the nature of the social context, both interpersonally and culturally. Such extensions of the approach will be illustrated when practicable in the following chapters.

As indicated earlier in this chapter, this particular approach to cognitive mechanisms, analysing multi-dimensional discrimination performance in individuals, is a new development for any part of psychology. It relates closely to many other psychological ideas, ancient and recent, but so far has been applied almost exclusively to the psychology of eating and drinking. Indeed, both the reason for developing this approach and the practicality of developing it over the last decade or so rests on the regularity of our habits of dealing with relatively well-understood materials and information, namely foodstuffs, their sensed qualities and their nutrient compositions. The psychology of food thus may shortly be providing a basis for further advances in many other areas of psychology and indeed in related social and biological sciences.

Chapter 2

Development of Appetite for Food and Drink

This chapter illustrates how a cognitive approach to appetite lends coherence to current information on the development of eating habits, food preferences and control of food intake in infancy and childhood and throughout adulthood as lifestyle changes and cultural exchange ramifies.

A new-born infant can show some basic signs of possessing an ingestive appetite. When awake enough, the baby will suck and swallow milk or other fluids brought to the lips. Reflexive though this behaviour may be, it shows a disposition to ingest. In addition, a crying baby can often be quietened by something to suck on. This effect is more reliable when the sucking yields some fluid, especially if it is sweet. It shows the satisfaction gained from these stimuli, another criterion of appetite for nutriment.

This chapter considers how the organization of eating and drinking develops from these early beginnings. Mainly we deal with development up until independent search for and preparation of food. Nevertheless, implications for lifelong appetite change are pointed out, including the effects of ageing.

The Mechanics of Ingestion

Ingestion is a complex set of movements that are initially under inherited control. Yet ingestive movements rapidly come under learned control and quite early may acquire some cognitive shape.

Sucking is normally the earliest form of these movements, but forms of sipping and biting can be carried out as soon as required, while chewing of solids after a fashion can be done within a few weeks. Nevertheless, as well as teeth being necessary for mastication of harder materials, the successful eating of some materials involves development of skill in subtler movements of the tongue and jaws. Lettuce is supposed to be disliked by young children: that may be because it is tricky to chew effectively or pieces of leaf stick on the palate and create a nasty feeling. Closing of the lips and breathing need fine control for fully efficient consumption of fluids and wet solids.

When the milk reaches the back of the mouth, it is literally vital that it goes down the throat into the stomach and not down the windpipe into the lungs. Older infants develop reflex swallowing movements by which the epiglottis separates the body of fluid from any air in the mouth and sends the fluid down the oesophagus, while a jet of air goes up the back of the nose (giving a small concentrated sample of aroma to be smelt). We may choke when this motor pattern gets disorganized, perhaps because it is not triggered properly in the normal way by a ball of fluid in the pharynx (you feel you have to swallow) or because breathing for speech has disrupted it. Indeed, the risk of choking is increased because the back of the human mouth is uniquely large as part of our capacity for making the wide variety of sounds we use in speech. So it is highly adaptive that in earliest life human infants do not have to use the epiglottis but milk can pour straight down the throat without crossing the opening of the trachea.

Rooting

When a hungry infant is touched on the upper or lower lip, on one corner of the lips or perhaps on the cheek, the head turns in the direction of the touch (Sainte-Anne Dargassies, 1977); the lips may part too. This helps the baby to cooperate with anything that the mother does to bring the face to the breast and the lips to centre around the nipple.

Then, when the lips are touched symmetrically, they close and if a good seal is formed the baby begins to generate a series of pressure reductions with the tongue and cheeks. Hence, a newborn infant's reflexes enable the nipple to be grasped in the mouth and sucked efficiently. Some mammals eject milk into the pup's mouth but the human breast simply makes milk easier to suck out in response to the stimuli of suckling.

The delivery of fluid into the mouth has a dramatic influence on the sucking movements, showing them to be under sensory control. From birth, a baby given a pacifier (a dummy teat) will give half a dozen very rapid sucks over a couple of seconds, wait several seconds and then give another burst and so on indefinitely. This is known as non-nutritive sucking. Similar lip and tongue movements occur while the young babies are asleep. These bursts of rapid rhythmic movements of the mouth parts are reminiscent of the lapping from a pool or bowl of water or licking from a spout shown by adult animals such as dogs and rats but they would be difficult for a human adult to imitate. Non-nutritive sucking movements may occur towards the end of a feed but the sucking of fluid most of the time takes a very different pattern. Each suck is more protracted, taking up to a second or more. One suck follows another immediately or with irregular pauses. This pattern is constrained by the transfer of liquid through the back of the mouth and may be controlled by the sensory feedback or anticipatory cues (feed-forward) from the pulses of fluid leaving the nipple and passing down the throat.

Successful Feeding

Every human mother knows to put her baby to breast. This results from information picked up earlier in life; there is no need to invoke a motivational system of inherited skills, let alone personal memories from infancy. Despite the natural anxieties and imagined unique difficulties experienced by first-time parents, most breast-feeding is unproblematic.

Nevertheless, it does occasionally go wrong. The simple snags are evidence against a tightly coordinated reflexive system. The less obvious disruptions show up the complex reflexes on which infant feeding is based like all other behaviour.

A simple example is the baby's upper lip getting folded over between the nostrils and the breast. This stops the baby breathing while suckling and sooner or later that makes the whole process of breast-feeding aversive to the baby, if the nurser does not do something about the interference.

A subtler problem is lack of infant-nurser interaction during the feed. Mum may be taking insufficient interest in what seems to interest baby. Albeit variable, there are social reflexes of returning looks with gaze, smiling, cooing and touching. It is just as natural but not universal to intervene by gentle shaking or poking to wake the baby when dozing off at the breast (or bottle). If the baby or the mother is rather more passive than most, too little milk may be taken, crying and night-waking may become more frequent and the mother's milk supply may decline.

All shapes and sizes of babies and bosoms are adequate to clamp on and deliver the goods! Some cultures put honey on the nipple for the newborn baby but the incentive for the rooting and suckling reflexes is not needed. Little fluid is delivered for a few days following the birth but that colostrum is concentrated in substances which prepare the digestive tract for serious work and initiate protection against infection; the neonate has plenty of fat reserves and can be left to sleep most of the time for the first day or so on the outside.

Biological Regulation of Feeding

Wah! Infant Hunger

A baby can generally get fed when necessary, if the mother or someone else able to feed is within reach. At times when the digestive tract is empty and probably also partly triggered by an endogenous rhythm, the infant will be alert and active and very likely exercising all its muscles: arms, legs, face and diaphragm pulse away, producing the picture and sounds of distress or what even gets over to an adult as frustration and anger.

Hungry crying may sound different from crying from other causes. It can be imagined how the pattern of wails differs between a stabbing pain such as wind or a pin and persistent discomfort such as cold or abrasion. However, lack of food can lead to pangs or an ache of hunger in adult experience. If time pattern and loudness do not distinguish hunger cries from other distress, that leaves the sound spectrum. Lack of food and a desire to be fed can readily be attributed from knowledge of when the babe was last fed and the habitual feeding pattern. Such attributions may be reinforced by the infant's reactions when the caregiver responds, with distress sustained by a pain but soothed by anticipation of feeding.

This 'hunger' includes thirst or, rather, the infant is unlikely to have distinct dispositions or forms of distress while milk is providing sufficient food in ample water, any excess of which is easily excreted. It is only following birth, though, that feeding as well as watering are by mouth. So it is not impossible for some functional distinction to be expressed. Infants do not appear to discriminate milk from water for several months. Although it is said that hunger and thirst may be distinguishable at four months, a genuine differentiation remains to be established between needs for water and for food (e.g. energy) in selective behaviour towards liquids and solids or non-caloric and caloric fluids.

Physiological Effects of Suckling

Several components of the process of feeding a baby contribute to soothing the symptoms of distress. Crying is stopped by the stimulation of being picked out of the cot and its restart may be inhibited by some contrast between lying in a cot and being held in arms, such as warmth from another body. Sooner or later, acquired anticipation of being fed plays a role. The movements of sucking provide alternative activity, if not more. Sensory stimulation from the milk is certainly important. The taste of sugar and the feel probably of fat are major quieting influences in other baby mammals; they even have pain-killing effects (Blass, 1987). Given the other effects of sweetness considered later, the limited direct evidence justifies the belief that oral stimulation by milk inhibits distress in the human baby.

This quieting does not just permit the infant to stay attached to the nipple. It ensures a steady rhythm of sucking. The eyes open as the muscles around them relax from crying; with the baby held in the arm at the breast, this makes eye contact with the feeder very likely. In addition to social and learning effects, this opportunity to attend to something else interesting presumably helps completion of the feed, by keeping the infant alert in what otherwise might become a rather soporific activity.

Milk accumulates in the stomach, of course, as the feed progresses. There is normally some tone in the muscles of the stomach wall and, just like down the oesphagus from the swallowing movement, waves of contraction pass across the stomach towards the pylorus where it joins the duodenum, the uppermost part of the intestine. Thus, pressure maintained in the stomach and those waves pump any gastric fluid in globs into the duodenum. However, the start of feeding relaxes the stomach and so the pressure difference may be reduced and pumping slowed for some while. A little of the feed may be passing down the upper intestine but the vast majority of it stays in the stomach. The resulting volume stretches the gastric wall. In very young rat pups, if passage of material from the stomach is prevented, the feed stops no sooner or later and it can be stopped as quickly by material infused into the stomach as by swallowed fluid. It seems, therefore, that only gastric distention stops the feed. Purely gastric satiety may be operative in the young human infant.

In adults (of several mammalian species) satisfaction of hunger also brings drowsiness, particularly if the meal is large. This suits adults during their sleep period. A more modest feed may leave the baby alert and contented, thus opening up opportunities to do more than sleep and be fed. Another obvious pattern following a feed during the day is a brief rest or even a nap and then involvement in social and physical activity, like play or an outing.

The separation of breathing and swallowing during suckling is imperfect and so considerable amounts of air can go down the throat into the stomach. Some air mixed with the milk can pass into the upper intestine. If such air gathers into a bubble of a size stretching the wall of the digestive tract, that is painful. Poor digestion can also produce gas in the lower intestine, generating discomfort known as colic (from its source, the colon).

By gentle patting on the middle of the back, gas in the stomach can be eased up to the junction with the oesophagus through which it is released, reducing the risk of intestinal gas and relieving any discomfort built up in the stomach. Burping baby may even overcome some premature satiety from distension or distraction, in which case feeding can continue for a while longer. However, gas and liquid may not be well separated in the stomach. Also, the oesophageal sphincter is not discriminating in what fluid it lets pass. So the infant may regurgitate small amounts of milk, even without any back-patting.

Emotional Context of Infant Feeding

Freud and succeeding generations of psychoanalysts have attributed profound consequences for adult emotional life and personality to the mother–infant interactions during feeding at the breast, as well as during later interactions such as over toilet training. Such ideas can be very influential on the fantasy life and interpersonal relations of a psychoanalysed adult but it is technically very difficult to determine how realistic they are for what actually happens in the infant's mind.

There is obvious scope for drastic misinterpretation of correlations between early experience and adult behaviour. The simplest sort of error is to assume from similarity between the pattern in infancy and the pattern in adulthood that the former causes the latter; an equally logical initial interpretation is that an infant's genetic inheritance determines both infantile and adult patterns.

More likely than either of these extremes, as we shall see for food preferences, is some form of developmental continuity having primarily neither genetic nor experiential determinants. The infant develops a pattern of its own from a series of interactions between genes and environmental structure, perhaps with a considerable contribution from random accident. This developed or epigenetic pattern then 'channels' future selections from the environment and the workings within genetic constraints, which may serve to maintain some of the early pattern.

That is, while consisting entirely of nothing material that has not come from interactions of the genes with the environment, the individual to some degree imposes her or his own structure on perception, action and the environment. To that extent, a developed person can be autonomous and capable of making choices that are to some extent self-determined, rather than entirely determined by isolatable factors in genetic endowment, cultural upbringing or current context that have the same effects on everybody.

Affect During Suckling

Delivery of milk into the mouth of even the newborn infant appears to have a positive emotional impact, beyond its soothing and even analgaesic effect. Certainly a taste of sugar on the tongue elicits a slight opening of the lips and perhaps a little sideways stretch, reminiscent of a smile or smacking of the lips. The tongue may protrude and withdraw, as in lip-licking. This looks like pleasure to the adult. It is certainly different from the sucking or chewing movements that directly prepare and deliver material to the back of the throat for swallowing. Other infant mammals show similar movements of the lips and tongue in response to the taste of sugar. It is a reflex that can be organized solely within the brainstem in the rat and occurs in human infants born without a forebrain (Steiner, 1973). Chiva (1985) suggested that these responses do have incipient subjective and communicative functions and so the feeding process provides the beginning of emotional development.

Gentle stroking and soft but firmly backed touch, provided in the course of feeding, appear to be comforting and pleasurable. Warmth to the skin may also soothe and even contribute to pleasure, at least at ambient temperatures in temperate climes. Infants appear to come to expect to be fed when laid down in the arms in the usual feeding position: after some days, a baby may mouth and root if the breast or bottle is not presented immediately. Within a week or two of birth, infants that are always clothed become distressed on being undressed and calm down when clothes are put back on.

Milk itself is accepted from a bottle with the most enthusiasm if it is at body temperature, not cooler or warmer. It is not clear whether this depends at all on previous experience of milk at body temperature from the breast.

Visual and auditory interaction also play a major role. The mother's voice or at least noises like it catch a baby's attention within a week or so of birth. Since the eyes are open while the feeding infant is alert, whatever innate face recognition categories exist are applied to the nurser's features from the first feed. The role of this eye contact in bonding may be more important initially on the mother's side, in giving a pleasing sense that the baby is attentive and interested in her; this is functionally important for baby, probably not so much in keeping the feeding session going – there are plenty of other reinforcements and control of session duration – as in helping to ensure that mother comes promptly to feed the infant when sustenance is next needed. Crying is a nasty sound and so adults have incentive to stop it. However, to ensure that the noise is stopped in a way that benefits rather than harms the baby, it is also important that a source of distress is attributed by adults who can do things to relieve the need.

Food Perception and Eating Habits

Congenital Recognition of Food and Food Sources

The crying, rooting, sucking and quieting of a newborn baby add up to the smooth performance of a well-informed search for and uptake of food. This system of abilities is presumably built into connections within the brain between innervation of receptors and muscles of the trunk, head and mouth. Is this use of environmental information sufficiently sophisticated to justify attributing to the neonate some knowledge of where to search and the perception after some fashion of teat and milk? Once we have determined what information is actually being processed, this is an objective conceptual issue about proper use of the word 'perceive', i.e. know through the senses, by capacities dependent on the genes and individual learning. There is no space here to discuss such issues – see, for example, Booth (1976) and Bloor (1983) and conceptual analysts they cite. The answer turns on whether criteria of performance that could be considered to justify attribution of knowledge are met in this case; it does not depend on granting that there are particular contents of the infant's consciousness – rather, the other way round.

We have seen that, when in a state of readiness to be fed, the neonate can discriminate where around the mouth a contact has been made. The sucking pattern differs between a dry teat and one that is delivering liquid. Sucking is also affected by the temperature and taste of the milk. The newborn infant may be able to discriminate a lactating woman from one who is not and may show familiarity with the mother's smell or movements. All these could be experience-independent reflex patterns of stimulus and response but that does not rule out the possibility that their performance is sufficiently sophisticated to satisfy the criteria for being regarded as perceptual skill.

Learning to Eat

Like all motivation (the cognitive structure of action), eating and drinking involve skills of both movement and sensing.

Considerable parts of the motor skill of ingestion are preorganized by intercon-nections within the brain (Chapter 8), such as biting just strongly enough to break a lump of food without the teeth banging hard together or flicking the food under the teeth from one side of the mouth to the other during chewing without biting either the tongue or the cheeks. Nevertheless the broader and initially more delib-erate ('voluntary') aspects of eating movements have to be learned, no doubt re-inforced by comfort, speed and social approval. Preventing dribbling and not showing other people half-chewed food require the same skills of mastication with lips closed. Breaking up hard pieces of food so that they are comfortable to swallow demands persistence and care as well as strength of jaw.

Most learning to eat is perceptual, however. Foods begin to be distinguished from non-foods and better and better from each other. Events in gut and tissues become recognized as relevant and so we gain learned control of eating to some degree. Interpersonally and emotionally significant aspects of feeding occasions also acquire influence over the ingestive behaviour and the desire to eat and drink. Our eating habits are largely driven by recognition of the mutual appropriateness of the edible and potable materials available, the time, place and social meaning of the occasion and the state of one's insides.

Despite their integrality, we can try to consider food, social context and bodily state separately. The general application of the cognitive approach of this book to the learned development of eating is outlined below and then, to end the chapter, some particular issues of life-long appetite development are considered. Visceral perception is considered against this background in Chapter 3. Details of the social perception of eating are covered in Chapters 4 and 7 on a similar developmental base. First now we consider the development of perception of food identity and quality.

Learning to Recognize a Foodstuff

Before we turn to a general theory of the development of food preferences, let us look at some specific examples that have been studied and some of the wider implications of those research results.

Learning to Eat Salted Food

Development of a liking for salt in foods provides one of the more easily investigated models of perceptual learning about foods.

Receptors in the mouth that are sensitive to sodium ions mature quite late in mammals that have been studied closely. A very young baby may not refuse formula that has been made up by mistake from salt instead of milk powder or sugar and the result can be fatal. Yet after some months, an infant may make a face to a drop of salt solution on the tongue if it is strong enough.

An infant's liking for salt can be tested by comparing the intakes of unsalted baby cereal and a lightly salted version, offered on separate days as the first course of a regular meal such as in the middle of the day. Some breast-fed four-month-old infants who had just begun to be given solids by their mothers all ate more of the slightly salty cereal (Harris, Thomas and Booth, 1991). Yet infants who had continued on breast milk until five or six months ate the same amount of the two cereals in tests when started on solids. This contrasted with six-month-olds who had been on solids for a week or more. Their intake of salted cereal was greater than unsalted intake in direct proportion to the number of times they had been given food containing an appreciable amount of salt in the previous seven days (Harris and Booth, 1987). This indicates that experience of salt in food induces a liking for the taste. Therefore, Harris *et al.* (1991) argue, the simplest account of the whole pattern of data is that babies get to like the very low level of salt in breast milk if fed exclusively on it from about four months, at which age infants begin to be able to taste low levels of salt and, they suggest, there is an innate preference for saltiness in that range that can then begin to be expressed and modified by experience. More babies need to be tested to establish this suggestion, including those younger than four months.

Simply getting to like the taste of salt, at least at low levels, is only the beginning of the story though. By twelve months of age, infants are quite put off a food without salt that they are used to eating with salt added. Harris and Booth (1987) tested infants of that age with mashed potato instead of baby cereal. If unsalted potato was given first, they still ate somewhat more salted potato presented on a subsequent day but the difference was much less than when the salted potato was tested first. That is, the taste of salt had become part of the whole sensory experience of potato and its omission created a temporary reduction in interest in that food.

Our animal heritage raises a question about any food-specific selection or avoidance and a craving or revulsion, learned or not. Does the sensory preference or aversion serve any nutritional requirement? In the case of a craving for salt or any disposition to select salty-tasting materials, the question is whether this helps to meet a need for sodium ions and/or perhaps some other mineral (chloride, calcium, magnesium, potassium, etc.).

A taste receptor for sodium and either an innate preference for its stimulation or the capacity to learn to like it might well have had some selective value but it seems impossible to gather the evidence required to calculate the advantage to the human species. The dependence of sodium preference on current sodium status, on the other hand, has yet to be investigated in human infants. Adult and young rats depleted of sodium switch from aversion to preference for strong salt solutions; indeed, undergoing depletion in infancy potentiates the rat's intake of salty-tasting fluid later in life.

The tragic case of a small boy who ate rock salt is always recounted in this context. He was taken into hospital and not allowed to eat the salt. He died because his adrenal glands were not secreting enough of the hormone that stops the kidneys letting all the circulating sodium ions pass out of the body in urine. Nevertheless, his craving for salt, or his tolerance at least of the nasty taste and emetic qualities of concentrated salt, could have been a habit he had developed by stumbling on a way of reducing the malaise of adrenocortical insufficiency. This is not evidence for an innate sodium appetite in the human species.

Careful examination of salt preferences in substantial numbers of adults who had been deprived of (or loaded with) sodium casts doubt on influences on salt taste preference from current bodily sodium status as distinct from recent tasting of low or high salt diet (Beauchamp *et al.*, 1990). However, detailed investigation of a small number of adults whose sodium intake was controlled by tasteless capsules has provided some indications of a genuine sodium appetite, i.e. increased liking for a salty taste when depleted of sodium (Huggins *et al.*, 1992).

Learning to Drink Sweetened Water

Drinks and foods containing sugar invariably have other aspects to consider such as a colour, an aroma or another taste. Even confectionery made just out of compressed sugar ('boiled sweets') is given fruity flavours. The cheapest varieties of lemonade are not mere sugar in water but also contain fruit acid and carbonation. So, a plain sugar solution is not generally recognizable as a real drink, nor is table sugar by itself a normal food.

However, babies in some families are given plain sugar solution to drink be-tween milk feeds. Beauchamp and Moran (1984) found that one-year-old American infants who had been given sugar water when they were younger liked plain sweet-ened water better than those who had not been brought up on it. This difference persisted to some extent at two years of age. Presumably a young child by then is likely to have had some experience of flavoured sweet drinks such as juices, colas and sodas.

Thus it seems that sweetness is expected in the materials it has been experi-enced in before. Even though the congenital preference for sweet things is likely to persist in the primitive brain connections, the contextualization of preference still occurs and indeed begins to take hold as soon as experiences of sweetened materials are provided.

Juices and, later usually, purées of fruit and vegetables are sometimes given to suckling infants instead of milk formulae or water. Like plain sugar solution, these juices are generally accepted at once. This may largely be because they are liquid, like milk, but the sweetness of fruit and some vegetables would also contribute, as may the minerals if the salt taste receptors have matured enough. The importance of fluidity is indicated by the adverse reaction of infants a few weeks old to pastes that are not sweetened, such as baby cereal (Wolff, 1987).

Learned Liking for Milk?

Tastes are more readily manipulated in naturalistic experiments than are other orally sensed characteristics of foods, namely chemical irritation as from pepper or ginger, thermal properties, tactual patterns, aroma up the back of the throat and even sounds such as scrunching cereal.

The visual appearance of foods and food sources can be controlled quite readily. Wolff (1987) found that sight of the bottle alone created no reaction in hungry bottle-fed infants until two months of age, and then only if it was removed after a feed had got under way. Only by 5–6 months did sight of a bottle between feeds elicit mouthing movements and then not reliably.

The early acquisition of food colour preferences remains to be studied. Adult monkeys learn to feed from a black or white syringe according to the glucose or saline it delivers and that liking satiates as more and more of the fluid is tasted and swallowed (Burton, Rolls and Mora, 1976). Perhaps a baby fed milk from a transparent bottle would get to like drinking white fluid. It remains to be seen how early we learn to like the orange colour of juice from oranges or the purple colour of blackcurrant juice.

The taste of milk sugar and of the minerals in the whey and the aroma from the small fat-related molecules that milk gives off are also important in good quality milk. This aroma is presumably part of what a baby smells on a lactating woman. Without an appropriate amount of salt and perhaps some lactose too, heavy cream diluted in water does not taste like real milk.

The relative importance of taste and smell in food preferences is often exaggerated, however. Texture and temperature can also be crucial.

When milk is pushed around at the modest speed it is in the mouth, it resists those pressures slightly more than water does: that is, it is a bit more viscous. The molecules of milk protein (casein) dissolved in the whey, together with submicroscopic clumps (micelles) of casein and the generally somewhat larger globules of cream in suspension, all tend to cling together. If the milk is pushed hard, though, the molecules cannot hold on to each other and so viscosity goes down at higher speeds. The pressure receptors in the skin of the mouth somehow pick out some of the resulting changes over time in the shape of the tissues in which they are embedded to help create a sensation of thickness or richness (to which taste and smell also contribute).

The globules of cream are important because skimmed milk feels as thin as water and creams feel thicker than milks. The creamy texture is more than just the effect of fat globules on viscosity, though. They also create a sense of smoothness (Kokini, 1985; Richardson and Booth, 1993). This smoothness in addition to the thickness (Mela, 1988) is crucial to the accuracy of judging by touch how much fat is in the milk (Richardson *et al.*, 1993).

Thus, if the suckling infant's oral mechanoreceptors are sufficiently sensitive and tactile pattern perception is sophisticated enough at that age, it would be possible to learn to recognize and to like the texture of cream during the weeks of breast or bottle feeding. There is no evidence for a congenital preference for creamy texture. There is no functional reason to expect innate recognition of fat in milk either. Any fluid enables suckling to work. A baby that rejected the breast for not providing the feel of a fatty milk is not going to survive to hand on those genes for recognizing and preferring cream. The deliciousness of the creamy feel of mousse, ice cream and cream filling (on top of their sweetness as often sold these days) could well be an acquired 'taste' also, picked up early in childhood or whenever those foods are served as treats or filling desserts and differences in the feel of the fat globules are noticeable.

Infants suck faster and longer at a bottle when the fluid is at body temperature, not cooler or warmer. Those younger and older Americans who like to drink a glass of milk reputedly prefer it straight from the refrigerator rather than at room temperature: such 'warm' milk may even be revolting. The preference for milk at body temperature in infants and a preference for cold milk from later in childhood might well both be acquired simply from experience with such temperatures. There is an intriguing issue, though, whether the change also involves interactions with other sensory qualities of milks, a culturally based distinction between babies' milk and milk for 'big boys', or other factors.

Development of Food Identification

Taking note of these examples, we can now turn to a general account of learning to recognize foodstuffs.

Since recognition requires a comparison of the present with the past, it must be founded on memory. Being able to name or select a food correctly requires much more than learning its name or its use; it requires learning enough about the perceptible properties of the food to be able to distinguish that food from others. This is the psychological case of a very broad principle, that good performance by a system requires mediating mechanisms that are well adapted to the tasks the system tackles. So, an important basis for the cognitive approach to food and ingestion taken in this book has been research on how we and indeed other intelligent species learn quantitatively about stimuli such as foods and food sources and how we put what we have learned into memory for comparison with upcoming stimuli.

Psychologists and indeed neurophysiologists have long studied the basic processes of learning, mostly in benign animal experiments using highly controlled and physically simple stimuli. Unfortunately, the research traditions of animal learning and memory neurophysiology have developed separately from the psychology of human perception and cognition, which have tended to use physically complex or even symbolic stimuli (such as words). Recently some overlaps of interest in both mental processes and brain mechanisms have become increasingly apparent but the primary interests of animal and human psychology remain divergent.

Nevertheless, an intimate link was pointed out nearly 40 years ago (Shepard, 1957) between animal conditioning of arbitrary and isolated stimuli and the tradition of human psychophysics, also studying responses to physically simple stimuli out of context. Learning in animals and psychophysics in people both concentrate on single abstract stimuli in one sensory modality, such as a colour, a musical tone or lines at different orientations or spacings. Both of these traditions within psychology have largely ignored the problems of the multi-dimensionality of object recognition and the normally contextually relative nature of perception and knowledge. Indeed, they remain isolated from cognitive psychology in any realistic sense. Yet Shepard's link provides a high road to characterization of single features at the basis of holistic recognition and indeed the identification of discrete causal processes in any science.

This is because the connection concerns the quantitative characteristics of single features. When coupled to a performance approach to ratings, rather than the subjective approach, Shepard's idea provides a way of integrating contextualized learning about food, i.e. the phenomenon of configurally conditioned ingestion, and recent work on multi-dimensional discrimination and the combination of features into recognition of objects.

Learned Analysis and Synthesis

The requirements for distinguishing a food from others with which it might be confused can be divided into two sorts. There has to be analysis of discrete features, determining their size or intensity. There also has to be synthesis of features into an integral percept. In other words, the perceptual pattern for each feature has to be recognized and its level measured and the discrete features' patterns have to be combined into the overall response.

This task might or might not be carried out at all levels in a strict sequence, such as analysis followed by synthesis. Within a sensory modality at least, it is conceivable that analysis follows synthesis. It seems likely though that each sense and each type of coding is analysed before intermodal synthesis occurs.

Also the distinction between analysis and synthesis is not absolute. A feature at one level can be an integral of more primitive patterns, all the way down to receptor-driven channels of information transfer, such as the red pigment in the eye or one type of bitter receptor on the tongue. An integral percept can be a feature for a higher level of integration, all the way up to the menu of food and drink for a celebratory dinner or a chocolate-coated, cream-filled wafer in its wrapping with brand name, nutritional and compositional information, customer service address and price.

At the higher levels of analysis and synthesis, the cognitive processes have been created by learning from experience. Indeed the learning of appropriate responses to combinations between food flavours and states of the digestive tract was the first experimental demonstration of situational integration or appropriateness in eating (although it was not quantitated). The importance of appropriate levels for features of food was brought out dramatically by the first demonstration of the acquisition of food preferences by association with the effects of their energy contents. These basic learning effects will now be considered for their implications for the characterization of food recognition mechanisms.

The Learned Stimulus Strength

Rats were found to come to prefer whatever particular level of sweetness was associated with the effects of maltodextrin (partly hydrolysed starch: short-chain glucose polymers) or of glucose solution that was not so hypertonic as to be aversive (Booth, Lovett and McSherry, 1972). Even the innate preference for greater sweetness could be reversed by this acquired preference for the taste of an energy-providing food. When a high level of sweetness was associated with a lower concentration of glucose polymers than the concentration associated with low sweetness, high sweetness was consumed in smaller amounts than low sweetness. Thus, even rats are able to learn to recognize the appropriate level of sweetness to eat in order to get the most energy. All sorts of flavours paired with polymeric glucose, particularly in predigested form, become strongly preferred by rats (Sclafani, 1990). Similarly, young children get to like flavours paired with higher concentrations of starch-derived glucose polymer (Birch, 1987).

This learning to recognize a food is not restricted to sweet taste and carbohydrate reinforcement. The overwhelming of the innate sweetness preference was mentioned as dramatic evidence for the strength of the learning mechanism. As we have already seen, babies get to like the levels of salt that they are repeatedly exposed to. Odour and texture preferences can be reinforced by the effects of good-quality protein in rats (Booth and Simson, 1971; Baker and Booth, 1989) and in people (Booth and Gibson, 1988). Toddlers' preference for pudding flavours are increased by fat hidden in the dessert (Johnson *et al.*, 1991; Kern *et al.*, 1993).

Two aspects of preference are shown by these findings. One is that the reinforced sensory characteristic is preferred over another less reinforced or unreinforced stimulus. Another is that a particular strength of the reinforced characteristic – the level that has been reinforced – is preferred over higher and lower strength. In animal learning experiments, these two aspects have been called extra-dimensional and intra-dimensional learning. The two aspects can be theoretically related by considering the strength of the learned response in relation to the level of the conditioned stimulus (CS). The particular level of the particular stimulus that has been conditioned will evoke the strongest response. Higher and lower levels of the stimulus will not seem the same as the conditioned stimulus and so will elicit less strong responses. To the extent that the response to one stimulus is the same as the response to another, animal learning psychologists say that the response 'generalizes' from one stimulus to the other. Hence this decline in response strength as the stimulus level becomes lower or higher than the CS is known as an intra-dimensional stimulus generalization decrement.

Shepard (1957) pointed out that the gradient of intra-dimensional generalization decrements in learned response to a stimulus corresponded to human judgments of dissimilarity of a test stimulus from a standard. Assigning quantities to similarity or dissimilarity is however an ill-specified task. What is to be compared and how much difference counts as a given degree of (dis)similarity is left to the assessor. Worse still, if numerical ratings are used instead of positions in space, the response requires the processing of the number system onto the dimension of difference being rated. So recent successes in developing a theoretical account of similarity and recognition (e.g. Shepard, 1987; Ashby and Perrin, 1988) are likely to be several steps removed from the fundamental processes of recognition performance.

Instead, one can consider the discriminative performance of preference for different strengths of a learned stimulus. The bigger the difference between the learned strength and the test strength, the greater the number of just discriminable differences there will be between the two strengths. The decrease in preference should be proportional to that discriminability, above or below the trained strength. This gives an isosceles triangle of recognizability as a food and hence of degree of preference for the test item. This has been observed many times in adults when biases on expression of preference are avoided. It remains to be tested in young children, let alone infants.

Learned Integration of Features

Psychologists working on animal conditioning have long drawn a distinction between two ways in which a pair of simultaneous signals might evoke a learned response after that pair of stimuli had been conditioned (reinforced) by association with some significant consequence. This involves a more complicated cue than has been usual in classical conditioning. In Pavlov's laboratory, generally a buzzer would sound before food was squirted on the dog's tongue, or perhaps a light would predict food. After a series of such pairings, the dog would start salivating to the buzzer or the light, as the case may be, but would not salivate to a cue that had not been reinforced by food. However, a number of interesting questions about what the dog will learn can be asked if the buzzer and light are switched on together just before the food. The conditioned stimulus then becomes what is known as a compound of two stimulus elements.

After conditioning, a compound stimulus might have an effect which is no more than the sum of the effects of each element when presented alone. In this case, the observed response is presumably the result of separate processing of each of the stimulus elements.

Alternatively, the compound stimulus might have a greater effect than the sum of the effects of its elements. At the extreme, turning on the buzzer and light together might induce salivation but presenting either the buzzer or the light alone has no effect at all. One way in which learning theorists have thought about this is that a third stimulus emerges during conditioning. Hence the response is the sum of the effects of the buzzer and the light and also the effect of a stimulus that is quite different from either the buzzer or the light, although it is made out of a combination of them. Emergence of an effective combined stimulus after reinforcement of a compound stimulus is known as configural conditioning.

There has been surprisingly little study of configural conditioning. Any compound conditioning procedure of course looks complicated when it is still a struggle to understand what goes on under various regimens for conditioning simple stimuli. Yet compound stimuli, while still highly artificial, are a big step closer to most everyday situations. We do deal with buzzers and lights, of course, but we also have to learn many stimuli composed of multiple elements. No amount of study of unidimensional stimuli can ever give us a hint of how stimulus dimensions are combined. Yet even the study of a mere two dimensions may be sufficient to give us some basic principles of how three or four or perhaps larger numbers of features are integrated into the response to an object.

Oddly enough, one of the few examples of configural conditioning provided the solution to the most basic problem of food intake control: how can the decision to end a meal be influenced by the energy content of the food before it has been digested and absorbed and begun to be used in energy metabolism?

Conditioned Satiety

Infants compensate to some extent for overstrength formula by cutting back on the intake they accept (Fomon, 1974). However, it is not clear how much this is due to a stronger sating effect at the first and every meal or whether the effect depends at all on learning to anticipate shortly subsequent satiating effects from a rich-tasting formula.

At two years of age and over, toddlers can learn to moderate how much they eat of a distinctively flavoured meal spiked with a substantial level of glucose polymer (Birch, 1990). The only mechanism that has been suggested for such learned compensation of meal sizes is a conditioned loss of interest in eating when food items and partial fulness recur in a combination that previously has been followed by oversatiation or a bloated sensation. This phenomenon was called conditioned satiety, because it is a learned loss of preference for at least some foods which depends on a degree of repletion, which fits the general definition of satiation of appetite for foods.

The toddlers compensate better for the glucose polymer if they are persuaded to think about what is going on inside them: they are given practice at a game of filling a transparent doll's stomach with marbles (Birch *et al.*, 1987). Therefore this learning may depend on awareness of the transient bloating effect of higher concentrations of the predigested starch, which appears to mediate the conditioning of food-specific satiety (Booth and Davis, 1973; Booth, Mather and Fuller, 1982).

Learned Appropriateness

The initiation or termination of eating of particular foods may also become contextualized to the social situation or time of day. The food is appropriately attractive or satisfying. Birch, Billman and Richards (1984) found that toddlers were beginning to acquire the adult sense of the appropriateness of breakfast cereals to breakfast time. In a further study of adults, Kramer and colleagues (1992) could find no evidence of a palatability effect but saw a postprandial satisfaction effect of eating cereals at breakfast time.

Other examples of feature integration in food recognition were given in Chapter 1, but the evidence from early life is limited to the above fragments.

Liking for Sweetness in Foods and Drinks

The taste of sugar is a highly salient feature of many foods and drinks in the industrialized world. This theme will therefore recur throughout this book. Here we will use the liking for sweetness to illustrate a detailed application of the above theory of learned recognition of foodstuffs and of the contexts in which they are liked.

The case of sweetness is theoretically interesting for developmental psychology because it is the only definite example of an unlearned liking from the oral senses. The interaction of this innate preference with preference learning is also practically important. The interaction provides part of an explanation why sweetness is so important to food in industrialized countries. This interaction also gives reason to think that foods and drinks are sweeter than they need to be to get all the pleasure we want without the risks to which some uses of sugars expose the teeth and the waistline and the expense and worries of artificial sweeteners, detailed later in Chapter 7.

Why Do We Consume So Many Sweet Things?

About 10–20 per cent of the calories consumed by Western countries come from sugars. The British and Swiss are among the highest consumers, a lot going in (with fat) as chocolate. Cane or beet sugar (sucrose) is mostly added to foods and drinks, as are glucose polymers, glucose (in Europe) and fructose (in North America). Fructose and glucose both come from fruit. Milk and yogurts contain lactose but it is not very sweet.

Above a few percent, sucrose will contribute a noticeably sweet taste to a food or drink. Some adults at least have found a sugar dessert confection or a strongly sweetened drink to be unpleasantly sweet for them. Of course, even if food designers provided the median of the amounts of sugar most preferred in a food or drink, 50 per cent of consumers would have too much (though a good number of them may not object or even notice). However, there is reason to suspect that many items are sweeter than they need to be for maximum popularity, because of faults in preference measurement and failure to allow for the effects of the innate sweetness preference on the development of likings for foods and drinks new to the individual.

A theory of the cognitive mechanisms within choices of sweet foods and drinks opens up possibilities of better understanding of likings for sweet things and more accurate estimation of what people want immediately and in the longer term. Attention to the decision mechanisms regarding sweetness of foods and drinks clarifies the determinants of consumer demand for sweetness and intakes of sugars and substitute sweeteners and enables measurements of discriminations between more and less preferred sweetnesses.

A simple theory follows from what has been said thus far. This invokes two mechanisms.

First, we are born with a mechanism by which a sweet taste can facilitate ingestion. As with any reflex process, the stronger the sweet stimulation, the stronger the ingestive response would be if the reflex was operative uninhibitedly. That is, the innate sweet preference function should be a continuously rising graph of preference from taste threshold to either receptor saturation or maximum attainable response.

However, the reflex does not operate throughout life without interference. There is also a general mechanism of coming to like the characteristics of the foods and drinks we become familiar with, and indeed we come to prefer most the familiar strengths of those characteristics. This learned preference should therefore rise to the familiar level and then, unlike the innate function, fall again at higher levels (for more details, see Chapter 1).

The influence of sweetness on a person's choice of an item should therefore be an interaction between these two cognitive mechanisms, in combination with all the other momentarily salient determinants. The more thoroughly learned the liking for a material, the more effectively the learned preference for a particular level of sweetness should suppress the unlearned greater liking for greater sweetness. However, if you present someone with a somewhat unfamiliar item, then the congenital reflex may break through and the net result be that the overall preference does not decrease above the most preferred level. A new product is liable to evoke this pattern in an adult, as also is a non-drink or non-food such as plain sugar water (Thompson *et al.*, 1976) or sugar crystals. Many foods and drinks will be novel or relatively unfamiliar in at least some respects to a young child. Thus, the sweeter these initial offerings the more likely they are to be accepted. On the other hand, if less initial enthusiasm is managed somehow, the lower level of sweetness will become familiar and liked in such items in future and, via channelling effect, tend to be selected for the indefinite future. The sweetness will help to reinforce the appetite for that drink/food in the circumstances of use, e.g. whenever feeling a bit dry or peckish, in need of reward or comfort, it is time for sensation or fun or it's just there.

More Than One 'Sweet Tooth'

The contextualization of food sweetness preferences will depend on the individual's eating habits. A close examination of most-preferred levels of sugar in some foods and drinks and of reported choices of sweet over non-sweet alternatives in English adults has provided evidence for two distinct sets of foods and drinks that some people prefer sweet. One set includes a fruit drink and vegetable soup. The other set includes hot drinks, dessert sweets and chocolate. The latter group of people presumably have a habit of taking snacks and desserts and taking them with lots of sugar. The former group may still have snacks but of fruit rather than confectionery. Such habits could go back to childhood, as just described, or the unconventional snacking habit may be the result of efforts to eat more healthily (Chapter 6; Conner and Booth, 1988; Conner *et al.*, 1988b).

Appetite in Young Children

The principles of familiarization and social or nutritional association appear capable of explaining much of the development of eating motivation through childhood and into adult life. However, some apparent anomalies must be considered.

Food Preferences and Aversions

A young child by and large accepts what is provided, gets used to it, and is reinforced for accepting it by social participation, the removal of hunger pangs, a comforting sense of fullness and warmth and unconscious after-effects of nutritional improvement signalled via the gut wall, liver metabolism or receptor systems in the brain.

Finickiness and being choosey among foods may sometimes be due to a sensitivity to nasty tastes, such as some bitter compounds, difficult textures or irritants. It may be a neophobic tendency, perhaps cultivated by insufficient exposure to variety earlier or pickiness about food on the parent's part. It could be self-assertion: I'm a baked-beans boy or the peanut-butter-and-jelly king.

Children are commonly seen to eat foods out of the home that they adamantly refuse at home. This illustrates the social character of eating. The emotional meaning of a piece of cheese at home where one likes just bread and jam is quite different from the same cheese on a toothpick from a pile from which one's playmates are grabbing handfuls at a friend's birthday party. It would not be surprising if the child even thought that the cheese tasted better at the party.

Some children worry their parents by rejecting a wide range of foods or eating what appears to be a very small amount. However, if the child is growing normally, there must be enough being eaten and it is in a decent nutritional balance. Persistence in occasional offers of small amounts of other items and encouraging a sense of adventure when eating out will maximize the chance of eventually widening the range. If the child will eat only ham sandwiches and chocolate, it may not be ideal but it is not necessarily at all unhealthy: maybe the child would get to like some fruit if served with chocolate sauce; perhaps toasting the bread or putting dressing on the ham would widen the palate.

Young children particularly may feel unwell for a day or two and lose their appetite. If they leave out a food and then get well, the illness should not be blamed on that food: it is likely to be pure coincidence, because intolerances and allergies to specific food constituents are quite rare and very often grown out of.

Initiating an Eating Bout

From a very young age, we are liable to eat a tidbit that is offered or that we come across in the course of other activity. The more difficult issue is what causes us to ask for food or make opportunities to eat. The usual presumption is that an empty gut and the metabolic changes that follow the end of absorption will dispose the weaned infant to want to eat and make verbal or other signals of desire for food.

However, socialization to the family's eating places and times can provide alternative or augmenting signals. It can seem sufficiently long since one last ate or the time on the clock approaches the habitual hour. Others may be eating or going to get food.

The disposition to eat can be focused on a particular food and may then become compelling on attention. This might be called a craving. Again it may arise simply because the occasion is appropriate and it has been a relatively long time since that food was eaten.

None of this need reflect digestive or metabolic need or signals. Addictions may have metabolic bases in some cases, such as cigarettes, opiates, stimulants and calories. Yet even these cravings can intensify or recur from purely social or emotional causes, just like other appetites such as for sex, play, gambling, driving fast or paddling in the sea.

Meal-Eating Habits

What, when and where eating occurs is more than just an aggregation of food preferences and initiated bouts of eating. Complex cognitive and behavioural structures are established for eating situations, commonly centred on the construct of a meal or its variants such as a snack, 'a bite to eat', a barbecue, a banquet and so on. .

Eating habits develop first from practices in the home. Then visits to other families' homes and to play group, school and other social groups may widen the repertoire, as do vicarious experiences of people eating in TV programmes and advertisements.

The traditional meal, seated at a table with other members of the family or friends, persists in homes, outside eating places and in media presentations. However, the readily available packet foods have made eating possible almost anywhere, not only seated reading, watching events or travelling but also while walking around the house or down the street. The habits are generally acquired by joining in with siblings, parents, peers at pre-school, older children and other adults, as well as models of all those types seen in TV commercials and other media presentations.

The complex interactions between psychological, cultural and technological processes can be illustrated by British television commercials for small portions of fish in batter, but stored frozen and ready to grill, not needing deep frying. These 'fish fingers' are sold primarily for children's early evening meals in the home but are eaten at any meal, including breakfast, and by adults as well as children when convenience and lightness are at a premium. Advertising of one major brand of fish fingers has been centred on an avuncular seaman. This emphasizes the natural origin of the food. It goes over as friendly enough to the child while being reassuring to the adult who will make the purchasing decision and probably most of the serving decisions, even if the child asks for fish fingers in the supermarket or at mealtime. However, the portion is sometimes broken open in a commercial, to expose chunky white fish under the batter. This is in line with the British insistence on cod or haddock wrapped inside the deep-fried batter in the traditional fish and chips. The commercials do not show the ketchup that replaces the salt and vinegar, nor do they call attention to the fat in the batter that is necessary for grilling.

Appetite in Adolescence

Eating habits diversify further as children become partly independent of adults, have some money to spend as they wish and spend leisure in groups meeting at clubs, on the street and in eating places.

Grazing

The adolescent is often physically very active and at times is also growing faster than at any other period of life except the first few months. Therefore individuals differ greatly in how much food they need and one individual can vary over time as well. Feelings of hunger and occasions to eat may recur six or ten times a day, unlike the conventional pattern of three meals a day, and often skipping breakfast and skimping lunch.

If an adequate amount is eaten on each occasion, its after-effects are likely to moderate appetite at the next snack, both in theory (Booth and Mather, 1978) and as observed in young children (Birch *et al.*, 1991). The likelihood of overeating may even be less than with meals forced to be further apart in time.

Food Preferences

Children's preferences as measured in research to date do not match those of their parents at all well, despite the commonalities of genes and environment. This is true of toddlers (Birch, 1980) and of student-age offspring (Pliner and Pelchat, 1989).

This could be because checklists, rankings or ratings of food names or even food samples are not actually measuring the strengths with which alternative food-stuffs are preferred over each other. However, even if preferences are being measured adequately, it may be quite unrealistic to assume that the similarities of genetic endowment and early eating environment should be reflected in preferences.

Foods are often presented in different forms and contexts to infants and toddlers from those offered to older children, let alone served by the adults in the family to themselves. Some of the foods are entirely different. Then children are offered foods in other homes and in nursery and school groups that may differ in recipe and type from that presented in the home. Older children select a further variety of items in the shops and eating outlets that they frequent with or without one or both parents. Also, both teenagers and adults select foods and get to like them for many purposes besides family eating, such as at celebrations and parties, for lunches raising money for famine relief or at the latest eating or drinking place. There is not necessarily therefore any 'family paradox' in very low correlations between food preference scores of parents and their offspring at any age.

Body Perception and Eating

From the effect of doll modelling seen by Birch, it seems that children acquire the idea of filling the stomach very early in life. In students, ratings of filling and fattening expectations from foodstuffs are highly correlated. By the age of 10 or even 8, some children who are not overweight are concerned about their shape and have begun to act like dieters. (Chapter 7 goes into this in more detail.)

Children naturally tend to become self-conscious about their appearance and the shapes of their bodies when they change rapidly. Culturally and personally significant diversity in shape and size becomes highly visible when growth spurts and secondary sexual characteristics develop at different ages and in different ways. Comparisons with young adults that a teenager would like to emulate become more direct as full height is approached. There may be ten years between puberty and full maturation of physique.

A stigma is attached to being fat among quite young schoolchildren, contributing to teasing and bullying. A large part of this stigma is attributions of laziness and greed about food. A belief that eating too much makes you fat is acquired at a very young age. When slimming and dieting loom so large in adult life, it is only to be expected that pre-teens take on those preoccupations and practices, just as they can pick up cigarette smoking or substantial consumption of alcohol if available and presented relevantly to the child's self-image. Even eight-year-olds can become sufficiently preoccupied with dieting to be too strict on their eating; as a result, they are so hungry, emotional and ill-equipped to resist temptation that they will continue eating after having been tricked into taking a snack (Hill *et al.*, 1989). This is a replication in children of the experimental test for 'breakdown of dietary restraint' that has often succeeded in adult dieters (Herman and Polivy, 1980).

This stigma on fatness is paradoxically and viciously strong for the sex whose shape is naturally more rounded. The reasons for this pressure on women to be slim are considered in Chapter 4 but it can be literally fatal for some young girls. Even when the female teenager is take into hospital, brought up to weight and counselled on her emotional problems, up to one in four later dies from starvation amid plenty, other forms of suicide or increased susceptibility to disease. This extreme reduction in food intake is based on an intense preoccupation with avoiding fat or any appearance or feel of fleshiness on the bones, so that muscle is also called 'fat'. The size of the body is regarded as unrealistically large, particularly relative to clothing sizes, such as the waist measurement of jeans that are judged to fit well (Fuller, 1980; Booth, Fuller and Lewis, 1981). Other difficulties with growing up and a perfectionist, obsessional, depressive or dramatizing temperament may also be preconditions for this self-starvation based on loathing for normal shape. Nevertheless, practices of severe dieting, such as having only green salad for main meals and eating in tiny mouthfuls ('like a bird'), can become habitual when sufficiently motivated initially. Hunger pangs decline during prolonged starvation and the pleasures of eating are forgotten. Indeed, they can be compensated to some extent by the pleasures of preparing food for others and watching them enjoy it: the family may refrain from pressing a self-starving young woman to eat while she cooks for them.

The prevalence of distress, disease and death from this disorder of eating, as well as of the stress and health risks from less compulsive and less 'successful' dieting, would presumably reduce if there was more respect for diversity of shape and even admiration for individuality in different aspects of appearance. Mass communications and large-scale manufacturing and marketing may continue to develop ways of meeting minority interests better and provide alternatives to the average item or least unpopular activity. Young people, particularly women, currently suffer most from dieting and its disorders. However, dieting as well as exercising appear to be taking a hold among younger men now. The cult of slimness cannot be undermined merely by educating the young. Adult culture will have to change as well and the gender discrimination behind much of the concern with shape be removed too.

Appetite in Older People

Age brings longer and sometimes wider experience of all aspects of life, including the uses of food and drink. Eating habits continued into later life are therefore liable if anything to have become more strongly engrained. Unless used to trying new things when younger, an older person may have very fixed food preferences. This may not always be good for the health, because the older style of diet was not so balanced nutritionally or even perhaps some nutritious items are no longer available or have become expensive. Lifelong habits may not be entirely appropriate any more because the useful intakes of some vitamins and minerals may go up in older people while energy requirements may decrease. On the other hand, what someone has lived off and enjoyed for half a century can in general hardly be unwise enough to warrant interference.

Yet age is also liable to bring cause for changes in eating habits. Sometimes health deteriorates and a change in diet is called for to sustain recovery or help ward off worse. Widespread changes in the food supply to support healthier eating in general, without special health claims or premium prices, can help ease such changes later in life.

Retirement from a paid job can bring to an end a substantial part of a person's social and physical activities. Other roles may or may not be developed instead. Occasions to meet and have a drink or meal can become much fewer. The result can be loss of some of the incentives to eat in amount and variety. At this time too, income usually decreases without as much of a reduction in outgoings, when offspring have long since become independent and the family house paid for; indeed, while still a senior employee without major domestic expenditures, an older person may be living better than ever and eating out and buying expensive foods and drinks, whereas moving onto a pension may constrain the finances even for shopping for ordinary meals at home. On the other hand, pensions and other post-retirement income can be good enough and time to travel and socialize so much greater, that life has never been better.

With age also comes increasing liability to a variety of mild or sometimes serious physical and psychological problems. Maybe some of these arise from normal ageing but injuries and illnesses obviously take their toll. Mobility, hearing, sight, smell or recent memory may decline, affecting shopping, cooking and maybe the enjoyment of food. Losses of ability, of social contacts and roles and of loved ones may become unmanageably depressing. A general hopelessness and helplessness often comes with a physical inertia and a loss of interest in the simple pleasures of life. So, for example, appetite for food is often less during clinical depression or normal grieving. Nevertheless, many older people remain as upbeat and energetic as most younger ones do when trouble strikes; eating well is a good coping or compensating strategy and diet is not the slightest problem.

Do Defects in Flavour Perception Affect Appetite?

A particular possibility among this array of conceivable changes in appetite mechanisms in older people has attracted research attention recently in both psychology and nutrition. Declines in the senses of smell, taste and texture may reduce food preferences and so prejudice nutrient intake.

Unfortunately, all the data on this possibility are very indirect. It is still not widely realized that sensory influences on everyday food choice and intake in an individual can be estimated at all, let alone with relative ease and accuracy if the specific issue is properly conceived and appropriate tests divined.

Thus groups of older and younger people are compared on nutrient intakes and/or sensitivities to particular taste or odour compounds that have been estimated by standard methods which are rather rough and ready and so only suited to comparisons between groups in any case. This ignores the great individual differences in food preferences and dietary intakes, and the complex sequences of changing cognitive processes that determine the food selections that cumulate into average nutrient intakes.

Alternatively, sensory thresholds and reported food likings or frequencies are compared. These are not measures of sensory influences on an individual's choices among foods either. The only directly relevant information is the effect of differences in a sensed constituent on a person's choice of a food, relative to other influences on that choice. The effect depends on the relation between the individual's sensitivity to that constituent and how distant the available item's characteristics are from that person's ideal level for that attribute of the foodstuff.

Only if such relations can be established for some particular food choices would there begin to be evidence whether sensory deficits affect nutrient intake. If insensitivity to bitterness does not affect a person's choice between cabbage and other vegetables not containing that sort of taste, it is unlikely that the sensory deficit is affecting intake of green vegetables, let alone of roughage or vitamins in them.

The discriminativeness of preference among levels of a tastant has been measured in one or two experiments comparing different ages (Booth, Conner and Gibson, 1989; Gilmore and Murphy, 1989) but further methodological development is needed to relate such measures to everyday eating.

Further Reading

The following books consider practical implications of research into the development of appetite in infants and children.

St. James-Roberts, I., Harris, G. and Messer, D. (1993) *Infant crying, feeding and sleeping*, New York, Harvester Wheatsheaf.
Satter, E. (1987) *How to get your kid to eat . . . but not too much*, Palo Alto, CA, Bull.

Chapter 3

Physiological Influences on Appetite

Ways in which the body might influence the mind to affect decisions about eating and drinking are considered from a psychological viewpoint.

Do We Eat from Need?

Everybody assumes that a lack of nutrients excites appetite. In the biomedical sciences, it is taken for granted that thirst comes from messages that a lack of water in the body sends to the brain and that hunger arises from signals of need for food. It seems equally obvious that a full stomach reduces interest in food, or at least in some items if not all foods and drinks.

Indeed, so incontrovertible have these ideas seemed that even the psychologists have long regarded hunger and thirst as biological 'drives'. Depending on the theorist, a drive has been defined as the operation of withholding food or water, the resulting physical state of tissue deficit or a general excitation of behaviour that has been induced by the lack of water or food. A great deal of attention was then paid by psychologists of learning to the question of how a generic arousal can produce specific behaviour. Not only do we and other mammals suck or bite after food or water deprivation; our ingestive movements can be selectively directed towards the water or calorific materials we need. Physiological psychologists tended to ignore this theoretical problem, however, and assumed that water deficit produced water intake and energy deficit produced food intake without worrying how the behaviour was organized to achieve such outcomes. The psychologists of animal behaviour believed that they had debunked drive theory by showing that rats work hard for the mere taste of saccharin. Physiological psychologists sidestepped that point by imagining that our species survived by getting all the calories needed at critical times from sweet-tasting things. That however is a most implausible principle around which to build the brain (see Chapters 1, 2 and 8).

Similarly, in medical physiology, hunger, thirst and satiety were defined as bodily sensations caused by the state of the stomach, mouth or blood. When it was realized that people sometimes ate without stomach contractions and drank without a dry mouth, 'general' sensations had to be invoked; these were thought of as unconscious products of brain activity, rather than conscious experiences generated from stimulation of the periphery.

A more sophisticated medical concept is that of a sense of thirst, hunger or satiety. This is a judgment of what is needed by the body that does necessarily rely on awareness of a bodily sensation. Indeed, a 'sense' of something does not have to be conscious, although in medical research that awareness is presupposed as part of a general presumption that psychology is only about the contents of consciousness. A sense of thirst or hunger is the ability of the water or food intake or the verbally expressed desire for water or food to match the extent of depletion or repletion with some accuracy. This is to construe the rating of thirst or hunger and indeed the ingestive behaviour as psychophysical judgments. That is realistic so long as the presumed internal stimuli are indeed specific to lack of water or energy and can be distinguished from other events inside and outside the body, just as the usual stimulus that the psychophysicist presents has to be unconfounded by other information.

Nevertheless, despite this widespread presumption that we know very well when our bodies need food or drink, a surprising number of experiments on people eating normally (and indeed on experimental animals too) have failed to show influences specifically on ingestive appetite from the actions in the body of ordinary foods and drinks, or of a lack of nutriment.

The cognitive approach taken in this book provides one basis for seeking to reconcile these discrepancies in the research literature on the physiology of normal appetite. On this view, acts of eating and drinking behaviour result from the integration of information from foods and drinks, from the eating or drinking occasion and from the state of the body, all with reference to past experiences of those sources of information. Thus the effect of the current signals from the body may be strong or weak but in either case it will be highly contingent on other current influences.

Hence, influences on appetite from the digestive tract or from the tissues of the body might easily be overwhelmed when the circumstances differ greatly from usual, because the physiological influences depend on that wider context. Another possibility must be considered, though, once we have allowed adequately for these confoundings and interdependencies: this is that current bodily state often has no influence on appetite. Rather, the effects of current external influences may depend to some extent on what they have meant for the body in the past but current bodily state has no effect in familiar circumstances.

In either case it will not be easy to get evidence for what in fact are major physiological influences on ingestive behaviour, if they exist. Investigators must measure all the major momentary inputs to the cognitive processes controlling ingestion and analyse that causal structure in ways that allow for the eater's learning history. Current influences from tissue depletion or food in the gut may only be reliably measurable in the context of familiar eating environments and habits. Instead or as well, we may have to measure the body's messages to the brain at the time when they exert their influence by reinforcing those habits and environmental cues that exert all the immediate control. Major physiological influences will then only be detectable when new learning occurs as a result of changes in the contingencies between perceived aspects of eating occasions and their neurally monitorable physiological consequences.

The long-standing and wide-reaching separation between biological and cognitive sciences has prevented these complexities from being tackled very effectively to date. So there are rather few data that are both physiologically and psychologically interpretable concerning the bodily influences on normal human hunger, thirst and satieties for water and food. One view of the existing information is offered below, first dealing with the appetite for water and then addressing appetite for food.

Thirst and Its Satiation

A healthy adult will begin to complain of thirst when the osmotic pressure ('tonicity') of the blood is raised by lack of water (Wolf, 1958). This osmotic effect is readily created by infusing a hypertonic salt solution – that is, one that has a higher osmotic pressure than the blood normally has (isotonic). This is a remarkably sensitive mechanism. A rise in tonicity by as little as 2–3 per cent can be enough to trigger what a person rates as a strong desire to drink and an immediate drink of water in a hitherto water-sated human being, monkey, sheep or rat.

An even more impressive facet of this cognitive performance of recognizing the state of one's body is the fact that the relationship between the rated strength of thirst and the osmotic pressure of the blood is close to a straight line (Robertson, 1991). As we saw in Chapter 1, this means that we can measure how good thirst ratings are at discriminating between blood tonicities, regardless of exactly how the ratings were done. This is a psychophysical function, just like a plot of sweetness intensity ratings against sugar levels. From a linear regression, we can estimate the proportional change in tonicity that is halfway between being so large that it is certain to alter the thirst rating and so small that it makes absolutely no difference to the degree of thirst. From Robertson's data, thirst ratings seem to be able to distinguish blood tonicity differences as low as a fraction of a percent. Such acuity compares very well with the external chemical senses such as taste where Weber ratios go down to as sensitive as about 10 per cent at best; such discrimination is more of the order of visual acuities.

However, this tightness of control of drinking behaviour by a rise in osmotic pressure of the blood may be exceeded by the brain's response to the same change as an indication of a need to conserve water (as well as to take it in). The antidiuretic hormone (ADH; also called vasopressin) increases the kidney's efficiency at getting water back from urine as it filters from the blood. ADH is secreted from the base of the brain both at a lower osmotic threshold osmolality and also in a more precise straight line.

This greater sensitivity of ADH secretion than of thirst is generally interpreted as adaptive: it may be less costly in the wild to start concentrating the urine than to risk an immediate search for water. However, that interpretation would bear further investigation. Thirst thresholds are very variable. Indeed, they no longer appear to be higher than those for vasopressin secretion when thirst is rated at frequent intervals (Thompson *et al.*, 1981). Thus it is conceivable that the vigour of a person's or experimental animal's call for water could be trained to discriminate finer differences in level of the osmotic cue from the blood. In other words, maybe our sense of water depletion, like a hunter's use of the nose, can become more acute than it is in the uses to which we normally learn to put it.

Indeed, a question has been raised about the universal assumption that the desire for water is an unlearned response to a rise in blood tonicity that has somehow been preprogrammed into vertebrate brains (see discussion following Booth, 1991a). As mentioned in Chapter 2, there is no evidence that human babies have a preference for consuming water specifically when depleted only of water until an age of several months. By that time, they are likely to have had experience of correction of water deficit by a fluid such as milk, juice or water and of differences between those contingencies and the rather effective removal of hunger by solid foods for example, as well as by milk. Conclusive physiologically controlled behavioural evidence for congenital thirst is similarly lacking in experimental animals, which contrasts with the case for innate sodium appetite in rats and sheep. Yet we know that human babies and rat pups can learn such discriminations in external sensory modalities from the earliest days after birth. Hence the onus of proof can be placed on those who claim that the mammalian appetites for water and energy are inborn.

Thirst Without Water Deficit

There is another reason for examining the possibility of roles for learning in drinking in response to water deficit. So far as the evidence goes, it seems that most human drinking occurs without an appreciable rise in the osmolality of the blood (Phillips *et al.*, 1984). Nevertheless, some of this so-called 'need-free drinking' might well in fact be indirectly controlled by need. There may be inherited mechanisms or learnable processes by which drinking can anticipate and prevent a water deficit that would otherwise arise in those circumstances. Hence research into learning from effects of drinking on water deficit might uncover ways in which the need-free desire to drink has been established by past experience.

For example, drinking is associated with the eating of meals in people and in some domesticated animals. The digestion of food draws considerable volumes of fluid into the gut. Absorption increases the osmotic pressure of the blood and increases the amount of water required by the kidneys to excrete waste products. Thus, most meals create demands on body water and so drinking before and during a meal can prevent a deficit and may even avoid a deficit-induced thirst. There are inbuilt anticipatory mechanisms (Kraly, 1990) but eating-induced drinking may be learnt too.

Some drinking away from occasions of substantial food intake may also be need-anticipatory. Drinks are often taken in the middle of periods of work or leisure activity. Sometimes the level of physical activity after the drink may be sufficient to increase water loss through the lungs and perhaps by sweating. Protein metabolism puts extra demands on excretion and hence body water content (Fitzsimons and Le Magnen, 1969). In such circumstances, the between-meal drink may be partly motivated by a wish to avoid thirst that is expected to arise when fluid is not so conveniently available.

Thirst for a particular type of water source could also arise from a sense of frustration or malaise. If someone remembers liking a particular drink but has not allowed themselves to indulge in it and now feels the situation requires it, then that item may become strongly desired; we feel a craving for it. It is commonly said that the desire for a beer rises sharply at the moment the pubs open towards the end of the day.

A more esoteric example is the fashion there once was for eating ice, to which people suffering from anaemia were particularly disposed. Lack of iron is unlikely to create a water deficit or a deficit signal. A slight malaise or change in sensory input might however induce a dependence on sensual excitement that could readily be satisfied by chewing pieces of ice. Such a habit of consuming a non-nutritive material is called pica. Someone compulsively managing subtle symptoms in this way may not be able to describe what is going on. People do not have to be aware of the origins of their cravings for them to be 'psychological' in this way, rather than being specific innate responses to a determinate signal of need. After all, a need-driven desire to drink can 'come from nowhere' after a meal or work in low humidity or perhaps as the blood caffeine or alcohol goes below the habitual level.

Need-anticipatory drinking could also arise by processes unavailable to attention. Recognition of water deficit or its imminence would then be like recognition of a face, a colour or a smell. Even a bodily sensation that we call one of thirst might in fact be an epiphenomenon or an illusion and no part of the processes that actually excite an interest in water consumption. Dryness of the mouth is certainly not necessary for a current water deficit to cause drinking. People and animals with poorly functioning salivary glands still take adequate amounts of water without drinking all the time.

These issues cannot be addressed simply by asking people questions when they have been made water-deficient or want to drink as a result of other influences. To make progress in cognitive physiology, all potential influences, both cognitive and physiological, must be separated from each other, i.e. varied in a way that prevents their strengths being correlated.

Blood tonicity after hypertonic saline infusion correlates with ratings of dryness of the mouth and unpleasantness of oral sensation (Phillips *et al.*, 1985). Volunteers also say that they have drunk enough water when these sensations go away. However, as well as slowing the loss of water through the kidneys, plasma hypertonicity reduces the flow of saliva. This thickens the mucus in the mouth, creating an unpleasant sticky sensation which is attributed to drying out. Therefore the correlation between dry mouth and thirst could reflect parallel effects of the water deficit. Hence it is not evidence for a causal contribution of the dry sensation to the desire to drink.

Experimental drying of the mouth by peripheral agents that do not affect blood tonicity might also provide evidence for a role of the dry-mouth sensation in thirst. However, a failure to find such evidence out of the context of normal drinking and water deficits may only reflect the artificiality of that test. There is no reason at all why the desire to drink should not emerge directly from the brain's processing of the osmotic signal, unmediated by any external loop such as the sensing of some effect of water conservation or preparation for intake.

Illuminating variations in mouth wetting might be more feasible under normal conditions. The dryness is only briefly reduced by wetting the mouth. People suffering from medical conditions involving chronic dryness of the mouth also get only slight relief from drinking. The normal dryness only goes when water is absorbed, correcting the osmotic pressure of the blood and restoring salivation.

A feeling of a refreshed mouth after a fruity tasting drink may provide a research opening (S.J. French *et al.*, 1993). Acids are a strong unlearned stimulus to salivation. Hence, wetting of the mouth may continue for a while after such a drink has been swallowed, while the water in the drink will have independent effects considerably later. Even if this mouthwetting after-effect of sourness is slight, it is so prompt that it may dominate the memory of the thirst-quenching power of that drink.

Non-osmotic Thirst

A water deficit could in principle reduce the volume of the blood and of the fluids between cells in the tissues of the body: this is called hypovolaemia. In some animals, it causes drinking. A preference for salt as well as plain water shows up in hypovolaemia; this is functional, because it replaces fluid missing from the blood at the tonicity and sodium concentration that it should be.

However, water deprivation may not induce hypovolaemic thirst in people (Rolls, 1991). Exercise does initially (Greenleaf *et al.*, 1977), as fluid is transferred to the active muscle cells. However, temperature also increases and at this early stage thirst is inhibited rather than stimulated. Sweating and, of course, any bleeding will also deplete the body of fluid. Nevertheless, there are several pints of fluid outside cells to cover incipient water deficit without raising blood tonicity. There is no clear evidence for thirst in people who lack water in the absence of a rise in osmotic pressure of the blood.

Slaking of Thirst

Drinking commonly reduces the desire for fluid or a wet food and sometimes completely eliminates it for a while. This water-specific satiety may well be under some physiological control. The control does not have to be strong, however, because a substantial excess of water is readily excreted. The adaptive value of any inherited water-satiety signals would be to limit the time spent drinking at a waterhole with predators around.

A rapidly consumed drink cannot be brought to an end by removal of the signals of water deficit that may have instigated the thirst: there has been no time for much, if any, water to be absorbed. Furthermore, the water deficit has drawn on all 'reserves' of water in the tissues and gut and so the act of drinking or its sensory effects cannot trigger a release of substantial amounts of water in anticipation of replenishment from the drink. Hence, thirst has declined to a major extent before the osmotic pressure of the blood has been reduced below the thirst threshold.

Dogs lap up water very fast and have been popular experimental subjects for physiologists of fluid intake. It was soon discovered that a dog used to the experimental conditions will take a drink that is remarkably similar in size to the water deficit that has been induced by infusion. The infusion creates signals that bear no relation to the time, activities and temperatures since the last drink. Yet the signals control how much the animal drinks. The reason may be that, like any of us, the animal has lifelong experience of restoring water deficits created by excretory losses and by breathing and panting (or sweating in our case). So it has had every opportunity to learn how much to drink in order to cover the usual deficit and hence get rid of the signals from it later when most of the water will have been absorbed or perhaps put to use in digestion of food.

This skill was dubbed 'oral metering' by the physiologists. Somehow the mouth measures the volume and tells itself to stop when appropriate. This however merely states the problem; it does nothing to solve it. How does the mouth measure drink volume? How does it know the right amount?

Do the drinking muscles get fatigued? Do the oral sensations from water become boring? Does the dog (or do we) count the laps (or sips) or swallows? Does the dog time itself, given a constant rate of drinking? There is some recent work on rats drinking saccharin solutions (for their sweetness, though, not for thirst) that seems to have excluded all these possibilities except counting swallows, or perhaps licks or bursts of licks (Mook and Wagner, 1989). Presumably rats, dogs and even we do not count swallows in numbers. Perhaps somewhere in the brainstem a neural circuit becomes more and more excited as swallow follows swallow in rapid succession and sufficient excitation shuts down the facilitation of drinking by the deficit signals.

However, thirst is not reduced purely by swallowing movements. Swallowing food did not reduce drinking in dogs (Ramsay and Thrasher, 1986) and seems not to in us. Yet the swallowing of hypertonic saline transiently reduces thirst ratings (Seckl *et al.*, 1986) and dogs on a water-deprivation schedule drank the same amount of isotonic saline in a test in which they usually received water (Thrasher *et al.*, 1981). Maybe the mechanoreceptors in the back of the mouth distinguish whether fluid or solid is being swallowed and a learned or unlearned inhibition of thirst occurs accordingly.

There are limits to the amount of a food or a drink that a person will consume on a given occasion that arise solely from the sensed characteristics of the material, such as its flavour (Rolls *et al.*, 1980). This item-specific satiety might be explained by a form of habituation or boredom. Alternatively, it could reflect the learning of a normal amount to consume. For example, volumes familiar from common drinking vessels could provide units in which drink volume is metered. This might be the information from memory that is used by a 'swallow counter' when visual cues are not available.

Even determining what is metered in drinking would still leave unsolved how the right amount is decided. A switch mechanism of the sort just described could do the job without additional complications, if more drinking-induced excitation was required to overcome the thirst from stronger deficit signals. If the appropriate number of swallows, time of drinking or degree of boredom or fatigue has to be decided in some other way, then the oral meter needs calibrating. 'Calibrational learning' has been invoked to explain the navigational skills of birds and bees. So something of the sort would not be so extraordinary in order to navigate the waters of the body. Nevertheless, this idea is really just another name for a mystery. Testable mechanisms should be specified and indeed the simplest possibilities excluded first if possible.

Associative learning involves relatively simple mechanisms, seen even in animals without backbones. In one form of learning a response tendency (like ingestion) becomes stronger when associated with a reinforcing consequence. One of the more straightforward sorts of associative learning that could provide control of the quantity drunk would be the reinforcement of extra drinking by a shortfall in the water yielded below full relief of the deficit. Drink flavour preferences can apparently be conditioned by association with water yield in water-deprived rats (Revusky, 1968; Booth, 1979b). Alternatively or as well, overdrinking may already have been punished by uncomfortable fullness, say; this aversive consequence might be reduced, and hence the learned moderation of drinking extinguished, as a result of something like faster emptying of the stomach when a large water deficit is signalled to the brain. Resolution of such issues demands a conjunction of physiology and analysis of the cognitive processes controlling behaviour. However, this combination of expertise has yet to be developed in human research or in experiments on any other species.

Such conditioning effects are not constrained to one stimulus modality, such as the number of fluid swallows. In combination with a throat signal, or even instead of it, the size of the drink might be decided by a conditioned response to a cue from the stomach. For a given level of muscular tone in the wall of the stomach, the tension in the gastric wall will be determined by the volume in the stomach. Hence gastric distension can provide a good measure of drink size.

The amount in the stomach does indeed help to stop a water-deprived rat or monkey from coming back to take some more water within a few minutes of finishing the first drink, as shown by draining the fluid from the stomach (Blass and Hall, 1976; Maddison *et al.*, 1980). Nevertheless, it does take a few minutes for the animal with an empty stomach to start drinking again. This indicates that signals from the mouth or throat are sufficient initially. Furthermore, dogs used to drinking after water deprivation drank no more in the first hour when water was drained from the stomach than when it was not (Ramsay and Thrasher, 1986). So the stomach is not always involved.

It would be a mistake, though, to suppose that the mouth and throat were not involved at all when a gastric cue contributes to preventing a return to drinking. Delivering the water directly to the stomach via a tube bypassing sensations and movements in the mouth and throat may not be as effective as the combination of oropharyngeal and gastric cues. This could be a threshold effect of addition between the two sources of satiety or its could be a learned coordination between mouth and stomach cues. Only careful behavioural physiology could determine.

At present, the evidence from drinking is consistent with the standard concept of an overlapping succession of satiety factors. First there is only transient stimulation of the mouth and throat and memory of that stimulation or activity in the past. Then there comes a rather more prolonged satiety from stomach and upper intestine. Finally, after a delay but then sustained, there is satiation (or simply lack of thirst) from the circulation and tissues. This is an additive sequence, without amplification of earlier effects by later effects as in a metabolic cascade. However, this picture of the physiological control of slaking of thirst could change as soon as possibilities of learning processes (Holland, 1991) or cognitive control of drink size and thirst induction (Booth, 1991a) are adequately examined.

Hunger and Its Satiety

Physiologists and ecologists share the working hypothesis that, after water, energy is the requirement that is most urgently served by foraging and ingestion. Unfortunately for understanding the psychology of eating, however, both sides of biology have developed approaches to food intake that neglect the behavioural processes involved.

Function versus Mechanism

The ecologists have developed theories of optimal foraging. These attempt to estimate how adaptive in natural selection different strategies of using feeding sites and food materials would have been. In principle, these theories use overall reproductive success (inclusive evolutionary fitness) as the criterion. Nevertheless, more practicable intermediate criteria of adaptiveness are often used, e.g. the efficiency of a foraging strategy in net yield of metabolic energy. A bird that hovers over flowers to gather nectar and a dock labourer in a poor country on a subsistence diet share the problem that they spend almost as much energy getting food as the food provides.

Concepts from economics are also applicable to animal foraging (Collier, 1980; Lea *et al.*, 1987) and of course to human food choice (Moskowitz, 1983). These ecological and economic analyses are unquestionably worthwhile enterprises. Indeed, they are essential to advances in our understanding of interactions between species and habitats, since observations of actual evolution are so fragmentary.

However, the optimization approaches do not have to attend to a biological question that is no less legitimate: how does the individual animal decide when, where, what and how much to eat? A preoccupation with evolutionary fitness or economic logic has distracted some investigators from the fact that issues of mechanism are also there to be addressed.

The physiologists have also created a diversion from mechanistic investigation by developing their own sort of functional explanation. This is the notion of homeostatic regulation of the internal environment, which has become central to integrative or whole-organism physiology. The homeostatic approach thinks of food (or water) intake as output from a natural system that functions similarly to thermostatically controlled air conditioning built by human engineers. Indeed, one of the homeostatic functions that has been suggested for food intake is maintaining constancy of body temperature (the thermostatic theory of feeding control: Brobeck, 1947/8). A more modern version invokes regulation of food intake by the measurement of heat production by metabolism in the body, minus the work done by muscular activity (ischymetric regulation of food intake: Nicolaïdis, 1974, 1984). The homeostatic theories of hunger that are in all the textbooks invoke a metabolic variable related to a macronutrient, i.e. glucose for carbohydrate metabolism (glucostasis), amino acids for protein (aminostasis) or triglycerides for fat (lipostasis).

The regulated variable is often said to be concentration in the blood but this is unrealistic. Mayer (1955), for example, insisted that the glucostatic theory was not based on blood glucose concentration (which, after all, as he pointed out, can get very high in diabetes without preventing hunger) but on the uptake of glucose into a tissue that served as a satiety/hunger sensor. The lipostatic theory (Kennedy, 1952) invokes the level of triglycerides stored in adipose tissue, signalled to the brain by some unspecified factor in the blood. Again, the concentration of the fat-store signal need not be the regulated variable: it could be rate of uptake or some neural action that depends on other factors such as glucose metabolism.

The homeostatic concept is scientifically useful only so long as it is used to seek out the mechanisms by which any such regulation of the internal environment is achieved. Instead, a lot of research has been and continues to be directed at demonstrating (or refuting) the mere occurrence of good regulation. Often, it is not even homeostasis that is investigated: no hypothetically regulated internal variable is measured; rather the cumulative intake of energy or of some particular nutrient is expected to recover from imposed restriction or excess and this recovery or compensation is called regulation. Such observations tell us nothing of how the system works. At best, they provide no more than phenomena to be explained.

The issue is, given that intake does respond in some way to a disturbance, by what processes does that response come about? The identity and even the existence of a regulated variable are issues that can be left on one side while we study the mechanisms actually operative in given circumstances where something systematic is happening. It does nothing to advance our understanding of the mechanisms of intake control to postulate a fixed or sliding value of an unmeasured internal variable that is compared in some unspecified place with the current value to produce unknown corrective actions that result in the observed response. This 'set point' language is vacuous, as are the phrases 'homeostatic behaviour' and 'regulatory response', when they are used as no more than labels for differences in intake observed between presumed degrees of need.

Metabolic and Gastrointestinal Control of Hunger/Satiety

To be of scientific use, then, a theory that food intake serves a regulatory function must specify testable hypotheses as to the mechanisms involved. What processes excite and/or inhibit eating in ways that might help to steady an observable physiological variable?

The strength of various candidate corrective mechanisms of hunger and satiety can be measured by the extent to which the regulated variable is kept constant. Assuming that storage or loss of a nutrient does not vary, intake compensates for changes in intake that would disturb the availability of that nutrient in the body. This was the use originally made in freely fed rats of the concepts of 'behavioural caloric compensation' (Booth, 1972a) and 'energostatic' control of food intake (Booth, 1972b). The mechanism being manipulated to affect food intake was the flow of any source of metabolic energy from absorption to its oxidation in the liver. This was achieved by waiting for the volume and osmotic effects of the energy loads to decline sufficiently for their only effects on food intake to be exerted as a result of absorption. The strength of satiation was measured in terms of the number of calories by which food intake went down by delaying meals and reducing their size. The differences in cumulative food intake were completed before the second meal, even after the largest loads, and approximated to the load within a short while after the end of absorption (Booth and Jarman, 1976).

Unfortunately, the notion of caloric compensation of intake was taken up as a measure of the 'regulatory response' to a food or food constituent, instead of using experimental designs capable of distinguishing among possible mechanisms by which the compensatory effect was induced. Theoretically meaningless (and potentially health-endangering) statements are made that the intake of fat or starch or sugar or this or that substitute is or is not well compensated (or indeed stimulates intake). A food or a food constituent cannot have a fixed effect on intake.

The fundamental scientific question is, rather, what excitatory or inhibitory mechanisms are stimulated by specified actions of food under specified conditions. The practical question for human health is what the effects on eating are during the opportunities that actually do arise while those hunger and satiety mechanisms have been activated.

The technique of measuring such appetite mechanisms by compensatory intake showed that the rat could be satiated by the full range of sources of energy while they were being absorbed (Booth, 1972b; Panksepp, 1971). This was evidence that all the homeostatic theories of food intake control could be combined. Only one main theory of hunger and its satiety was required, based on the net rate at which the liver was currently producing energy or taking in metabolic fuels and exporting them to other tissues (Booth, 1972a,b; Booth and Jarman, 1976). This proposal that use of energy supplies satiated eating connected with Russek's (1963) theory that liver glucose controlled hunger. Biochemists had long recognized that the liver 'spared' glucose for the brain by oxidizing any substrate, including fats, alcohol and non-glucogenic amino acids. Hans Krebs was awarded the Nobel Prize for formulating the tricarboxylic acid cycle by which any nutrient could be oxidized to produce the cellular energy 'currency', ATP. So the rate of hepatic ATP production was suggested as the basic 'energostatic' variable. (Since the idea is not regulating the amount of energy but measuring the rate at which energy is produced in cells of the liver, i.e. cellular power, a better word would be 'cytodynamometric'!)

The theory was that net energy flow to the liver is regulated by a boost in the desire for food when energy production decreased and by an inhibition of eating when power throughput increased (Booth, 1972a,b, 1976; Booth, Toates and Platt, 1976; Friedman and Stricker, 1976). Different aspects of the Krebs cycle have subsequently been invoked (Russek, 1981; Langhans *et al.*, 1983; Tordoff and Friedman, 1988). Also, anticipatory control of hepatic metabolism seems to be involved (Smith, Hoffman and Campfield, 1993), producing a dip in blood glucose before spontaneous meals. Nevertheless, the general idea is now widely accepted that metabolic control of eating centres around metabolic integration by the liver.

INTAKE MODELLING

Physiologically realistic calculations based on the energy-flow theory simulated the patterns of meals around the clock that are observed in rats under a variety of conditions (Toates and Booth, 1974; Booth, 1978). Rather disconcertingly, when the parameters were adjusted to values appropriate to a notional sedentary human adult, the computer simulation 'ate' breakfast, lunch and supper of reasonable sizes at close to the usual times (Booth and Mather, 1978)! This is not really support for the idea of strong and direct physiological control of human eating, however. It is consistent with the more realistic idea that a culture's norms for eating meals are liable to adapt to the requirements of the average adult. An important idea emerged from these rough theoretical calculations. The way that the stomach empties controls the flow of energy to the liver and so is the key to the timing of hunger and (less directly) to its suppression by eating. Predictions about gastric emptying rates made from the timings of meals on the basis of this modelling were subsequently confirmed (Newman and Booth, 1981; Duggan and Booth, 1986).

HUMAN MECHANISMS

Experiments directed at metabolic mechanisms of hunger and its satiety in human adults were run in parallel to the rat experiments. Unfortunately, the most readily observed effects of carbohydrates on eating and on what people say about food were not clearly distinguishable in origin between the upper intestine and the circulation to the liver. Most subsequent experiments on human food intake and ratings have not been designed to distinguish mechanisms at all, however. Also, although physiologically ambiguous, those old experiments did indicate some common circumstances where no satiety mechanisms are operative (Booth, 1981, 1988a). So the results will be summarized below.

Satiety Mechanisms

It is crucial to any experiment on internal mechanisms not to present the manipulation of nutrient contents in recognizable foods. Identifiably different foods have differences in culinary role, cultural stereotype and personal experience attached to them. They are therefore liable to be expected to have different satiating effects, as De Graaf and colleagues (De Graaf *et al.*, 1992) have recently confirmed. This point has not generally been recognized in work on the satiating effects of different foods, thus vitiating the interpretations offered in terms of nutrient composition. Indeed, evidence for such effects of beliefs about recognizable foodstuffs has been observed in some of the experiments that confound food identities with effects inside the body. Satiety ratings immediately after the meal, before substantial absorption is likely to have begun, showed the same pattern of differences between foods as the ratings taken an hour later (Rolls *et al.*, 1988); the effects observed after a further delay might therefore arise from expectations of the foods that had been eaten, rather than from postingestional effects of their contents. The conventional uses of the foods would create greater and more enduring satisfaction from a meal of pasta than from a meal of confectionery, for example, even if the carbohydrate and energy contents were equated.

Effects of protein on hunger

In one of the first experiments using disguised nutrient compositions to get at metabolic mechanisms of hunger (Booth, Chase and Campbell, 1970), suppression of food intake was sought after protein had been digested and absorbed. This was because some of the carbon in the absorbed amino acids might be held in muscles for later cycling to the liver as a source of energy. There was indeed evidence that protein was better than a mixture of carbohydrate and fat at keeping hunger at bay after absorption was likely to have ended.

Over shorter intervals, protein and carbohydrate disguised in gels do not appear to differ in their satiety effects (Geliebter, 1979; Sunkin and Garrow, 1982). However, protein (like starch too) often comes in particles. Some pieces of meat might be large and tough enough to take longer to get out of the stomach and/ or to be digested in the upper intestine. This principle was used to run the first adequately designed test since 1970 for the late satiating effect of protein. There was evidence for a hunger-suppressant effect of protein three hours after eating, in that larger and tougher pieces of lean meat (mostly protein) were more satiating at that time (French *et al.*, 1992).

Protein in food is very likely to be suppressing hunger also while it is still in the digestive tract. Receptors for digestion products of proteins have been detected by recording of electrical activity in nerve fibres going to the brain from the wall of the upper intestine in some species (Meï, 1985). They could inform the brain's control of eating that a source of energy has been ingested or even specifically of its proteinaceous nature, to guide protein-specific appetite (Deutsch, 1987; Baker *et al.*, 1987; Deutsch *et al.*, 1989). However, there is no direct evidence implicating intestinal protein-related receptors in eating.

Such receptors are known, though, to be important in adjusting digestive se-cretions to the diet ingested. One way they do this is by triggering the release of a hormone that stimulates pancreatic juices and bile and slows emptying of the stomach; this is called cholecystokinin (CCK) and used to be named pancreozymin also. The secretion of CCK contributes to the early satiating effects of meals in rats, monkeys and people. Normally CCK seems to augment satiety by intensifying signals from stretch in the wall of the stomach, through both keeping food longer in the stomach and also acting on the vagus nerve's transmission of the signals to the brain (Moran and McHugh, 1982). Oddly enough, although protein is known to be a major stimu-lant of CCK secretion, much of the research on CCK-induced satiety has used sugar-rich foods and roles for CCK in effects of protein ingestion on eating behaviour have not been considered.

Effects of carbohydrate on satiety

Experiments aimed at identifying metabolic satiety effects of carbohydrate in human beings began by using glucose solutions, as the rat experiments had done initially and as was standard practice in hospitals at that time for tolerance tests of blood glucose. A prompt reduction in intake was seen, even using an unpalatable test food developed for the protein tests (Booth, Chase and Campbell, 1970). However, a large volume of concentrated glucose solution has osmotic effects that tear at the back of the throat and can be nauseating if any of the solution gets through the stomach into the duodenum insufficiently diluted (Cabanac and Fantino, 1979). It is hardly surprising therefore that strong glucose loads put people off food and even make the taste of sweetness unpleasant while the glucose is being diluted and absorbed (Cabanac, Minaire and Adair, 1968). These loads also decrease the pleasantness of food aromas (Duclaux, Feisthauer and Cabanac, 1973), not just intake of unpalatable food or the pleasantness of plain sweet water – which is not a drink or a food for most people and becomes boring anyway on repeated tasting, even without a nauseating preload (Wooley, Wooley and Dunham, 1972). The key point nevertheless is that the postingestional actions of hypertonic glucose are as irrelevant to the satiating effects of normal food in people as they are in rats (see above). They can-not be used to test for regulatory functions of the decrease in pleasure from sensations of eating (Cabanac, 1971). This requires a form of carbohydrate that contributes to normal satiety in its postingestional effects on attitudes to recognizable foodstuffs.

Whole starch, whether in particles or converted into a gel, generates textures in the mouth that cannot be masked effectively or matched by non-caloric material or even by preparations of other macromolecular nutrients. The differences between particles of starch and particles of cellulose, chalk or protein cannot be disguised to touch. Fortunately, partly hydrolysed preparations of starch became available in the late 1960s, technically named maltodextrins (MD) or sometimes (more casually) glucose polymers. Some versions contain little of glucose in the free form or of maltose (the two-glucose sugar). Maltodextrins are very soluble in water: a syrup can be made containing as much as 100 g in 100 ml. The solutions taste only of the glucose and maltose to the human tongue, which can be matched by those sugars or substitute sweeteners. However, even at quite low concentrations, MD solutions have a distinctive bulky texture, unlike the thin feel of sugar solutions. This is because the long chains of glucose molecules in maltodextrin tangle with each other when the solution is pushed gently by the tongue onto the palate. Fortunately this feel of 'body' can be matched by very low concentrations of non-caloric macromolecules such as cellulose gum. Thus we can make a variety of palatable versions of recognizable foods and drinks whose carbohydrate content is fully disguised to the human senses and approximates in molecular structure to the partly digested products of starch in the upper intestine. Maltodextrins were therefore substituted for (or compared with) sugars in all my physiological experiments after 1970.

Our search for satiety effects of carbohydrate metabolism in people using MD05 was carried out in 1970–3. We eliminated feedback from the amount remaining on the plate by offering an array of pairs of small sandwich pieces and yogurt and chocolate bar dessert portions and replacing an item as soon as one was taken from the pair. The serving and replacement could be done face-to-face by an experimenter or automatically by a multichannel machine: it seemed to make no difference to people who were not sensitive about their eating. A fruit-flavoured drink or water was provided. The rate at which portions were taken was calculated from the times recorded but no systematic effects of experimental conditions were detected (Booth, Lee and McAleavey, 1976), perhaps not surprisingly given that a variety of foods was eaten in these tests, as in normal life. In some of the later experiments, ratings were also made of desire to eat or not eat, of the pleasantness of eating named foods not presented for lunch, of how much would be eaten from a menu and of sensations in different parts of the body and of mood. Changes in all these ratings were closely related to energy intake across groups and so there was no evidence that the measures tapped different influences on appetite for food. However, changes in the pleasantness of familiar foods not being eaten was the most sensitive measure statistically (Booth, Mather and Fuller, 1982), indicating that people can tell us the energy content of their eating more accurately in the attractions of eating than they can in what they actually eat in a test lunch.

People who were used to sandwich meals and found the fillings palatable came to take their normal lunch once or at most two or three times a week. The first lunch tended to be smaller than later ones, but thereafter no effect of repetition was detected. Male students (getting a free lunch!) ate the biggest meals, but seldom more than 1200 kcal. Some women ate no more than about 200 kcal. People had to be excluded from group designs where the preadministered energy ranged nearly as high as their lunch energy intake.

The maltodextrin or control 'preload' was given in a syrupy lemon-flavoured drink or sometimes in a creamy coloured coffee or soup at the appropriate moment before lunch eaten at the usual time. The drink was served in a thick mug, to disguise weight difference. Someone who felt that their appetite was not affected by a thin nasogastric or orogastric tube could be loaded without drinking; also maltodextrin remaining in the stomach could be recovered by withdrawal through the tube, with a couple of washings to complete the recovery. Such tests showed that nine-tenths of a 70-g load of MD05 had left a stomach that had just emptied of breakfast in about 20 minutes (Booth, 1981). Blood glucose levels supported the assumption that maltodextrin was rapidly digested and absorbed. However, glucose concentration did not begin to rise in the blood until between five and ten minutes after a drink of maltodextrin, whereas blood glucose had already begun to go up at five minutes after a drink containing the same weight of glucose. This reflects the need for digestion of maltodextrin before absorption, unlike free glucose.

That delay in maltodextrin digestion has a subtler physiological implication that appears to be very important psychologically. A hitherto empty stomach will begin pumping maltodextrin into the duodenum without the usual restraint from receptors in the duodenal wall that are sensitive to glucose and other products of digestion (Hunt and Knox, 1968). Emptying of a glucose drink, on the other hand, will be immediately slowed by those receptors or even stopped for a while (Booth, 1972a; Booth and Jarman, 1976). Thus, in the five minutes or so while digestion of maltodextrin gets up speed, a considerable volume of the drink will accumulate in the upper intestine. All this can be rapidly digested and absorbed, whereas little of the glucose drink has been let through into the duodenum. Hence, from 5–10 minutes after the drink on an empty stomach, there will be a period of glucose absorption at a higher rate from maltodextrin than from glucose. This prediction is supported by the observation that the delayed rise in blood glucose after maltodextrin loading, catches up with the rise after glucose and overtakes it for a while. Hence, concentrated maltodextrin might send a strong stimulus to energy metabolism 10–30 minutes after consumption.

However, this signal is confounded by likely effects also in the upper intestine. The maltose released by digestion in its lumen and/or the glucose released from that maltose by the disaccharidases in its wall could conceivably reach high enough concentrations to have osmotic effects, despite the speed with which glucose can be transported across the wall into the bloodstream. For example, water might be retained or even drawn into the duodenum which is very sensitive to the stretch that would occur as soon as luminal volume expanded sufficiently; intestinal stretch strongly suppresses food intake in rats (Ehman *et al.*, 1971) and may be nauseating or painful. (Part of the initial rise in blood glucose after a concentrated glucose load may come from liver glucose release in a stress response, rather than from absorption.) Alternatively or as well, the glucoreceptors in the wall, that behave like a sort of osmoreceptor (Hunt and Stubbs, 1975), might sense an unusually high concentration of glucose and send a 'supersatiety' signal to the brain.

In fact, there was a readily visible suppression of intake after a load of concentrated maltodextrin, which lasted from about 10–15 minutes to 30 or 50 minutes or more after loading, depending on the size of the load and hence how long it took for most of the carbohydrate to be emptied, digested and absorbed. This prompt but brief satiety effect depended on the maltodextrin being sufficiently concentrated. It did not depend on load volume, down to a mere 7.5 g of MD05 in 15 ml of solution (Booth, 1981). This is consistent with the interpretation that this satiety effect results from rapid digestion of a bolus of maltodextrin that is initially dumped from the stomach (Booth, 1972c; Booth and Davis, 1973).

This unfortunately casts some doubt on the relevance of the effects of maltodextrin to the actions of starch in foods which is still contained in particles that will only slowly be penetrated by digestive enzymes. White flour and other refined starch, as well as sugars of course, may be able to form sufficiently strong solutions in the upper intestine to produce similarly rapid absorption when eaten on a near-empty stomach. They would have to be eaten at the start of a meal that is several hours after the previous meal because otherwise the duodenum will still contain digestion products that will prevent the stomach from dumping the starch.

Unfortunately also, as emphasized above, we cannot tell whether this effect arises from mechanical or chemical stimulation of the duodenal wall or metabolic stimulation of the liver (or some other tissue, such as in the brain). At least the larger doses of maltodextrin (and glucose) confound digestive with metabolic effects. However, 15 g must all have been absorbed long before 30 minutes were up for lunch to start in the above experiments. Furthermore, that suppression of intake had a mean value that was greater than the energy in the load. Hence there may well be in human beings as in rats (Booth and Jarman, 1976) clear evidence for a strong satiating after-effect of rapid absorption of glucose.

With that possible exception, however, this line of experiments was a failure as an effort to elucidate the physiology of human satiety. Nevertheless, some theoretical implications of the experimental results have increasingly emerged as of practical importance.

First, the efficacy of claimed assistance in weight control can best be assessed by understanding first how the alleged slimming aid might work. Properly controlled clinical trials are only worth the expense of investigation and trouble to the participants if they can be theoretically justified. 'Satiety tests' that do not elucidate the mechanism of action are useless because conclusions are limited to the conditions of testing which necessarily differ from those of clinical use (otherwise the satiety test would be a clinical trial).

The above research turned out to be directly relevant to one slimming aid that had been on the market for a long time. This is a sort of chewy fudge or soft toffee, composed primarily of glucose syrup (i.e. glucose made by hydrolysing starch completely). The recommended use of this material is to eat about 15 g of carbohydrate half an hour before a meal and thereby spoil the appetite at that meal and find it easier to eat less. Consumed by itself, this fudge would deliver a small amount of fairly concentrated glucose to the duodenum that would generate a satiety signal half an hour later strong enough to cut back intake by at least a little more than the energy in the fudge itself. However, the makers recommend that, in order to send glucose to calm the 'appetite centre in the hypothalamus' (a mechanism that does not exist: see Chapter 8), 'absorption is accelerated' by taking a warm drink after the fudge. Instead, by diluting the glucose, this drink will literally wash out the supersatiety effect.

Secondly, the human results are consistent with the results from rats that indicate that substantially satiating physiological effects of food last little or no longer than absorption. The duration of absorption and hence of the postingestional satiety is closely related to the amount of energy consumed (Hunt and Stubbs, 1975). Roughly speaking, an hour or so after its ingestion, 200 or even perhaps 300 kcal of carbohydrate is unlikely still to be acting on any satiety mechanism and so will not be compensated by a reduction of intake if eating occurs after that time. The practical implication is that one of the most fattening ways of consuming energy is in or with the drinks that habitually occur in work breaks between meals, more than an hour before lunch or supper (see Chapter 7).

Fat in hunger and satiety

The sensory qualities given to foods by fats have been impossible to simulate by non-caloric and physiologically inactive substances. Non-caloric oils would be needed to replace fats in baked goods but in any quantity are liable to motilize the lower gut. Appropriately sized and shaped particles of protein or cellulose may provide low- or zero-calorie substitutes for dairy creams but the more fat is to be delivered the less passable the simulation becomes. Adequately disguised high-fat loads have therefore not been available. Meals containing different levels of fat that do not seem obvious to the investigators have not been adequately measured for discriminability and attributions of fat content and satiating power by the eaters tested.

However, Welch, Read and colleagues (Welch *et al.*, 1988) have carried out some very productive experiments with healthy volunteers on close to their usual routine of meals. The approach was quite direct, to infuse fat through a tube to one of the sections of the small intestine: the duodenum is uppermost, next to the stomach, the jejunum is midway, below the entry of bile which is essential to emulsify fat for ease of digestion, and the ileum is next to the start of the lower intestine.

The participants were asked to distinguish between sensations of hunger and sensations of satiety, as well as discomfort, although they were not asked to describe the sensations they associated specifically with wanting to eat or wanting not to eat. There was no formal assessment whether hunger ratings measured a distinct process from satiety ratings but the two words behaved qualitatively differently with respect to the site of infusion and differences in their physiological effects.

Infusion of fat into the jejunum tended to induce sensations of satiety. This means that satiety will be sustained or increased as some of a meal containing fat that stays in emulsion in the stomach begins to pass through the duodenum. Since fat is a stimulus to secretion of CCK, mediation by that hormone was examined but it did not appear to be involved. Also, fat receptors may slow emptying of the stomach via CCK or other mechanisms, but there was no obvious relation to gastric volume either. It remains to be examined, however, whether appropriate gastric distension and jejunal fat levels act together to help create the normal quality and intensity of the sensation of fullness.

In contrast, ileal infusion of fat tended to delay the onset of hunger. It also suppressed the migrating motor complex, a powerful wave of contractions that passes intermittently down the digestive tract after the end of absorption, presumably to dislodge indigestible material and pass it to the bowel. This double effect of fat in the ileum is consistent with the idea that this contraction wave is the usual basis of hunger pangs. Neither the contraction nor the pangs are likely to start, therefore, until all the fat in the last meal has been absorbed or so little fat is being emptied from the stomach that it is all being digested and absorbed in the jejunum. Hunger pangs are therefore associated with an empty stomach, but this does not necessarily mean that the stomach is the sole source of the pangs, nor that filling the stomach with water will suppress the pangs of hunger for energy in the form of fat.

Physiology of Learned Appetites and Satieties

Hunger and the initiation of food intake have always seemed likely to the physiologists to have a gastrointestinal and/or metabolic basis. Satiation and the termination of a meal is more problematic though. The behavioural physiologist Le Magnen (1956), for example, pointed out that sufficient absorption is unlikely to have started by the end of a short meal to provide metabolic signals that could terminate eating by themselves. He proposed that sensory qualities of a food were used to anticipate effects following the meal that could be predicted from past experience, much like the association of flavours with delayed effects of poisons or nutrient deficiencies. Indeed, he showed in rats that odours, tastes, textures and colours that had been repeatedly associated with delayed administration of a concentrated glucose solution, the blood-glucose reducing hormone insulin or the appetite-suppressant drug amphetamine were rejected in choices offered with a control cue and induced a reduction in the size of a meal on diet marked with the conditioned cue (Le Magnen, 1969).

However, Booth (1972c) pointed out that this was not evidence of learned control of the process of stopping eating at the end of the meal. Rather, the observations could be attributed to a conditioned aversion to the food cue that was present from the start of the meal. That is, merely learned unpalatability could explain the rat's lack of persistence with eating. Just such a learned slowing of ingestion near the start of a meal has been demonstrated by close examination of the licking patterns of rats which have become used to taking meals from concentrated sugar solutions and other hypertonic liquid diets (Davis and Campbell, 1973; Davis, Collins and Levine, 1978; Davis and Smith, 1990).

To be evidence of the participation of food cues in the control of the satiation of hunger that ends a meal, Booth (1972c) argued, the aversion to the food would have to be confined to the later part of the meal (and presumably at least a short period following the cessation of eating). The first evidence for meal-end specific conditioned aversion was obtained by training with concentrated and dilute suspensions or pastes of starch (Booth, 1972c). Concentrated starch does not have the abnormal osmotic effects that had long been recognized from experiments on direct intake-suppressant effects of sugars (McCleary, 1953; see earlier in this chapter). Low-glucose maltodextrin became available while those experiments were being run. When hypotonic solutions of these partly hydrolysed starch preparations were used instead of whole starch, the learning of relative aversions confined to the second half of the meal became readily replicable (Booth and Davis, 1973; Booth, 1977a). Indeed, when sufficiently mild tastes or smells were used, this satiation could be associatively conditioned in rats by one experience of a dilute meal and one of a concentrated meal of MD05 having different flavours (Booth, 1980a).

After the first experiments, a more direct analysis was also introduced of the acquired change in flavour as the meal progressed. In a test meal after training, the rat was given repeated choices between the concentrated-paired and the dilute-paired flavours in the same intermediate strength of MD05. When the same flavour had been paired with the effects of concentrated MD05 at the start and at the end of the rat's training meal(s), it was found that near the start of a test meal the concentrated-paired flavour was consumed more quickly by itself and preferred in a choice with a cue for dilute MD05, while towards the end of the test meal that cue for effects of concentrated MD05 was consumed more slowly and rejected in favour of a flavour cuing dilute MD05. Thus the learning of the relative aversion for the cue that predicted effects of concentrated MD05 was confined to the later part of the meal. Indeed, there was a learned preference for the concentrated-paired cue earlier in the meal. This switch from preference to aversion (or at least the loss of a strong preference) explains the termination of the meal on food having that flavour and, by the same token, the small-sized meal that results from experience with concentrated starch preparations.

This switch or decline in preference was not merely due to the eating of the same flavour throughout the meal. When an initial relative preference just as strong was created with pairing with concentrated starch, it may have declined somewhat but it was definitely not reversed as the meal progressed (Booth, 1977a). Moreover, the conditioned flavour does not have to be present in the first part of the test meal: the relative aversion to concentrated-paired flavour still appears when the flavour is first introduced for the second half of the meal (Booth, 1985; Gibson and Booth, 1992). Therefore the phenomenon is not simply a growing boredom or habituation to the flavour. Conditioned satiety has a mechanism that is quite different from the food specific satiety that can also develop during continued ingestion of a distinctive flavour.

The only remaining explanation for these findings is that the direction of flavour preference depends on the difference in physiological state between the early and late parts of a meal. The internally driven flavour preference has been learned from the distinctive consequences of the conjunction of a flavour and an internal state. It is not simply an increase in food preferences during hunger and a decrease during satiety, which could be produced by nothing more than unlearned general drive. Which flavour showed increased preference early in meals and decreased preference later in meals depended on which maltodextrin concentration it had been paired with. A flavour paired with dilute carbohydrate does not show a decrease in preference during the test meal (Booth and Davis, 1973; Booth, 1980a). Moreover, this dilute-conditioned preference also turns out to be dependent on internal state, both in rats (Gibson and Booth, 1989) and in people (Booth and Toase, 1983; Booth *et al.*, 1994). When a flavour paired with dilute maltodextrin during either hunger or satiety is tested in the state used in training, preference for that flavour specifically increases. Yet when the flavour is tested in the state in which it was not trained, no such preference increase is seen.

These effects illustrate that the flavour and the internal state are producing the same behaviour. There is no difference between the appetizing or hungrifying effect of dietary stimuli and the appetizing or hungrifying effect of internal signals, despite the traditional attempts to call the supposed pull from food 'appetite' and the supposed push from the body 'hunger'. This verbal manoeuvre has no mechanistic significance and so is scientifically misleading. Of course, the food (and the external environment) contribute to hunger (the appetite for food) and the body contributes separately. The different sources of influences can and must be analysed out but they both produce the one hunger or food appetite.

This also implies that, not only have internally driven flavour preferences been learned, but also flavour-driven internal signals have been learned. Some depletion signal has been picked out by the flavour paired with maltodextrin early in the meal. A repletion signal has been picked out by the flavour paired with maltodextrin late in the meal. That is the main relevance of conditioned appetite and satiety to this chapter.

First, these internal-state dependent conditioning effects establish the principle that physiological influences on ingestion may be learned. Possibly, as mooted earlier for thirst, all normal control of ingestion by bodily states has been learned. Furthermore, what is learned is a combination of dietary and somatic cues that is subsequently recognized to evoke facilitation or inhibition of ingestion. Thus, appetite involves processes of cognitive integration, as detailed in previous chapters.

Secondly, there is also the question which effect of maltodextrin conditions appetite to flavours during depletion and how it differs from the effect that induces the opposite change in behaviour during repletion. Suffice to say in this context that it appears that metabolic effects condition preferences and more extreme intestinal effects condition aversions (Booth, 1979a; Booth and Davis, 1973; Booth, Mather and Fuller, 1982).

Thirdly, these phenomena provide a methodology for identifying physiological signals. What is the physiological state with which learning has integrated the flavour? The answer can be obtained by observing the effects of physiologically specific manipulations on the learned momentary dietary preferences. Very little use has yet been made of this principle. Gibson and Booth (1989) demonstrated that gastrointestinal distension could indeed serve as the cue for appetite and desatiation conditioned to the food cue by dilute maltodextrin in rats. This chapter concludes with a proposal of a cognitive approach to the physiology of appetite that builds on the extension of this technique outlined in Chapter 1.

Most foods except meat (and hence all recipes) contain appreciable amounts of carbohydrate. This carbohydrate would condition facilitation of eating that food (or drink) in the presence of an empty stomach, or even when the stomach is rather full, if the food is presented as a dessert after a first course that did not produce a prompt supersatiety. This would also be true for protein (Baker *et al.*, 1987; Gibson and Booth, submitted), for alcohol (in rats: Sherman *et al.*, 1983; Mehiel and Bolles, 1984) and for fat (in young children: Birch *et al.*, 1991). In this way, hungers will be learned for most or all foodstuffs. Thus an apparently non-specific hunger for food will emerge. Booth, Lovett and McSherry (1972) dubbed calorically conditioned sensory preferences 'trophophilia', the reverse of toxiphobia, the poison-conditioned sensory aversions to which psychologists have paid much more attention. Booth, Stoloff and Nicholls (1974) provided evidence that rat pups come to like whatever nutritious material they find on initial explorations outside the nest by this same process of hunger learning. Weingarten (1985) showed that the preference could be strong enough to start eating before the internal cues were appropriate when instead the preference had been conditioned to an external cue.

The bodily sensations that are part of the learned motivation may not be distinguishable between the nutrients that established them, largely because foods are generally mixtures of nutrients: so far, no difference has been established between the bodily sensations of protein-conditioned appetite and other hunger sensations. Hunger sensations of course seem very different from thirst sensations. There appears to be no work on the phenomenological differences between thirst satiety sensations and hunger satiety sensations. Perhaps a difference in the quality of fullness can be reliably described and pinned on the difference in gastrointestinal effects of repletions with water and energy.

Stunkard (1975) argued that 'Satiety is a conditioned reflex' on the same basis as Le Magnen, including the idea that somehow both food cues and gastric cues could become conditioned stimuli. Because hunger could also be conditioned, Booth (1977b) picked up on Stunkard's (1975) proposal by using the title 'Satiety and appetite are conditioned reactions'. The proposal by Booth and Davis (1973), firmed up from 1977 onwards, was that dietary cues and contextual cues internally or externally are conditioned in combination. All jointly predictive stimuli become elements in one compound conditioned stimulus. When the elements act as a unity in controlling the learned response, as proposed, the psychologists of learning call it a 'configural stimulus'. The standard definition of configural learning is in effect the emergence of a new stimulus. The combination of an empty stomach and a particular flavour now elicits a response that cannot be accounted for as the addition of the effects of the flavour alone and the empty stomach alone. Since ingestive responses cannot be measured without some dietary flavour and some state of the stomach, the evidence for configuration rests on the reversal of the response to a flavour when the gastrointestinal cue is changed between meal-starts and meal-ends. It is also supported by observation of emptiness taking part in inhibition of ingestion and fullness contributing to facilitation – conditioned de-appetent and de-satiating effects respectively.

We have considered learned appetites and satieties under the rubric of the associative conditioning of stimuli. This should not be taken to imply that all (or even any) learned ingestion is classical or Pavlovian conditioning of elicited respondents.

The experimental designs are cast in the framework of stimulus-stimulus association as a device to ensure strict analysis of the structure of the learned behaviour – which stimuli have acquired control of which direction of influence on ingestion. These designs do not determine whether the observed eating or drinking behaviour or disposition is an elicited movement pattern (respondent) or an instrumental act (operant) – less technically, the extent to which the interest in food and drink is involuntary or intentional. Experiments carried out thus far do not distinguish between unconscious associations and awareness of the contingencies. They can be interpreted in terms of changes in evaluation or belief, or different sorts of response that could affect intake or ratings, e.g. emotional reactions of pleasure or more reflective decisions as to what is wanted (Booth, 1991b). Thus it is arbitrary to opt between aversion, disgust and avoidance without distinguishing data or for pleasurable sensations rather than pleasing activity until criteria have been established to separate affect from desire.

Learned food-specific control of intake when full (conditioned satiety) has been observed in food intakes in human adults (Booth, Lee and McAleavey, 1976; Booth, Mather and Fuller, 1982) and young children (Birch *et al.*, 1987), in choice preferences in adult people (Booth, Mather and Fuller, 1982), monkeys (Booth and Grinker, 1993) and rats (Booth and Davis, 1973) and in pleasantness ratings (Booth and Toase, 1983). This appears to be an effect of readily digested starch in concentrated form that has been eaten in the early part of the meal, creating a mild bloated sensation shortly after consumption of dessert and so averting the eater from that dessert. The evidence for this hypothesis, in rats (Booth and Davis, 1973) and people (Booth, Mather and Fuller, 1982), is that when the concentrated maltodextrin is reserved to the latter part of the meal, the amount eaten of the dessert and the whole meal is not trained down as it is when the same material is included in the early part of the meal.

These mechanisms may well be operative with everyday menus of potatoes, pasta, pastry and bread, and perhaps readily digested fat too. Cognitive stereotypes and expectations can presumably be built up on accumulations of unconsciously conditioned reactions (Booth, 1987). Also experiences with changes in the body leading up to, during and following drinks and meals can be interpreted in the light of preexisting evaluative frameworks and beliefs arising from communication with other members of the culture. Expectations acquired from others might be supported to some extent by somatic symptoms or indeed aspects of one's own behaviour that are noticed. This then could strengthen and introduce more specificity into both the expectation and the self-perception, thus amplifying and individuating the bodily sensations by a process of autosuggestion.

Just believing that one meal was more satiating than another, quite independently of their carbohydrate contents, was sufficient to produce as marked a difference in ratings of hunger and the pleasantness of uneaten foods as a substantial actual difference in carbohydrate content (Booth, Mather and Fuller, 1982).

Physiology from Ratings

As for many cognitive issues, it is not much use merely asking people lots of questions or indeed just measuring their choices and intakes in everyday life or in laboratory tests with attractive foods. What is important is to exploit the sensitivity of quantitative description of states and attitudes where it can be used to test between alternative theories. Intake tests can never do this. Just taking ratings or physiological measures cannot either. However, ratings could help to elucidate the physiological bases of otherwise mysterious effects.

For example, 50 g or more of fructose by itself suppresses food intake more than two hours later (Spitzer and Rodin, 1987; Rodin, 1991), which is not seen after ingestion of the same weight of glucose, sucrose (a compound of fructose and glucose) or maltodextrin. Since glucose stimulates insulin secretion but fructose does not, the effect was attributed to subtle differences in patterns of insulin secretion, although insulin levels barely differed at the time of the satiety effect. In fact, the absorption of fructose largely depends on the presence of glucose also in the upper intestine. Doses of fructose above about 50 g are well known to produce lower intestinal symptoms because the fructose reaches bacteria which produce gas and osmotic distress. It would be crucial to assess abdominal discomfort as sensitively and specifically as upper abdominal fullness and the epigastric hunger pang, in order to determine whether the 'satiety effect' of large doses of pure fructose is in fact unphysiological in this way.

Memory of the last meal could also produce long-delayed after-effects. As well as the effect of food attribution at 20 minutes indicated by the results of Booth, Mather and Fuller (1982), Rolls *et al.* (1988) as mentioned earlier, saw what can be interpreted as memory effects after an hour. High palatability of a meal has been reported to raise the rated desire to eat shortly before the next meal was due (Hill *et al.*, 1986). This was interpreted as a physiologically mediated effect of palatability. That seems to assume that appetite ratings somehow bypass the mind, once the sensations in the mouth have faded. The observed statistical difference was only one in dozens that could have been tested and so, until the result is replicated, it cannot be accepted as firm. Even if the effect is real, we need to know whether desire to eat gives that result because it is merely more sensitive to effects on overall hunger than are other wordings or because it is dissociated from other appetite ratings under those circumstances and measures a particular facet of hunger or of the influences on it. Assuming that rating desire to eat is simply a sensitive measure of hunger, so far from being evidence of a physiological effect of palatability, the effect illustrates why Wooley (1971), for example, despaired of picking out physiological signals from cognitive effects: people are likely to be influenced by memory of what was in the last meal as well as when it was in looking forward to their next meal.

The late timing of an effect is therefore no indication at all that it arises from physiological after-effects of a meal.

Towards a Cognitive Physiology of Appetite

It is technically difficult, or at least very time-consuming, to make physiologically meaningful manipulations or measurements within the ethical constraints appropriate to human experiments. Nevertheless, the lack of advance in the physiology of human appetite is largely attributable to lack of attention to the necessary psychological theory and methods by biomedical research workers and even by psychologists interested in the topic.

Since the cognitive processes involved began to be elucidated in the early

1970s, biomedical research funding bodies on both sides of the Atlantic have failed to understand the centrality of learned co-ordination of gastrointestinal and metabolic influences with dietary and environmental influences in the control of food and water intake and what people say about drinking and eating. Most of the subsequent experiments on human eating and drinking, even by behavioural physiologists and biological psychologists, have collected data on food and drink intakes and ratings that are physiologically uninterpretable and have not been psychologically analysed.

The difficulty is to control and measure both learning processes and physiological conditions in ways that dissociate actual causation from confounding variables. The experimental conditions required to investigate the roles of learning processes in physiological influences on behaviour or subjective experience have unfortunately not been generally understood in biomedical science (or by many psychologists). Understanding of the mechanisms of normal satiety and appetite in people and laboratory species has advanced at a snail's pace by neglect of the cognitive character of the problems of investigating physiological influences on hunger, thirst and their satiation as identified in the mid-1970s.

The Cognitive Paradigm

The fact that internal influences on hunger, thirst and their satieties are integrated with dietary and external influences by the processes of learning has profound implications for research into physiological factors in eating and drinking. The momentary context of any gastrointestinal or parenteral signal triggers memories that have a major influence on subjective experience as well as overt behaviour.

Effective qualitative analysis will depend on the context being close to some familiar situation: diets cannot just be provided without regard to what they mean to each eater. Quantitative analysis, such as a dose-response relationship between a nutrient concentration and an ingestive measure, will require measurements that enable calculation of the cognitive integration of that internal signal with the salient food stimuli and other simultaneously effective internal or external cues as well.

Investigating the physiology of satiety forces attention onto the fact that the internal state is changing all the time during and after a meal. Sooner or later, investigators realize that satiety mechanisms cannot be measured purely as cumulative intake or lack of it, such as a meal size or an interval between meals. The interactions among influences towards the end of the meal and continuing after it have to be considered. This requires analysis of the ways in which the instantaneous tendency to eat depends on food characteristics and external situation as well as on processes within the body.

Momentary rates of consumption, compared between foods and external and internal contexts, can provide some evidence. The only illustration of this to date is J.D. Davis's work on rat's rates of licking sugar solutions, compared between different sugar concentrations and particularly between different postingestional consequences of drinking such as osmotic effects of an unabsorbable sugar (Davis *et al.*, 1978) or learning effects of draining some of the sugar from the stomach (Davis and Smith, 1990). Unfortunately, these postingestional manipulations are not physiologically normal and sugar solutions are not maintenance diets on which rats can be brought up. A considerable amount of work has been done on rates of eating and drinking in experimental animals and healthy and distressed human beings but unfortunately the different influences on eating have been confounded and the different characteristics of the cumulative intake function (initial rate and rate of slowing, when slowing is observed) turned out to be correlated (Kissileff *et al.*, 1982) and so not attributable to separate factors.

Momentary choices between foods have been used more effectively to identify physiological influences on ingestive appetite, as illustrated earlier in this chapter. Relative intakes of two diets over periods of 1–2 minutes or even as long as five minutes in a rat taking more than ten minutes to complete a meal showed effects of the internal difference between the early and late parts of a meal, both when the diets were presented together and when they were presented separately on different occasions (Booth, 1972c, 1977a, 1980a; Booth and Davis, 1973). In people, these dispositions to choose between foods can be expressed verbally as well as in selective eating behaviour. Each food can be rated in turn for liking, preference or how pleasant it would be to eat it right then. The ratings are no less (or more) valid measures than brief intakes of the tendency to ingest: validity depends on the test stimuli and context to which the individual is responding (see Chapter 1). Parallels to the rat data on maltodextrin's differential conditioning of relative preferences between hungry and satiated states were obtained in people using differently flavoured yogurts presented before or after lunch (Booth, 1985; Booth and Toase, 1983).

Recognition of Sensations Related to Ingestion

Similarly, quantitative answers to readily comprehended questions about bodily sensations could in principle be highly sensitive to physiological influences on appetite. It depends whether a distinct pattern of neural input can be recognized in association with the specific desire to eat or drink or not to eat or drink. If this objective identification can be learned, then a private sensation has been created that should be expressible concretely and symbolically. The verbal expression might be in terms of some theory of influences on appetite, such as emptiness and fullness of the belly. Nevertheless, the physiological signal that is being recognized might be chemical stimulation to cells in the wall of the intestine, the liver or the brain. A pain can be referred to a place in the body different from the source of stimulation. A flavour identified by smell is commonly referred to taste in the mouth. Similarly, the epigastric pang might come from contraction anywhere in the upper gut or even a lack of energy input to the liver and the feeling of comfortable fullness might depend as much on lipid stimulation of the jejunal wall as on distension of the stomach or duodenum.

Hunger pangs have traditionally been attributed to gastric contractions but the association is far from tight. The migrating motor complex that passes down the digestive tract at intervals after most absorption has been completed is likely to affect stretch receptors all through the upper intestine as well as the stomach. Read (1992) suggests that this wave is the basis for the epigastric pang, in which case gastric contractions will not necessarily have a one-to-one relation to the sensation's occurrence.

An additional possibility is that central reflexes contribute to the hunger and satiety sensations (Booth, 1980b). The output of the autonomic nervous system from the brain is influenced by the metabolic receptors in the brainstem and hypothalamus that were originally thought to influence eating behaviour. This autonomic outflow modifies metabolism in the liver, hormone secretion from the pancreas and other glands and the muscle tone of the stomach. Hence the central autonomic sensors could affect visceral activity in ways that alter peripheral signals and so create distinctive sensations. The blood glucose dip before meals could be the result of a cooperative interaction between such a central-peripheral loop and the slowing of absorption: in effect, the brain sharpens the signal that might otherwise change too slowly to be readily detected in the array of information entering the brain from the body. This role of the brain might be acquired, in other words an expression of conditioned appetite for food. Also the dip might be programmed to vary round the clock, for example to facilitate the taking of meals during the alert phase (F. Smith *et al.*, 1993). One possible corollary is that the dip does not cause hunger by itself but, rather, the onset of search for food is that consequence of central integration of information in which the dip plays a critical part once the main causes of hunger are operative.

Measurement of Determinants of Sensations

Quantitative judgments have to be made on dimensions defined by reconstructable anchor points or standards. The intensities of bodily sensations labelled hunger, thirst or satiety are not on scales that can be adequately anchored on abstract quantitative words like 'extremely', 'very' or 'strong', any more than precise judgments of sweetness or creaminess can be made without reference to particular sweet or creamy items that are familiar (Chapters 1 and 2). We can judge better how strongly we currently desire to eat and even how intense a bodily sensation of hunger, thirst or satiety is, while we are in a given state of the body and social situation, if we also have a familiar food or drink to think about. The situation can then be recognized more exactly and a realistic reconstruction made from memory of the distance of the current situation from a precise standard most validly and precisely judged by the reconstruction from memory. This verbally expressed quantitative comparison of thoroughly reality-anchored entities is not an elaborate conscious calculation either. When set up properly, it should be as easy and unreflective as eating and drinking itself. It is merely the verbal expression of the learned integration of all influences on the tendency to ingest (see Chapter 1 on cognitive theory of appetite).

The liking for a food is an expression of hunger – that is, one aspect of the global pattern of eating appetites and satieties. The logic of appetite sensation measurement is the same as that of assessing the sensory quality of a food or drink material. Recognition of the best quality is most accurate when the perception of the test item is compared with the memory of its most familiar or preferred version, and when both are considered on a standard menu and within a bodily state and social situation that are also readily recognized (see Chapter 5, on food design). Smells and textures cannot be assessed out of context and it is much more difficult to judge tastes, colours and sounds in the abstract than has traditionally been assumed in research on the senses.

.   Similarly, to characterize the physiological bases of a particular bodily sensation relevant to eating or drinking as precisely as practicable, the effect of a measured physiological manipulation (disconfounded from any other influence on appetite) should be judged on the strength of the desire to eat with reference to familiar foods presented in a familiar menu and in a familiar eating situation. It is not enough to ask questions for quantitative answers about particular sensations recognizable as those of normal hunger, thirst or their satiation. The cognitive structure through which the person can make the requested judgement must be supported as realistically as possible.

Thus, we could estimate the influence of a physiological factor more accurately if we have in the data a basis for calculating its integration with some important non-physiological factors in appetite. Hence, a good way to measure the most delicious sensation of fullness would be by simultaneously measuring the most filling sweetness or creaminess of, say, a cheesecake dessert against the background of a meal at a time of day and in a social context where a definite sort of satisfaction is required.

In the same way, the most appetizing emptiness of the stomach or upper intestine will depend on the eating context and the foods on offer. Hence the intensity of the hunger sensation, as well as the strength of the overall desire to eat, will be best measured by the attractiveness of particular foods in an at least verbally defined situation and, to be most effective, an actual situation where eating would be usual. This is why, as mentioned earlier in this chapter, the pleasantnesses of named familiar foods were the most sensitive measure of the satiating effects of the actions of ingested maltodextrin (Booth, Mather and Fuller, 1982). Ratings of the strengths of a 'sensation of satiety' or of described sensations such as upper abdominal fullness or oral satisfaction discriminated between after-effects of disguised high and low concentrations of maltodextrin less reliably or even not reliably at all.

Conclusion

Research nominally on satiety over the last decade has not tackled the necessary cognitive psychology and visceral physiology. Analysis of the behavioural mechanisms of satiation has been replaced by measurements of the effects of food consumption on energy intake and on self-descriptions that correlate with intake. Satiety has been variously 'defined' as a private experience incontrovertibly measured by a rating using that word, as a parameter of food intake measured in units of energy content or even as a property of the food itself, such as its satiety value or satiating efficiency. These uses of the word all neglect the scientific issue: what are the processes by which eating an amount of that food in specified circumstances affects behaviour during whatever opportunities to eat arise subsequently?

A cognitive physiology of appetite will require testing of specific manipulations of visceral processes by direct administration or disguised variations in food composition. A succession of tests in adequately disconfounded variants of a familiar eating situation is needed to identify the quantitative structure of influences on an individual's appetite and the relevant bodily sensations. Progress in such work will require intensive collaboration among cognitive psychologists, medical physiologists and food technologists to develop realistic theories of the physiology of real-life appetite and the methods to test among proposed mechanisms.

Further Reading

Classic recent texts on the physiological controls of nutrient intake are listed below.

Physiology of Thirst (for Water)

FITZSIMONS, J.T. (1979) *The physiology of thirst and sodium appetite*, Cambridge, Cambridge University Press.

RAMSAY, D.J. and BOOTH, D.A. (Eds) (1991) *Thirst: physiological and psychological aspects*, London, Springer-Verlag.

ROLLS, B.J. and ROLLS, E.T. (1983) *Thirst*, Cambridge, Cambridge University Press.

Physiology of Sodium Appetite

DENTON, D.A. (1982) *The hunger for salt*, Berlin, Springer-Verlag.

Physiology of Hunger (for Calories)

BOOTH, D.A. (Ed.) (1978) *Hunger models: computable theory of feeding control*, London, Academic Press.

LE MAGNEN, J. (1985) *Hunger*, Cambridge, Cambridge University Press.

NOVIN, D., WYRWICKA, W. and BRAY, G.A. (1976) *Hunger: basic mechanisms and clinical implications*, New York, Raven.

THOMPSON, C.I. (1980) *Controls of eating*, Lancaster, MTP Press.

Chapter 4

The Soul of the Diet

Cultural constraints on and diversification of food and drink are considered in this chapter in terms of the cognitive processes involved.

Cultural Determinants of Eating and Drinking

Our social background is the source of many of the details of the mental processes in our habitual choices among foods and drinks and of when, where and how to consume them. No doubt there are some personally felt options, at least on occasion for some of us. Yet mostly these are between alternative culturally shaped eating or drinking patterns.

Thus, it is reasonable to take the position that virtually all of the normal immediate organization of a person's eating and drinking originates from the practices and outlooks of the groups with whom that person interacts and has interacted since infancy (Chapter 2).

Biology and Culture

This idea of cultural determinacy may be very puzzling for someone who believes that there are some quite strict biological controls on human intakes of water, energy and perhaps other nutrients. The prime example is the supposedly homeostatic control of eating by body weight. How can caloric intake (and indeed physical activity) be subject to the vagaries of culture and yet the energy content of the body stay constant in most adults to within a few kilocalories per day? (This argument assumes that constancy of body weight is not achieved by changes in metabolic efficiency. There is in fact no evidence for the sometimes huge changes in heat output that would be necessary to burn off overeating: Garrow, 1977.)

No answer to such puzzles is generally accepted. Indeed, some biologically oriented scientists appear to find the idea so challenging that they are disposed to discount the scale of cultural influences or even to deny that they are involved at all in, for example, the physiology of weight regulation. Certainly the implications of cultural factors in eating for the design of research into genetic or physiological factors in body weight are usually ignored. Yet arguably it is just this neglect of cultural aspects by biomedical research on eating that is one of the main causes of slow progress in understanding how mechanisms in the human body do contribute to the observed degree of control of body weight and other regulatory functions (compare Chapter Three).

Those who have addressed these issues about human culture and human bodies are far from resolving them, even in broad theory, let alone in empirical detail. Nevertheless, some suggestive principles have emerged.

Psychobiosocially Integrated Systems

First, as for other areas of human life, it is unrealistic and hence scientifically unproductive to set up a polarity of biology versus culture (or, in more of a cliché, nature versus nurture). Secondly, progress is obstructed rather than promoted by neglecting the cognitive organization of behaviour and experience or trying to analyse it out of existence in favour of either physiological mechanisms or cultural processes.

These approaches are doomed because biology and culture interact in the mental dynamics of an individual's behaviour. Hence, cultural and biological causation do not operate in totally isolated spheres and the study of psychological causation is critical to a realistic understanding of what makes people tick.

Biology Through Culture

One theoretical principle that is worth developing on the above basis is that biological control could be exerted in and through culturally determined eating habits. The biological mechanisms and historical processes of survival could be major constraints on social norms of food use or crucial factors in the cultivation of particularities in a norm.

For example, unhealthy or just physiologically suboptimal exploitation of the ecology by a human group's dietary practices could prejudice the maintenance of that group in competition with others and in the reproduction of successive generations. At the other end of the scale, a group might survive and succeed in an environment where others fail, because a food or a food use has become culturally important to that group and just happens to be nutritionally beneficial.

The Mexican tortilla has been proposed as an example of this latter process (Katz, 1981). Maize flour is cooked with lime to make this type of bread. It has served for centuries as the main source of energy for groups living at the subsistence level in Central America. The heating in alkali makes the vitamin niacin more available from the corn and also releases for digestion more of the essential amino acids which are low in proportion in corn. Beans help to complement the amino acid pattern of corn but the bean crop may fail when it has nevertheless been possible to harvest sufficient corn. Hence, it is suggested, the distinctive texture and flavour of tortillas became the preferred staple diet. Intergenerational transmission of the habit sustained the liking for tortillas although beans, other vegetable crops and even meat are now often available and their consumption removes the need for the essential nutrients released by the action of lime.

There has been a tendency by some in anthropology to look for complete explanations of food's roles in society in terms of such biological requirements on subsistence in small groups or of economic structures in larger groups. Examples include the sacred cow in India and the traditional Jewish food laws. Other anthropologists have countered by pointing to the conceptual and social functions of the eating habit or the attitude to food that is at issue.

The facts may not lie at either extreme. Something like the psychoanalysts' concept of 'overdetermination' may be relevant. A particular practice may be sustainable purely on a psychosocial basis or purely on a bioeconomic basis but may as a matter of historical fact have been sustained in both ways (and been all the more stable for that reason).

Even more likely, the biological and the cultural influences operate at different times and at different levels. A religious or ideological imperative may initiate a practice and economic structures may sustain it in later decades or centuries. Or, vice versa, a nutritional requirement may sustain the group that has a certain dietary practice but, if the requirement disappears, ethnic identity may maintain the practice still.

Biological Substructure to Culture

Another important principle is that some instances of biological control through culture may not be evident as social phenomena; the process may not be salient to members of that society or to people from other backgrounds. Such processes will be hard to identify. The disparity between the social and physiological structures involved may also make such a theory almost impossible to establish definitively.

A possible example of this sort emerged from quantitative simulations of basic physiological and learning mechanisms in human food intake control (Booth and Mather, 1978; see Chapter 3). The computer model of an adult human being 'ate' similarly sized meals while getting ready to go to work in the morning, in the middle of the day and after returning from work for a quiet evening. One interpretation of this theoretical deduction is that some culturally normal aspects of eating habits are roughly tuned to the average physiology and ecology in that society. For example, the pattern of three substantial eating occasions per day, that has been traditional in countries located in regions of the earth having temperate or cool climates, may distribute the average energy requirements through the day in a manner that maximizes the opportunity for automatic controls on energy intake to operate within the individual. As those calculations also illustrated, fewer meals per day could compromise both unlearned compensation of over- or under-intake from meal to meal (recently evidenced in children: Birch *et al.*, 1991) and also learned control of meal size and so prejudice health and vigour by accumulation of over- or under-weight. More frequent meals could permit good compensation but, until convenience foods came into wide use and 'grazing' during work or leisure activities became normal as well as feasible, more than the three meals breakfast, lunch and supper were hard to fit into daily schedules.

Because of the possibilities both of overdetermination or change in function and also of biological functionality at a level that is not obvious in the social structure or the personal concepts, it is doubtful whether it is worth seeking a biological need for every anthropological or psychological phenomenon to do with food and drink. This chapter therefore will focus on the more obvious cultural determinants of eating in industrialized countries, leaving aside the issues of biological fitness until we have some research results that put empirical constraints on sociobiological speculation about eating habits.

Psychology and Culture

Psychologists are expected to help investigate possible explanations for sensual craving and delight, the soothing effects of food and the distress of disordered eating. They have also been deeply involved in research on bodily influences on hunger, satiety and weight. In addition, however, people use foods and drinks as social tools and cultural symbols. What is going on in their minds during interpersonal exchanges involving food is no less a concern for psychology than are sensations and emotions.

This is not to blur the distinction between the eating and drinking customs of a community and the actions and mental mechanisms of individual members of that group, interdependent though those two sorts of processes are. These customs and the whole culture in which they are set are the proper subject matter of exclusively social sciences, such as the social anthropology, sociology and economics of food. Moreover, biological and nutritional anthropology and the ecological and engineering sciences are crucial to understanding an industrialized society and are also quite distinct from psychology. The technological history of the gathering and hunting and the cultivation and husbandry of plant and animal life and of modern farming and domestic and industrial food processing is rich in specific constraints and opportunities for the culture surrounding food and drink.

Nevertheless, eating and drinking customs also have their psychology. There are no customs without the processes involved in their practice by particular individuals living within that society. While there could be no cultural psychology of food without the historical, social and technobiological processes of food production and use, there also would be no communal activities of search for and consumption of food without the perceptions, reactions and actions of acculturated individuals.

Hence the generalities and idiosyncrasies of food preferences and aversions and the reasoning and emotions of weight control and eating disorder on which psychologists and other behavioural scientists have lavished so much attention in recent decades are no more than a modest fraction of the scope of the psychology of food use. Indeed, the usual research approaches to likings, dislikes, affect and thinking about food have been curiously asocial. The collection and interpretation of verbal data or food intakes have been handicapped by blindness to the cultural context of the intra- and interpersonal processes that the data reflect and depend on. A person's mental processes and behaviour have been treated as though they float in a vacuum, occasionally colliding with another person. This is not peculiar to food research. Cognitive psychologists and other laboratory experimenters on human behaviour and words in other fields have been accused of separating the mind from the social environment and regarding culture as entirely the creation of an unchanging individual human nature (Jahoda, 1992).

This chapter is intended to illustrate for industrialized societies how psychological processes that operate generally enable individuals' participation in cultural practices towards food that have been particularized by ecological, technological and socioeconomic history. This is a form of cognitive anthropology, in the sense of empirical analysis of evidence from human words and acts as to the social meaning of what is in people's minds. Within psychology, it is perhaps closest in approach to the study of social representations (Fraser and Gaskell, 1990); however, that part of social psychology has yet to address the sociality in eating and drinking.

As well as opening up the vista for behavioural nutrition, development of a cognitive anthropological approach could strengthen the theory and methods of social and natural scientists and practitioners of food and nutrition. Social nutrition and the food business have both long recognized, nominally at least, the individuality of the operation of the food culture and market (Bass, Wakefield and Kolassa, 1979; Ritson *et al.*, 1986). However, this recognition has generally been at the level of the anecdote and journalistic interpretation of aggregate statistics. Here we seek data that enable direct diagnosis of the diversity and generality of the actual mental processes operating consciously or unconsciously in people's purchasing and ingestion of food.

No attempt is made in this book to review the relevant data and theories (let alone methods) of the cultural disciplines (or the natural sciences). These are highly developed and any scientist who wishes to do serious research on behaviour towards food should acquire a decent overview of the nutritional anthropology and sociology, the food business and the technology of agriculture and food that is relevant to the population from which individuals will be sampled. Some general texts for these fields are listed in the bibliography at the end of this chapter and these refer on to the more technical original monographs and reports on particular topics.

Culture Through Psychology

From a psychological viewpoint, cultural determinants of eating behaviour operate broadly through two routes. The individual may be participating in a social activity with which opportunities to eat or drink are involved, perhaps in distinctive ways. For example, someone at a feast calls for a toast and everybody raises and takes a drink from a wineglass. Alternatively, a person may construe the foods or drinks on offer as more or less appropriate to the situation as a result of past acculturation into such a construction of those foods' uses. One would not risk causing offence by raising a glass of water instead of a wineglass, even if the wine in one's glass was finished.

Both the interpersonal and the internalized routes may operate simultaneously. Indeed, normally they will act in conjunction. The distinction becomes evident, though, when the requirements of the social role conflict with the personal construal. The teetotaller might raise the champagne to his lips but not sip it. The wine buff finding himself (like 'a fish *in* water'?) at the annual dinner of an Alcoholics Anonymous group may feel very odd drinking toasts in apple juice.

Thus, food and drink are used as cultural tools and symbols quite as much as they are to satisfy cravings, ward off hunger pangs, soothe emotional distress and ingest materials for sustenance. Yet these latter sensual, emotional and nutritional motives as well are highly culture-bound. In the USA, it might be peanut butter and jelly (jam) that some pregnant women sometimes crave, whereas in the UK it might be kippers, with or without marmalade.

We shall therefore be considering the 'soul' of the diet (its psyche) as those mental processes of food acceptance that either recognize the eating as social participation and exchange or, with more or less discrimination, sense the cultural appropriateness of the eating. In either case, what is involved is the objective but fallible identification of how a culturally defined situation fits to a more or less restricted range of eating or drinking behaviour. Consumption of food and drink is being considered in this chapter as an inherently social performance, whether in public or in private. Like the rest of the book, this cognitive social psychology will be limited to affluent countries.

Custom and Rationale

The social structures and processes in which foods and drinks play their roles are widely varied in character. Furthermore, an ethnically plural yet partly integrated society, which is both post-religious and undergoing religious revival, must be expected to be a melée of interchanging familial, companionable and affiliative functions of food.

Yet the distinctions between different sorts of cultural entity should not be blurred. A potentially open ethico-political system cannot legitimately be treated as a documented ideology. A flexible religion should be distinguished from a rigid cult. The institutionally formalized and sanctioned ritual is not the same thing historically as an informal symbol of status, celebration or friendliness.

Yet the cognitive processes mediating individuals' practice of these anthropologically distinct procedures may be indistinguishable. Religious values and social mores may differ little if at all in their modes of operation within the mind of the individual member of a subculture. On the other hand, differences in sociocognitive style between individuals may be large, even when they are all operating within a single social dynamic.

One Man's Myth is Another Man's Position Paper

Myths, taboos, superstitions, fads and quackery are all distinct categories of social phenomena. There is also a real polarity between folklore and professional consensus.

Experts and official bodies purport to draw sharp distinctions, though, between particular popular beliefs and practices and scientific facts which the populace should be informed about and educated to use. However, the individual citizen may have some legitimate doubts about a fundamental difference between today's official facts and doctrines and the myth or taboo that is now pilloried as error, although in some cases was once officially sanctioned.

This relativism is a psychological and cultural fact. So it behoves officialdom and science to get off their high horses and join the battle on foot for the beliefs and values of the citizenry, alongside marketeers, entertainers and moralizers and friends, colleagues and neighbours. The power to construct regulations, make official pronouncements or distribute information pamphlets is not power over citizens' hearts and souls and eating habits.

In any case, the cognitive analyses sit loose to the institutional sanctions on incorrect behaviour: the psychology of beliefs takes no position on the criteria for objectivity of belief, let alone the truth of any particular beliefs.

Food as Tool and Symbol

The psychologically most basic fact on which this chapter is based is that eating or drinking can be a means to some quite different end from self-sustenance. The food or drink can literally be instrumental to an achievement or it can serve in itself as symbolic.

The objective can be a natural physical consequence of the ingestion. For example, someone might eat the last portion in the communal dish so that none is left to throw away. However, even in such a case, the food consumption might be either a tool or a symbol (or both). That piece of food might have been cleared up partly or entirely as a tool to avoid waste. On the other hand, eating the last piece may have had symbolic content. It might have been intended and/or seen by others as an expression of appreciation of the host's cooking. Conversely, such an act may be a gaffe or an insult, for example where a culture of affluence requires hosts to overprovide and guests to acknowledge the plenty.

Whether a particular instance or even a recurrent type of instrumental use of food is genuinely symbolic is not necessarily an answerable question. Nevertheless, it is worth trying to treat the question of symbol or mere tool as an objective empirical issue, even though the matter can be treated in other contexts with literary flourishes that are entertaining or even instructive. That is, a psychologist should be cautious about attributing symbolism to a food use. From a scientific point of view, it is too easy to wax lyrical about deep meaning in eating practices.

This is partly a purely psychological issue as to what cognitive performance was involved in the action. Could an informed participant in the user's culture read a meaning in the act beyond what it achieves physically?

However, symbolism in food use is also an ethnographic issue. Indeed, this anthropological question must have a positive answer for it to be possible to answer the cognitive question (and, it should be added, vice versa). The question is whether that act in those circumstances amounts to the expression of a symbol for that culture.

These twin criteria provide a discipline on speculation for those who wish to distinguish empirical understanding from literary imagination. It should be noted that this is not a positivistic position: the objectivity is not based on access to uninterpreted data but on intersubjectivity and mutual evaluation of individual behaviour and cultural activity. It should also be noted that these scientific standards do nothing to undermine other values possessed by speculative accounts of the meaning of behaviour in a culture. At the very least, such stories can be fun. In addition, they may accelerate an outsider's acquisition of a better appreciation of what it is like to be a member of the society about which the story is spun.

Nevertheless, a story that is based on thin observation should be taken with a grain of salt. It cannot be uncritically assumed to give an account of actual structures in the functions of the institutions of the group or in the mind of even the most sophisticated member.

The objectivity of the issue is illustrated by the fact that a story can be told back in the society that was imaginatively represented and induce a change in their culture as a result. Indigenous peoples may dramatize their traditions for tourists and, in the case of food, serve up an inauthentic but acceptable version of what is expected. The story may even be 'tried on for size' by members of the society about which it was told. It may seem an intriguing and even plausible meaning for the food to more innovative or exploratory users.

Those who go to a Freudian psychoanalyst have Freudian symbols in their dreams and Jungians come to see the collective unconscious permeating all human activity. From popular expositions of Freud's books, it became commonplace to make sexual associations to the shapes of non-sexual objects. So, for example, a food marketer may present a picture of a stick of chocolate or, better, someone licking a cream eclair in an attempt to exploit potential phallic association. The symbolism does not have to be taken seriously to have some effect. This is a use of food as a symbol in the course of using the symbol as a tool to sell the food. This account can be extended to use of food and drink directly as a tool in the preliminaries if not the culmination of a sexual encounter.

Foods and Drinks as Tools

Any use of food is liable to be a means of self-expression. The self-expressive function is however hard to separate from more strictly instrumental functions which are bound up with what is being expressed, such as a social emotion or an ethical concern. So uses of foods and drinks as tools will be considered according to what they are intended to achieve over and above an expressive effect.

Food in Interpersonal Manipulation

Food is often served as an expression of affection for a person or of pleasure in their behaviour. It may indeed help to strengthen the bond emotionally and to encourage affiliative behaviour, so long as the gift of food is viewed as appropriate in type and scale by the receiver. In young children, preference for a food is reinforced when it is used as a reward (Birch *et al.*, 1980). So perhaps the giving of food by host or guest reinforces further expression of that sort of hospitality and reciprocity.

Refusal of the food served may be an attempt to gain attention. Equally, refusal to eat may be an attempt to punish the provider or to express anger or frustration. These strategies may be more common in young children or severely challenged people because their verbal communication is inadequate to the situation or has proved ineffective and the food-provider is perceived as strongly committed to having the food accepted.

Efforts are often made to encourage children to eat by offering a treat of some sort (such as a favourite dessert or some desired activity) to reward extra intake or the consumption of a disliked food. Such instrumental uses of food have been investigated experimentally and found to be counterproductive in reducing longer-term preference for the rewarded food (Birch *et al.*, 1982, 1984).

Conforming in a distinctive choice of drink or food may be a strategy open to a newcomer to a group as a means of ingratiation and a way to gain a sense of belonging. For established members of the group, nevertheless, such a choice is more likely to be symbolic (if it is more than purely habitual) and to serve as part of a sense of identity of the group, rather than being instrumental.

Meat Eating and Avoidance

Flesh foods are treated through particularly complex and diverse cognitive structures. The dominant tradition in many industrialized countries is to regard meat as a prestigious food. If it is too expensive to have at the main meal(s) every day, then a substantial serving is *de rigueur* for a special occasion. Yet there is also the vegetarian tradition in which meat eating is regarded as morally depraved. Deliberate meat avoidance may still be somewhat deviant in the West but it has a long and respectable history and is rapidly becoming normal among younger generations.

MEAT PRODUCTION MORALITY

This controversy is primarily ethical, at least in the minds of vegetarians as expressed in the rationales they give for avoiding meat. They do not expect to kill off cattle farming by refusing to buy beef or to stop hens being raised in batteries by avoiding chicken. Rather, meat is a symbol to them of objectionable human exploitation of other species. The prestige of meat is deplored as an expression of human arrogance and brutality. Vegetarians could not live with themselves if they ate meat: 'vegetarian' is not just a recipe; it is a self-concept. Liking meat is also a self-concept, if only in reaction and even though meat-eaters do not think of themselves as carnivores or speciesist oppressors, as professing vegetarians may call them.

Meat eating and avoidance are also instrumental, however.

NUTRITIOUS?

Lean meat provides the highest quality of protein and has a moderate fat content with a desirable unsaturated fatty acid composition. On the other hand, a mixture of plant foods, from beans and root vegetables to green salads, provides a wider range of essential nutrients, can be lower in fat content and is rich in fibre and antioxidants.

Thus, health motivation can be important in either tradition. Both these sectors of the food industry try to use healthy images to promote their products. It would however be both ethical and prudent to appreciate that genuinely moral positions cannot be undermined by health arguments, even if they did clearly favour the other side.

There are then some functions either of 'red meat' or of 'complex carbohydrates' and 'vegetables and fruit' that are cognitively, socially and physiologically less clear.

SATISFYING?

Among meat-eaters, beef is regarded as heartier than chicken or fish, with perhaps some divergence of opinion over pork and lamb. Much beef is indeed chewier than chicken and it may satiate for longer because the stomach, like the teeth, takes more time to break it down for digestion (French *et al.*, 1992).

There has been a tradition that men need beef more than women do. It remains to be investigated, in men or women who feel that way, how much this feeling is based on an image of 'red-blooded' masculinity, a notion that the tougher food to chew is more appropriate to the more muscular sex, or perhaps from a requirement from bigger bodies for a somewhat stronger or more prolonged stimulation of visceral satiety signals. Those are questions for cognitive research, in relation to the relevant anthropology or physiology. It would be better to have them answered before speculating sociobiologically whether a modern male preference for beef harks back to the hunting ages.

Battles over Eating

Parents tend to bring strong expectations to the feeding of their offspring, perhaps from the family culture in which they themselves were brought up. This can set the scene for battles to get a youngster to eat more or to choose foods more wisely. Young children may bring home food demands that seem nutritionally scandalous. Aversions or loss of appetite may come from nowhere. Teenage moodiness may push a plate aside.

It is unlikely (though not impossible) that the young one is sickening for something, let alone spiralling into anorexia or some chronic physical illness. If that were the case, pressure to eat properly is liable to exacerbate a loss of interest in food. A battle over food is unlikely to be productive. Even when immature, the psychobiosocial system is often a lot better than assumed at accommodating vagaries at one or other level without going right off the 'rails' of either biological or cultural growth.

Appetite for food does tend to decline during illness, disproportionately to the reduction in activity when confined to bed and inappropriately to the heavy energy requirements of tissue repair after injury. Light, sweet or otherwise attractive foods and drinks are traditionally regarded as important to tempt the appetite during convalescence, especially for children. There appears to have been no investigation whether such strategies are appropriate to the cognitive structure of 'poor appetite'. Furthermore, the need for food cannot be judged by the amounts generally expected to be eaten or even by the individual's past habits; protracted weight loss or slowed growth are the only criteria. Thus, a young person suffering from cystic fibrosis may be nagged for eating too little when no thinner than many fast-grown teenagers and not in fact falling behind the personal growth track.

Loss of interest in food in the elderly, after injury for example, puts them at risk of unintentional autoeuthanasia ('losing the will to live'). Again, it would be counter-productive to try to enforce eating. These days in hospital, intravenous nutrition is considered in such situations.

Fasting and Hunger Strikes

Food can be used as a tool by a total refusal to eat. Water is drunk but nutritive fluids may also be refused.

Hunger strikes use food as a tool of political protest or moral persuasion. Suffragettes and other prisoners with a point to make do this violence to themselves, either because no stronger form of protest is available to them or because non-violent protest seems ineffective and violence against others is in their view precluded.

Another objective of refusing food may be more a mental or spiritual purity. Holy men and mystics fast and pray as part of a self-punitive style of moral discipline. In India before independence, Gandhi could meld such religious traditions with mass politics by turning ascetic living into a well-publicized fast to attain a specific outcome.

Fasting provides examples of psychobiosocial integration. The physiological penalties are balanced by or even turned into cultural rewards in the faster's mind. Visible wasting of the tissues and/or the avoidance of plumpness by repeated or prolonged fasts signals a strength of conviction and may exert a moral pressure on others. The digestive movements that give rise to hunger pangs may perhaps decline but, even if they do not, the faster seems to adapt to them and may be able to reinterpret the sensations as something other than pains removable by eating; then they no longer instigate or aggravate the desire for food. During a prolonged fast, the brain adapts to using ketones as fuel from the breakdown of body fat and this may have some cognitive effects, such as subjective symptoms or changes in mental performance.

Purification of the body, rather than the mind, may be the objective of food-refusal or of highly selective eating in small amounts or special foods. This lay physiology is current in the notion of 'clearing poisons out of the system'. There is no scientific validity in implicit analogies such as rinsing out an empty barrel nor in interpreting a reduction in stools as an index of successful purging. Nevertheless, if respected figures teach the benefits of such a diet and some hours with an empty small intestine make one feel better, the practice will be self-reinforcing.

Athletes may fast to meet a requirement on weight, as in boxing, or to attain a shape, as in ballet (Garner and Garfinkel, 1980) or bodybuilding (Bolin, 1992). Water as well as food may be refused for a few hours, e.g. to weigh in, but obviously a high standard of athletic performance cannot be maintained without adequate amounts of water and energy as well as many other nutrients. Complete fasting is therefore unusual but a very strict restraint on eating may be maintained at certain times.

Dieting will be considered in Chapter 7. Its relevance in this context is the ideological fervour it can take on and the ritual extremes to which it may be pursued.

The worship of leanness may be regarded as too self-centred to merit ethical or political standing. Nonetheless it can gain all the fervour and outward practices of a conversion to a religion.

Self-starvation out of loathing for a normally shaped body may go out of control, probably because of physiological adaptations as well as emotional gains. In young people who are using food refusal to confirm their control of themselves, weight may go down to precariously lean levels (20–25 per cent below average weight for height), resulting in a syndrome that has been given the psychiatric diagnosis of anorexia nervosa. Women in their twenties are more likely to interrupt such bouts of starvation with a substantial meal, followed by attempts to get rid of the fattening calories by vomitting or using laxatives. If the meals get frequent and large a syndrome of bingeing and purgeing develops, whether or not the sufferer is underweight, overweight or in the normal range, which is diagnosed as bulimia nervosa. In these disorders of eating, food is wielded in clumsy desperation as a tool to shape the body.

Foods and Drinks as Symbols

Gifts

A gift of food is truly symbolic only if it is not seen as a reward or as reciprocation. It is 'the thought that counts'. The gift is unconditional, a token of love or personal affection.

The symbolism informs the selection of an item of food or drink that a guest may bring. Unless an understanding has been set up that a contribution to the host's larder would be appreciated, the most appropriate gift of food or drink is a non-functional symbol of friendship and appreciation. For example, it might be too small to serve at the meal or party which the guest is attending. It could be something to eat or drink by itself, not as part of a real meal. Confectionery can fit the bill rather well, as chocolate-box manufacturers well know. The gift is wrapped prettily, not like an ordinary food. Ideally, the item itself or the message attached to it has some shared personal significance.

Religious Symbolism

UNLEAVENED BREAD

Bread baked without raising by yeast is a key part of Jewish families' tradition of annually remembering the escape from Egypt led by Moses. Indeed, it is orthodox to clear all yeast out of the home at the time of Passover.

The evidence is that this is a pure symbolic practice. Its only basis seems to be the overt wish simply to relive the use of a longlasting food prepared for a journey into the desert. Support for this comes from the fact that the ban on yeast is confined to the period of the Passover celebration and so there is nothing wrong with leavening most of the time. Also, there are no severe religious sanctions on consumption of yeast, as there might be if it had more than this specific role. The effects of a small amount of yeast enabling the whole lump of dough to rise has been used as a religious metaphor for evil spreading through a society but this is no part of the rationale for the search for crumbs of leavened bread before the Passover starts.

Moreover, how the concept of subsisting on unleavened bread during the Passover is realized in contemporary and local conditions depends on the individual's upbringing and the custom of the household within a local synagogue and its section of Judaism. Family and synagogue leaders formulate an appropriate application of the symbolic principle. For example, when considerable quantities of conventional baked goods are kept under refrigeration, arrangements might be made to sell stocks that should not remain in the house to a Gentile, with a view to buying them back afterwards.

What matters is the type of food in the story. The point is to succour one of the taproots of Jewishness, a miraculous escape from slavery in Egypt. What counts as unalterable in the heritage emerges from the subcultural consensus, subject to theological argument, economic pressures and the dynamics of social influence, like any other custom.

COMMUNION WINE

For Christians, this is the blood of Jesus Christ, as he stated when telling his disciples just before his death to eat bread and drink wine in memory of his self-sacrifice. It is natural therefore for many Christian traditions to use red wine and indeed, because of the association of the crucifixion with the Passover, to use wafers of bread made without yeast. Nevertheless, yellow Communion wine is sometimes used. Christian denominations that avoid alcohol use unfermented grape juice if available or other red-coloured drinks such as blackcurrant. Not everybody is served with both bread and wine in some churches. The key words of the Communion ceremony are the body that was broken and the blood that was shed, solid and liquid spiritual nutriment. So perhaps the essence of the symbolism is a morsel to eat and/or a sip to drink and the details are ancillary.

Metaphor

Some symbolism in or, more usually, from food has become so trite (or deep) that it is now built into our language. Fieldhouse (1985, p. 198) lists metaphorical descriptions of people as sweethearts, the apple of my eye, a bad egg, a sourpuss, salt of the earth, being cheesed off, cool as a cucumber or hot as mustard and having a peaches-and-cream complexion. Someone can have a bitter attitude too, act sweetly, or speak in mellifluous tones; the plain English 'honeyed tones', though, lays it on too thickly and obviously and we are talking about flattery or cajolery, not just a sweet-sounding voice. Language can also be salty but that presumably refers to the taste not of food but of the sea in the talk of 'old salts'.

Elsewhere, Fieldhouse (1985, p. 56) mentions the use of the word bread to mean money. A challenge or activity in which someone thrives might be described as 'meat and drink' to them or their 'staple diet': the physical nurturance from food is metonymous for the nurturance of a full life.

Considering the ethnic distinctiveness of cuisines, it is no surprise that one group sometimes names another group by their foods, particularly when there are no distinguishing physiognomic features. Considering too the propensity for xenophobia and out-group stereotyping, it is not surprising that these culinary labels tend to be at least slightly deprecatory. Thus, some Americans used to call British people Limeys, because the British Navy once served lime juice to ward off scurvy, and the British used to call the French Froggies, out of amazement and horror at the idea of eating frogs' legs.

In virtually all these cases, experience with food has permeated our talk and thought about other areas of life. This diffusion is particularly striking from the consumption of sugary foodstuffs. The Greek word for pleasure, *hedone*, relates to the Greek for honey, *hedus*. The cognitive processes of a pleasure in the sensual thrill that may come from eating a sweet food are difficult to distinguish, though, from the pleasing character of the activity of satisfying a desire for a sweet food (Booth, 1991b). Be that as it may, we slide easily from using 'sweet' to refer to the sensation to 'sweet' as attractive (as we can move from taste as sensory experience to taste as liking or appreciation of quality). This pleasing quality is described not only in foods but also in other materials and objects and in people too as we have seen. At the opening of *Twelfth Night*, musicians are playing and Shakespeare makes the Duke imply that music could fill the ears for long enough to lose all its appeal, just as food becomes unappetising when the belly is overfull.

> If music be the food of love, play on.
> Give me excess of it; that, surfeiting,
> The appetite may sicken and so die.

This brings us to satiation: the cloying effect of sweet taste has not been separated very well in human experiments from the nauseating effect of swallowing too much sugar (Wooley, Wooley and Dunham, 1972). Eating enough of food with one set of sensory characteristics is sufficient to reduce the appetite for that food in particular for a short while (Rolls *et al.*, 1981). The immediate cognitive effects of the nausea on sensory preferences have yet to be measured, although it is the osmotic effects that concentrated sugars have in the digestive tract that reduce the pleasantness of sweet tastes (Cabanac and Fantino, 1977). Shakespeare was impressed by how loathesome the taste of sweetness becomes after eating too much honey, 'whereof a little more than a little is by much too much' (*Henry IV*). However, past experience may be important in such reactions. The osmotic effects in the gut condition aversion to the taste of the material that produced them, at least in animals (Booth, Lovett and McSherry, 1972; Davis and Smith, 1990): this also remains to be examined in people, although there is considerable evidence that gastrointestinal upset turns people off any distinctive food eaten some while beforehand (Rozin and Fallon, 1985).

Eating Motivation and Attitudes to Foods

Conventional eating and drinking practices shape the expectations, emotions and benefits gained by individual participants. Psychologists have attempted to find out what people want from food by getting answers to direct questions about their reasons for their choices from groups of respondents and then putting the data into one pool for multivariate analysis. Such a procedure can recover a consensus structure of motivation but only if sufficient number of respondents adhere to that structure. Such a structure of rationales that is held in common among a substantial proportion of respondents is likely to be conventional in the social group(s) sampled. Nevertheless, this approach may miss quite a lot of people who approach things differently.

Multivariate consensus modelling may therefore have some psychosocial validity. The conventional uses of opinion poll statistics have none. It is completely fallacious to tot up the frequencies of answers to particular questions and assume that the majority answers all come from the same people. Dividing respondents into subgroups who give particular pairs of answers (cross-tabulation) still tells us nothing necessarily about what was going on in any actual respondent's mind. The answers from each individual respondent must somehow be coordinated before the data from the whole survey are put together.

Social research is plagued with a confusion between validity of sampling and validity of interpretation. When one wishes to use survey data to estimate some output from a total population, such as candidates elected from a political party, the average per capita intake of fat or the norms for an I.Q. score, it is clearly important to survey a representative sample of the population in question. When quantitative research means estimating population quantities, then the sample must be large enough and adequately selected to permit reliable extrapolation from the part to the whole.

However, when the quantitation is of the determinants of behaviour, i.e. what is going on in the minds of members of that population, then validity of psychological measurement is the primary criterion. Representative sampling matters only if we need to know the prevalence in the population of a cognitive strategy and the survey can measure the strategy in each respondent. Consensus modelling and other conventional psychometric methods therefore require only psychological diversity in the survey sample. The usual multivariate models depend on correlations across the different respondents between the answers given by each person to different questions: diversity among individuals is necessary to bring out any across-person correlations that exist.

Despite its centrality to psychology since the statistical techniques were invented, psychometrics does not achieve the requisite individual measurement either. In fact, it makes the fundamentally invalid assumption that the structure of variation among individuals will be the same as the structure of variation within individuals, at least within the consensus. If we have no other source of evidence, then differences between people in the same situation (i.e. faced with the questions posed) have to be used in the hope that they reflect differences within each of those people when faced with different versions of the situations tested. Such within-person measurement has been strangely neglected by the science of the mind. It is essential in order to check at the very least this assumption that it is indeed a consensus among individuals that emerges from the correlations across respondents. Individual measurement can deal too with the people outside the supposed consensus.

Further fundamental problems about all survey techniques are that the questions impose ideas on the respondents and the answers are liable to reflect current conversation, entered personally and heard on the media.

Attitude research therefore has given a rather impoverished view of people's thoughts and feelings about their diet. When questions are asked about health, people can account for their food choice to some extent by the ideas around at the time. If they are asked what they like and what they can get, their answers account for their actions much better.

There is another major problem with the mainstream of psychological modelling of attitudes. The objective has been not just to get people to account for their actions. The aim of attitude research, often claimed to have been met by the models, has been to find out the cognitive determinants of the behaviour that respondents also report (Axelson and Brinberg, 1989). The idea is to identify the beliefs that need informing or the values to allow for in public policy on, for example, healthy eating. Instead, the results are likely to reflect what can be said secondarily to awareness of one's behaviour (Bem, 1972). The reasons people given for acting are socially acceptable justifications of their behaviour (Peters, 1954), not reports on what they are aware of among the factors that are actually causative of behaviour (many of which could be subconscious anyway in the case of normally unreflective choices).

Thus, even if it is sensible to try to separate the 'rational' from the 'emotional' (what is the difference in the mental mechanisms, as distinct from what they achieve?), simply asking people to vote for or rate conventional justifications is not the way to do it. That is 'direct' only in a naïvely muddled sense. A scientifically direct approach to the mental causation of eating, whether one classifies it as rational or emotional, would have to map the cognitive processes involved in a person's verbal or behavioural responses to observably varied situations (be they actual or described and imagined). Such data provide the basis for modelling of the cognitive processes mediating the effects of the observed determinants on the observed behaviour, the professed aim of attitude research.

Attitudes of Individuals

A first step towards determining the representation of culture in the cognitive processes involved in eating behaviour can be to look for relationships among the concepts that a person uses in talking about a common piece of behaviour towards food and drink.

A simple objective way of doing this would be to look for linear relationships among pairs of concepts. This approach has long been used to seek bivariate relations in individual differences within a set of data on multiple variables collected from many people. The resulting model of an apparent consensus expressed in a network of relationships is called a path analysis. An example is given for the beliefs, values, emotions and behaviour of dieting in Chapter 7.

We do not have to rely, however, on some consensus in the variations among respondents in their answers to a fixed set of questions. We can seek relationships among the answers to a set of questions from a person who has been asked about different forms of a familiar situation. Furthermore, both the situational variants and the questions can be phrased in the individual's own words.

Within-individual data can have statistical problems but the risk of running into these can be reduced. It is important to diversify the variants of the situation under discussion in ways that are acceptable to the respondent. (This helps the data to approach normality sufficiently in their distributions.) Also, apparently distinct

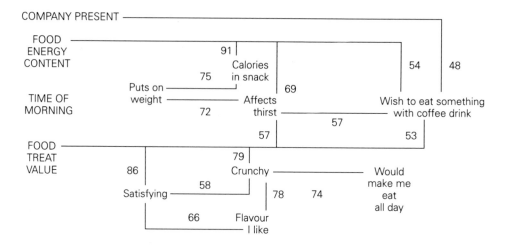

Figure 4.1 Correlation coefficients (×100) between concepts described in the words of a woman who has constant concern about her weight, as elicited in formalized re-interview after initial open-ended interviewing about her habitual morning coffee and biscuit(s) (see Tables 5.1 and 5.2). Capital letters: orthogonally varied descriptions of the whole situation (Table 5.2). Lower-case terms: personal tags (Table 5.1), rated in response to each overall described situation.

features of the situation that may influence the interviewee's responses should be varied independently of each other so far as practicable. (This reduces the bugbear of correlational analyses, multi-collinearity or confounding among variables. Where substantial correlations have not been avoided, these can be used to simplify the data by separate factor analyses of either or both the variations described in the situations or/and the variations in the responses given by the interviewee; the exhaustive version of this approach is called canonical analysis.)

An example of path-analytical modelling of a conversation with an individual about responses to variations in an eating and drinking situation is given in Figure 4.1 (Booth, 1992). This woman said in a preliminary interview that she always tried to delay her first intake of the day because she feared that even a drink would start her eating and she would not be able to stop. This fear and the temptations to snack are evident within the pattern of correlations in her ratings of situations that were described to her in own terms for factors that seemed from the initial conversation to be influential on her decision to have a drink and something to eat with it.

The standard technique in open-ended interviewing is simply to report what seems obvious to the interviewer. The words used may be subject to more formal treatment by some type of content analysis. This approach, by contrast, subjects the interviewer's hypotheses to a quantitative check by the statistical criterion of colinear association. (If only yes/no stimuli and responses were available, association statistics could be substituted for correlational statistics). The basic assumption is that causes and effects within the mind are straight-line relationships. This assumption has been substantiated under normal circumstances of food choice by the psychophysical techniques outlined in Chapter 1.

Indeed, the technique of within-individual path analysis just described is a form of individualized psychophysics. It has been adapted to exploring the possibility of a network of points at which two or more inputs are combined into an output (that may in turn be the input for one or more other nodes of the network). As a preliminary manoeuvre in tackling a network of relationships, the multi-dimensionality of the psychophysics at each node has been ignored. Instead, every variable has been treated as a potential influence on every other variable by multiple bivariate analysis. (Technically speaking, it is safest to replace the correlations in Figure 4.1 by partial regressions, to allow for collinearities: this means running a multiple regression onto each variable in which all the other variables are predictors.)

As is the case for conventional path analysis and indeed experimental investigations too, a confirmatory approach is much stronger than an exploratory one. That is to say, the interpretation is sounder if an hypothetical network was specified before the data were collected. To the extent that the postulated pathways show strong associations and there are no high correlations for pathways that were not predicted, the theoretical model is supported. Hence, this approach provides another discipline for qualitative research: a good report should contain a network diagram of the individual's attitudes to a typical situation. If an exploratory approach is considered, then the ideal should be recognized as enough data to run an automated scanning of all the interpretations that the data will bear (Glymour *et al.*, 1987).

Once a node in a network has been established as worth investigating further, then its apparent inputs can be tested as distinct features that combine to generate the output from that node, using the multi-dimensional psychophysical design. In fact, suitable multivariate data could in principle be given a psychophysical treatment from the start, testing the dimensionality of each node in the whole of a specified network. Where there are multiple outputs from a node, as well as multiple inputs, it would then be feasible to distinguish among different sorts of processing that might be involved in an integrative response to two or more inputs – namely, operating subconsciously, within sensual or emotional awareness and by the more rational use of shared meanings (Freeman *et al.*, 1993).

Commonalities and Diversity Among Individuals

The above approach is open to any features of or responses to situations that a person may mention in conversation or that the investigator may notice during non-verbal observation, and indeed to any situation commonly faced by one person and not others. Hence, an influence on one person's overall response may not be evident in the data from another person, even when faced with the same situation.

Nevertheless, everybody operates within one or more subcultural contexts shared with others. Therefore, many situations will be physically and socially the same for different people and so are liable to be approached with shared concepts in mind and to provoke at least some reactions in common. Even when the words used are not the same, discourse analysis can provide a case for identifying a concept used by different people. Given enough data, similarities in input structure to a node can be identified by statistical techniques.

In other words, individualized analyses can be used to identify consensus in attitudes where it exists but they do not force it on the data in the way that conventional attitude modelling has to do. Minority views and even a single highly idiosyncratic outlook can be mapped. Indeed, where there is no majority structure, several major types of approach to a class of situations could be characterized. Such an approach is obviously necessary if we are to be realistic about pluralistic societies.

Even more importantly, the experimentally designed interviews identify potentially objectifiable influences on people in well-specified situations. This gets round an even greater weakness in conventional attitude research – a lack of implications for action. The psychophysically based attitude modelling can interpolate predictions of how people will react to objectively specified circumstances, as well as making those predictions for any subset of individuals who share demographic, lifestyle or psychological characteristics of interest.

The Emotions of Eating

Development of a cognitive anthropology of food is as cramped as the rest of nutritional psychology by confusions about subjective experience and objective performance. Affect and social situation are logically and causally indissolubly intertwined. Yet most work on the emotional meaning of food is empty of cultural analysis.

The Nature of Emotions

The terms we use to label what are usually called emotions (or affect, in one sort of scientific jargon) are variegated and loose. In this situation, it is not wise to expect to define the concept of an emotion, let alone to develop a tight scientific theory of the family of phenomena. Certainly, the nature, causes and origins of emotions have been matters of great controversy in science and philosophy. The position taken here is therefore flexible and inexact. Also, it is limited to psychological aspects, leaving aside both biological processes and philosophical details.

It can be argued that, generally speaking, an emotion is identified by the objective social role normally played by the person to whom suffering of that affective experience is attributed (Coulter, 1979; Forgas, 1979).

One can also hazard the view that an emotion is typically caused by a breach of some normal expectation. That is, emotions result from frustration of motives, the socially attributed reasons for our actions (reviewed in the previous section of this chapter).

Given the human capacity for learning, we may expect consistent association of eating or drinking with an emotional situation to attach mood to the foodstuffs or beverage types used in that ambience. For example, we have seen how contented mood arises in the baby from the quieting effect of food stimuli, coupled with the tactile, thermal, olfactory and visual social stimuli from the nurser (Chapter 2). Presumably then, on an occasion when interpersonal comfort is lacking, for example during grief at a lost relationship or gloom at the failure to form one, eating can be a vicarious comfort. Eating or drinking the appropriate item might carry social memories, covertly if not explicitly, into the mood of the moment and alter it, at least to some extent.

In an effort to inform the targetting of food advertising more systematically than the creative intuitions of marketers, consumer research has sought to characterize emotionally or socially meaningful images carried by foods. Recently a social psychologist has used sought emotional meanings attached to the names of particular foods by word association (Lyman, 1989).

However, this method is liable to reveal more about American vocabulary and indeed current marketing ploys than the objective socio-affective roles of actual foods in real situations. Language is also full of cliché, empty metaphor and now meaningless etymological origins. It would be a good task for objective cognitive analysis to see whether the use of a food-originated term in a living language actually carries any food-related meaning in the mind of the speaker or hearer. Word association would be one way to explore that.

Psychoanalysts have speculated that adult emotion and personality are highly dependent on feeding and other experiences in infancy. An 'oral' person is generous to or dependent on others because indulged at the breast as a baby. However, this sort of theory has often been couched in such broad terms that it has been difficult to derive testable predictions (Kline, 1972). Such research as has been done has not addressed particular eating situations or types of food or drink, where indeed most transfer of learning from infant feeding might be expected.

To the extent that patterns persist from infancy to childhood and then into adult life, the causation is not necessarily from early feeding to later life. An infant's approach to feeding and other events may be characteristic from the start and that temperament might persist independently of its effects on interactions over food. For example, rather than cigarette smoking being a substitute for or reversion to suckling at the breast or use of a pacifier (dummy), the personality traits that dispose people to smoke, such as they are (Eysenck and Eaves, 1980), may have affected early orality.

Undoubtedly though, being fed and the infant–adult interactions between adults and infant or young child over food in early life provide many occasions and rich contexts for the development of differentiation and specificity among emotions (Chiva, 1985).

Emotional Eating

In the 1960s and 1970s, psychologists and psychiatrists doing research into obesity considered two main lines of theory, dubbed 'psychosomatic' and 'psychoanalytic'. These were primarily theories of emotional origins and bases of the overeating that fat people were stereotyped as indulging in. The soul of slimming will be considered in Chapter 7 but these ideas about emotional (over)eating provide a useful starting point for considering the cognitive development and structure of links between eating and emotions.

As the two terms indicate, these theories come from medical traditions. The so-called psychosomatic approach centres round the idea that social and emotional states causes bodily symptoms and in fat people these symptoms are hunger. The psychoanalytical approach is, roughly speaking, to regard overeating as a compulsion boiling up from emotional screw-ups very early in life in the interpersonal relationships between the infant and one (or both) of her or his parents.

From a scientific point of view, such ideas smack of magical 'explanation': the specification of cognitive mechanisms is crude and incomplete. Nevertheless, the lines of thought can be seen to relate to the longstanding distinction in the psychology of learning between classical, Pavlovian or stimulus conditioning (stimulus-stimulus association, eliciting involuntary responses) and instrumental or response conditioning (stimulus–response association, making the emitted responses intentional). The cognitive approach to eating and drinking taken in this book is founded on research into learned control of ingestion. The difference between stimulus and response conditioning or elicited and intentional behaviour in turn relates to the distinction drawn earlier in this chapter between food as symbol and food as tool. After stimulus conditioning, eating the food represents the emotion. After response conditioning, eating the food controls the emotion.

The advantage of this apparently behaviouristic conceptualization is that it ties down the design and interpretation of experimental and observational investigations to specifiable observables. In practice, however, neither the observable 'stimuli' or 'responses' need be at all physical. Indeed, they were percepts and emotions or intentions even in animal learning experiments, despite what the behaviourists argued (Hamlyn, 1956, 1991). Nor do the cognitive processes transforming perceived situations into emotional reactions or intended acts need to be confined to the barebone apparatus of association theory (e.g. Staats, 1975; Forgas, 1979): all that a cautious scientific approach requires is that more complex mental processes be invoked only when the evidence refutes a less complex explanation. As we have seen, psychologists not disciplined by such behaviour process concepts tend to commit overattribution fallacies.

EMOTIONALLY ELICITED EATING

A cognitive mechanism similar to the psychoanalytical ideas on emotional eating would therefore be an emotional state or a social situation that has come to elicit eating. The conditioned stimulus (CS) is socio-affective. The situations that normally are appetizing and help to elicit eating include lunchtime on the clock, a description or photograph of attractive food or an epigastric pang. Thus the emotional CS for eating can be confused with normal hunger (Bruch, 1969). Indeed, functionally speaking, that emotion is hunger for the sufferer from emotional eating.

The problem with this theory that eating may be emotionally elicited is lack of direct evidence that such classical conditioning can occur. In principle, a mood could become a CS for eating if paired with a consequence that already strongly elicits eating, such as the presentation of highly attractive food. Hence initially deliberate 'comfort eating' might become a more involuntary reaction to the need for comfort. However, such conditioning has yet to be demonstrated.

A more complex mechanism for classical conditioning of eating to emotion includes food in the CS along with the mood (Booth, 1987). While complicated, this is entirely realistic to the multi-dimensional character of appetite for food: we eat in response to perceived configurations of stimuli across several modalities (see Chapter 1). If we can integrate visual, gustatory and visceral dimensions, it seems reasonable to suppose we could integrate socio-affective dimensions also into the hunger complex (to coin a psychoanalysts' word!). A test for this sort of learning would be to look for dependence of a conditioned food preference on the socio-affective context of its acquisition. We looked for such mood-dependency of a food preference (conditioned emotionally, indeed) but could see no evidence for such configuring (S. Campbell and D.A. Booth, unpublished data, 1989). Such tests for emotional elements in eating CSs should be run on nutritionally and socially conditioned food preferences.

EMOTIONALLY INSTRUMENTAL EATING

Another way in which an emotional state or social situation could lead to eating is for the food to be expected to improve mood or to facilitate interpersonal interaction. In learning-theoretical jargon, the emotion occasions eating in this case, or the emotion is a discriminative stimulus for reinforcement of eating (it is the sign that distinguishes when reward is available for eating).

This is mood-control eating. The cake or chocolate is meant to cheer one up. The alcoholic drinks are meant to instil a party spirit. Awareness of an emotional need triggers ingestion of the materials which are expected by convention and past personal experience to meet that need.

The reinforcement of emotionally occasioned eating does not have to be a change in the occasioning emotion either. It might be some other emotional or social gain. It could be nutritional: indeed, it has been suggested that most emotional eating, including that in eating disorders, is classically conditioned or instrumentally reinforced by caloric satiation (Booth, 1987, 1989a). Spitzer, Marcus and Rodin (1980) pointed out that the reinforcement of stress-induced eating could even be cognitive or internal in the sense that the food simply distracts attention from an aversive emotional state. This could be an effective mechanism of negative reinforcement (strengthening the response by removing punishment) if the bad mood returns after eating, or even intensifies as guilt or anxiety sets in about having overeaten. The distraction is an immediate effect of eating on emotion and so, by a general principle of learning, it will have a more powerful effect than a comparable strength of effect after a delay.

It must be noted, though, that discriminative or occasioning stimuli are not distinguishable from conditioned or eliciting stimuli without very careful experimental design. By the same token, most pieces of human behaviour are probably a mixture of intentional and involuntary processes in variable proportions. For example, pairing of the consequence with the stimulus when it is being learned can be pitted against its unpairing from the response. However, this is not practicable with normal eating and drinking and is virtually impossible with emotional changes. In the formula *ABC*: antecedents, behaviour, consequences (where in this context *A* is emotion and *B* is ingestion), we may never know whether *B* follows *A* because *C* reinforces *B* or *A*.

Thus, it may not be very productive to pick away at the distinction between reactions and actions, or classical and instrumental conditioning (or symbol and tool), even for theoretical purposes, let alone to gain practically useful understanding. The important point to recognize is that development depends on the learning of processes that produce overt action specified by the external situation. The mind is not some ghost, revealed only by private intuition or clever statistics. We can see people's cognitive development in changes in how they deal with situations and we can read each others' minds objectively by a disciplined use of ordinary social intercourse.

Food and Mood

Biomedical and industrial interest in the emotions and eating has been focused on the idea that substances in foods and drinks may create or remove moods and alter social behaviour or intellectual performance as a result. In reality, emotions are deeply rooted in the perceptions and past experiences specific to the individual and the social role of current activity. Therefore the effects of eating and drinking on subjective state and social and cognitive performance are likely to have far stronger psychosocial determinants than chemical bases. We shall be unlikely to identify psychological effects of food substances (even on hunger and thirst motivation) until we have understood the cultural roles of the consumption of the food or drink item and the cultural and personal roles of its psychological effects.

Sometimes the cultural role of the food virtually is the mood. Enterprising abstainers can get into the party spirit without getting any of the party's spirits into them. Cups of tea can be as cathartic for a group of teetotallers after a funeral as a wake may be in a whiskey-using culture.

Expectancy Effects

Given the personally learned and culturally stereotyped roles of particular foods or drinks in certain emotional situations, it should be predicted that many items would not only be expected to affect mood and cognitive or physical performance but also often actually recreate the expected psychological effect to some degree, by directing attention to those aspects of the external circumstances or internal state that are of the anticipated sort. This is not a sheer effect of mind over matter, belief generating reality. It is the same process as auto-suggestion or self-hypnosis, when that works. The expectation, directed attention and active imagination are supported to some extent by a perceptible reality of roughly the right sort. This then strengthens the confidence, focuses the attention and feeds the imagination.

Even the powerful mood-altering drugs used in psychiatry probably have much of their specificity and therapeutic power by such auto-suggested (and prescriber-hyponotized) interpretation of less specific bodily or mental effects or even side-effects, like mouth-drying or other autonomic actions of anti-depressants (Thompson, 1978) or muscle-relaxant or sleep-promoting effects of anxiolytics. Digestion-prolonging effects of anti-depressants and some appetite-suppressants may con-tribute to their limited usefulness in treating bulimia nervosa and obesity (Booth, 1989a). If any of this is the case, milder and possibly less specific psychoactive food constituents such as caffeine or herbal agents or transmitter precursor uptake effects should not be expected to have pharmacological effects out of the appropriate social context and cognitive stance.

So, the measurement of behavioural performances or experiences is not the real difficulty in studying dietary effects on behaviour, despite a widespread mis-conception to the contrary. Answers to questions about personal viewpoints or momentary states of mind can be shown to reflect underlying determinants by the well-established criteria of multivariate psychometrics. Such adequately scaled in-struments provide valid and reliable expressions of differences in emotional state and in judgements of one's own ability.

The greatest difficulties arise rather in the design and interpretation of investigations of real-life psychological phenomena and, indeed, of the composition of the everyday diet as well. As in any other area of science, effective research requires a good theoretical grasp of the mechanisms liable to be involved and hence of the methods for getting evidence on their operation. There are no standardized tests for effects of diet on behaviour and there never will be, any more than there can be standard tests for dietary effects on children's growth or for consumer perception of food quality.

Food Cravings and Mood

Many ordinary people and scientists alike have assumed that cravings or appetite for foods must arise from nutritional deficits, hormonal imbalances or neurotransmitter levels that are corrected by substances in the foodstuff selected. Psychologists in recent years have raised a chorus of doubts about this presumption. The supposed evidence for wisdom of the body in creating appetites for foods containing needed nutrients has been severely criticized.

The basic criticism is that there is no evidence that the craved or selected food is recognized from its effects on the nutrient deficiency or hormonal imbalance, even for the case of the liking for the taste of salt (Beauchamp *et al.*, 1990). The behaviour is not specific for foods containing the substance supposedly controlling the selection and the bodily state is not one which is specific to the selection of those foods. It is therefore beside the point to investigate whether the nutrient appetite or substance addiction is mediated by mood changes, action on pleasure systems in the brain or non-conscious neural changes, because there is no biochemically selective behaviour to be explained.

Most cravings may be no more than recall of a distinctive foodstuff that has not been eaten for some time, when in a somewhat agitated state. Maybe sometimes the indulgence is permitted by a self-medication rationale, and this could be superstitiously or hypno-suggestively self-reinforcing. Alternatively, the more symbolic food would be excused by one's condition, such that pregnant women are reputed to act a little crazy or the bloating or cramps prior to or during menstruation are a syndrome of discomfort that certain foods can control. Such attributions can be cyclic (Rozin *et al.*, 1991).

A lot of attention has been given to suggestions that some sufferers from depression crave for carbohydrate-rich foods (starchy or sugary). The earliest source of this notion was how patients described the foods that they reported eating – as sweet or sugary. This is almost certainly to be culturally based, not biochemically. At that time at least, sugar was the great white evil and so any sufferer from mood disorder was liable to embroil it in their symptomology. Simon *et al.* (1993) found that eating-disordered women in France still showed abnormalities in sweet preference, while in America over the last decade abnormalities in cream preference have reflected the public disapproval of dietary fats.

Even when evidence for 'carbohydrate craving' is based on the nutrient contents of food observed to have been eaten, the investigators are misinterpreting a social phenomenon as a biological one. The foods having a higher ratio of carbohydrate to protein usually have also a high ratio of fat to protein (and to carbohydrate). It would be less inaccurate to say the craving is for fat-rich foods (Drewnowski, 1987). This was not done because of theoretical ideas that the high carbohydrate/protein ratio would affect the activity of the transmitter substance 5HT in the brain. Neither the nutrient nor the neurotransmitter is germane to the correct description of the craving. This must be in terms of the foods as they fit into the psychology of the cravers. Their eating habits and food concepts are shaped by their culture. In fact, the foods for which there is any evidence implicating 5HT (Wurtman *et al.*, 1985) are packet foods, like chocolate bars and potato crisps. The craving is for snackfoods. Emotionality about eating and indeed psychiatric disorders are also likely to be bound up with the snackfood readily available to tempt the slimmer to breach her or his diet and the disordered eater to binge.

Exactly the same can be said of so-called chocoholism (Hetherington, 1993) and the common craving for chocolate (Hill *et al.*, 1991; Rozin, Levine and Stoess, 1991). This media-hyped craze is a social phenomenon around the most popular snackfood, no more. There is no epidemic of addiction to chemicals in chocolate. Very few of those who feel out of control of how much they eat at a sitting or who actually do eat very large amounts at once are eating mainly chocolate: binges are on average diets (Tuschl *et al.*, 1990; Sobal and Cassidy, 1987). Even the sweet-toothed British eat much more potato or bread per head than than they do chocolate. It is just that chocolate is more salient, being thought of as a luxury rather than a staple, being eaten by itself more often than as part of a meal and by being tarred with the brush of nutritional naughtiness because of its sugar and fat contents – all cultural roles, not metabolic functions, pharmacological effects or individuals' specific needs.

Further Reading

There follow some major titles in the anthropology of food, which contain material complementary to this chapter.

ARNOTT, M.L. (Ed.) (1975) *Gastronomy: the anthropology of foods and food habits*, The Hague, Mouton.

BARKER, L.M. (1982) *Psychobiology of human food selection*, Westport CT, AVI.

BASS, M.A., WAKEFIELD, L.M. and KOLASA, K.M. (1979) *Community nutrition and individual food behavior*, Minneapolis, Burgess.

BELASCO, W.J. (1989) *Appetite for change: how the counter-culture took on the food industry 1966–1988*, New York, Pantheon.

BRUCH, H. (1978) *The golden cage: the enigma of anorexia nervosa*, Cambridge, MA, Harvard University Press.

BURNETT, J. (1989) *Plenty and want: a social history of diet in England from 1815 to the present day* (3rd Edn.) London, Routledge.

CHARLES, N. and KERR, M. (1988) *Women, food and families*, Manchester, Manchester University Press.

CHIVA, M. (1985) *Le doux et l'amer*, Paris, Presses Universitaires de France.

DEUTSCH, R. (1977) *New nuts among the berries*, Palo Alto, Bull.

DEVAULT, M.L. (1991) *Feeding the family: the social organisation of caring as gendered work*, Chicago, Chicago University Press.

DOUGLAS, M. (1984) *Food in the social order: studies of food and festivities in three American communities*, New York, Russell Sage Foundation.

FARB, P. and ARMELAGOS, G. (1980) *Consuming passions: the anthropology of eating*, Boston, Houghton Mifflin.

FIDDES, N. (1991) *Meat: a natural symbol*, London, Routledge.

FIELDHOUSE, P. (1986) *Food & nutrition: customs & culture*, London, Croom Helm.

FINKELSTEIN, J. (1989) *Dining out: a sociology of modern manners*, Cambridge, Polity Press.

FISCHLER, C. (1990) *L'Homnivore: le goût, la cuisine et le corps*, Paris, Odile Jacob.

FÜRST. E.L., PRÄTTÄLÄ, R., EKSTRÖM, M., HOLM, L. and KJAERNES, U. (Eds) (1991) *Palatable worlds: Sociocultural food studies*, Oslo, Solum.

GOODY, J. (1982) *Cooking, cuisine and class: a study in comparative sociology*, Cambridge, Cambridge University Press.

JEROME, N.W., KANDEL, R.F. and PELTO, G.H. (Eds) (1980) *Nutritional anthropology: Contemporary approaches to diet and culture*, New York, Redgrave.

LAWRENCE, M. (Ed.) (1987) *Fed up and hungry: women, oppression and food*, London, Women's Press.

MEAD, M. (1964) *Food habits research: problems of the 1960s*, Washington DC, National Research Council.

MENNELL, S. (1985) *All manners of food: eating and taste in England and France from the Middle Ages to the present*, Oxford, Blackwell.

MINTZ, S.W. (1985) *Sweetness and power: the place of sugar in modern history*, New York, Viking.

MORRIS, W.N. (1989) *Mood: the frame of mind*, New York, Springer-Verlag.

MURCOTT, A. (Ed.) (1983) *The sociology of food and eating*, Aldershot, Gower.

ORBACH, S. (1986) *Hunger strike*, London, Faber.

SANJUR, D. (Ed.) (1982) *Social and cultural perspectives in nutrition*, Prentice Hall.

SIMOONS, F.J. (1961) *Eat not this flesh: food avoidances in the Old World*, Madison WI, University of Wisconsin Press.

SLOCHOWER, J.A. (1983) *Excessive eating: the role of emotions and environment*, New York, Human Sciences Press.

Chapter 5

Design of Beverages and Food Products

The psychology of customers' uses of food and drink is considered from the point of view of improving the quality of match between what food businesses provide and what their customers use foods and drinks for.

From Gathering to Producing

Before urbanization, our ancestors used to range over the land, gathering plant foods and hunting terrestrial animals, birds and the fish from rivers, lakes or sea. Some of the spoils were eaten on the spot but much was brought home and usually cooked before eating. Plant extracts and fermented brews were also developed. Heavy crops of nuts or fruit and big game might have been shared within the larger group.

If too little food was available in winter, some of what would not decay had to be stored. Edible shrub fruit, grass seeds, tubers and even stems and leaves that could last the winter were cultivated. Also some animals were confined to a grazing range so that they could be kept available for meat and milk or eggs.

In recent millennia, villages were established around farms for the domesticated plants and animals, marketplaces for food (among other goods) and social areas or buildings where brews or meals were consumed. Elaborate cooking practices and food preservation techniques were developed and the products stocked up in communal as well as private storehouses. Rotting of food was slowed, for example by boiling and then covering the stew. Decay was virtually stopped by making water unavailable to the bacteria by techniques like baking in the sun or on a fire or adding salt. The stores and their outlets in stalls, shops and eating and drinking places therefore provided local communities with a wide range of raw plant and flesh foods, freshly cooked recipes and preserved foodstuffs. Longlasting foods and drinks could be transported over increasingly long distances where the demand for an item at the market repaid the costs with sufficient gain to the entrepreneur.

Thus, the cultivation of plants, the husbandry of animals and the preservation of foods were all scaled up from the domestic level in order to supply many local and even distant households from one batch. This enabled farmers, manufacturers and traders to earn their livings and freed more of the rest of the population to support themselves in other industries. Some of the villages were able to grow into towns and large cities. Over the last two centuries or so, many useful machines have been invented and sources of power discovered to drive them. This has enabled economically viable agricultural food production by fewer and fewer people. Mechanization of techniques of food processing and transport to local distribution systems of those products as well as produce more directly from the land allows whole regions or continents to be supplied by large specialized farms and factories.

The Need for Design

Each development of the food-supply system had to be self-sustaining by providing what people wanted to eat at a price they were willing to pay in a place they could get to. What most people most often want to eat for all or much of the time is from the range of things that they are used to. Thus the food shops and eating places had to provide items and combinations that were generally similar to those that a substantial proportion of the population were already consuming. At least any new variants had to be known to be eaten already by some other people and had to fit in with the activities of sufficient numbers to be saleable.

For this complex interaction between the supplier and the purchaser to remain viable, it has to be sufficiently near optimum for both sides. That means also that the supply–use interaction has to adapt to changing constraints and opportunities. On the production, manufacturing, distribution and retailing side that has developed in contemporary societies, that requires a sophisticated integration of technology and marketing. The contention of this chapter is that the supplier's design of foods and beverages has to be driven by information on the psychology of eating and drinking to be optimally efficient economically, ecologically, for the owners and employees of the supply organizations and for the population of individual customers.

How then do we combine the producing and selling aspects of a food business to maximum satisfaction all round? The balance between the supplier's needs and the consumers' needs depends on the many other factors besides customer behaviour that are involved in business in general and marketing in particular. We have to focus here on behaviour towards food, however. So we shall consider only one aspect of the problem, albeit as crucial as any and indeed arguably constitutive of the whole operation: there is no point in producing and distributing food unless it is eaten. This chapter is concerned with the elucidation of those foods and drinks consumers want within the range that might practicably be provided. Therefore, while broad technical, economic and organizational constraints are allowed for, detailed business considerations are not dealt with here.

What foods and drinks then do people want to buy? How can we get this market intelligence as efficiently as possible in a way that enables commercial organizations to see how to adjust their production and marketing processes as they see fit?

Determinants of Habitual Food Uses

Sufficient people have to want to use repeatedly a food item having a particular design for it to be an economic proposition. Hence the psychological basis for designing marketable foods will be the requirements that substantial numbers of individual eaters have on their recurrent use of such materials. These habitual uses of a foodstuff have to be quite popular or to become sufficiently popular quickly enough to help sustain the producing and marketing organizations.

This leads to a distinction between two approaches to food design and indeed to psychology generally (Chapters 1 and 4). The commonest approach is to use variations in behaviour across a set of people to estimate a universal (or at least predominant) pattern of requirements in which people differ only quantitatively – how much they want of this or that feature in the same basic product. For this classic approach to food design, research needs to be carried out on a large number of people and many empirical and statistical assumptions have to be made to extract a psychological consensus, especially if only responses to a few tests have been observed in each person.

The less usual approach, emphasized here, is direct estimation of the mental processes involved in a food use habit. The observations have to be repeated across various relevant designs within each individual tested and then a stable personal structure analysed out of that person's data. Repeated observations of an individual's actions towards personally relevant variants replaces the usual repetition of observations across people who are responding to a fixed set of designs. The generality or otherwise of any one person's pattern of requirements can then be tested in as many people as required by their diversity of patterns and the theoretical or practical objectives of the research.

This means that recurrent use by the individual is a technical condition for the direct psychological measurement of design requirements, as well as an economic condition for survival of a food item on the market. However, the individual research approach is better suited than conventional grouped observations to the development of products for uses by minorities that are growing or are large enough already. A prospective niche in the market can be fully defined only by personalized investigation.

Yet also a major market can only have its requirements precisely defined by detecting diversity using the individual approach. Then the measurements of the prevalence of use of each optimum design, needed to estimate the return from investment in marketing that product, can be properly designed to allow for diversity and avoid a false consensus.

Personal Exploration

Open-ended interviewing has of course long been used to gain informal information of the individual's view of situations. Ethnographic interviewing aims to identify broad patterns of behaviour, however, and is concerned with the culture in which the respondents live, rather than the individual's own behaviour in specific situations. Focused but open discussion in groups is frequently used in commercial consumer research but the aim is to generate ideas or flag problems, again not to detail the requirements of each or any individual in the group. The appropriate way to explore a person's requirements of a type of food in a particular context of use is open-ended discussion of that situation with the individual.

Many techniques have been used to tap individuals' thinking processes when deciding between products such as foods. One currently popular procedure in consumer research is called 'laddering' (Reynolds and Gutman, 1991). Interviewees are guided through statements of their hierarchy of means and ends, what they value in the benefits gained from eating a food with the qualities they ascribe. A more formalized version of essentially the same idea is used to elicit individuals' statements of their reasons for acting in terms of beliefs and values, as a basis for attitude modelling (Fishbein and Ajzen, 1975).

A major limitation of such approaches is that they lead respondents further and further away from concrete description of familiar situations and of their own actions within them. This is not necessarily getting deeper and deeper into their actual reasons for choosing between alternatives. It certainly misses influences on behaviour that are difficult to remember or may not even be conscious (Ericsson and Simon, 1980). Moreover, the further a person is in time or concept from actual events, the more they are liable to be using pleasing theories about themselves and reflecting the conventional reasoning in their social group (Anscombe, 1960). Crudely speaking, the behaviour may cause the professed attitude more than the other way round (Bem, 1972). The supposed ladder may be standing upside down!

A more realistic first step would be to get respondents to describe the variety of things they do in an habitual eating or drinking situation and to state what in the situation they think affects what they do. The exploratory communication, scene-setting or script-writing can remain at this relatively behavioural level, albeit purely verbal. It can be taken further by asking the respondent to say what it is about an influence that makes it affect them. This is one step up the ladder of reasons and values.

The interviewer next uses the respondent's own words to get precise specifications of potentially important aspects of the different foods and drinks, times, company, physical environment, mood and expected consequences that can occur in that situation. The interviewer enquires about aspects that are stated to be influential but also seeks examples of variation in any aspects that could in theory be important, even if the respondent appears not to have alluded to them. Theory also enters the interpretation of the respondent's statements that guides the interviewer's further questions and the criteria of precision that the interviewer applies when eliciting detailed specifications. Such theory could be intuitive but preferably it should be grounded in other evidence as to the sorts of things that happen in such situations.

Table 5.1 summarizes the results from one such exploratory interview.

Cognitive Formalization

The interviewer's (and indeed others') understanding of the respondent's statements can then be tested experimentally in one or more subsequent interviews. This can be done in a form of concept test, using only the respondent's words to describe foods and drinks and the context of their ingestion or purchase, depending on the objectives of the investigation. Alternatively (and usually at a more advanced stage), actual samples of the foods and drinks can be presented, preferably in physical contexts that are examples of the situations described (product testing in use or on display). In principle, actual movements of food selection or eating could be observed. In practice, it is much more efficient and need be hardly at all less valid to get the respondents to say what they would do.

To provide data that confirm or disconfirm the stated or hypothesized cognitive connections between words, a set of test situations must be designed (descriptively or physically) that differ in ways that appear to be important.

Table 5.1 Concerns evinced by a dieter about her mid-morning coffee and biscuits (see Figure 4.1).

Respondent's characterization units	Interpreted categories
Is a treat Is satisfying Flavour liked Is crunchy	Fun food
Makes me eat all day Puts weight on Number of calories in it	Danger food
Affects hunger Affects thirst	Thirst-quenching

Each important feature of the use situation must be represented by at least two different examples. Preferably the two examples should be high and low levels of the feature within a familiar range. Better still would be three or more levels of the feature if it is gradable. If the levels of each varied feature are approximately balanced over the personally acceptable range and the responses are allowed to operate in freely graded fashion over one clear dimension at a time, then the respondent's performance can be close to linear. That is to say, cognitive processes that affect each other are likely to be correlated.

The different levels of each feature should also be roughly equally spread over the test situations (e.g. half high, half low). Even more important, high and low levels of one feature should be fairly evenly split between both high and low levels of another feature (i.e. high–high, high–low, low–high and low–low in four tests). To put the point more generally, the tested features should be distributed orthogonally (with zero inter-correlations) over the test situations as nearly as possible. It is possible to get results if feature levels are confounded, i.e. correlated (collinear) or associated. However, for a within-individual analysis as with conventional multivariate analysis of grouped data, the stronger the collinearities the less reliable is the statistical clarification of sources of influence.

Table 5.2 gives an example of test situations that were described to the respondent of Table 5.1 in an experimentally designed interview. The features were selected on the basis of the initial interview (Table 5.1) to test the most obvious hypotheses as to what was influential on this respondent's behaviour in the situation discussed. The features of the described situations were intended to be orthogonally varied within the range of experience reported.

Variation in features that are actually important will have a systematic relationship to variation in what the respondent does. If the investigator and respondent understand each other and the respondent was correct in naming some reason, then that reason should relate to a feature and to behaviour. In other words the reason is a manifest or measured variable that appears to mediate the effect of the situation on the behaviour. Reasons may also relate to each other.

Links between pairs of variables can be identified by a set of multiple regressions, giving a matrix of partial regressions from every variable onto every other one. The highest partial coefficients calculated from responses to the tests in Table

Table 5.2 Hypothesized major distinct influences on the respondent's coffee-break behaviour, described in her own words (see Figure 4.1).

Time of morning
   Between 11.00 a.m. and 12 noon.

Flavoursome food item
   Highly flavoursome: pear; muesli biscuit
   Low flavoursome: rich-tea biscuit; chocolate chip cookie.

Calorific food item
   High: Muesli biscuit; chocolate chip cookie
   Low: Half a pear; a rich-tea biscuit.

Company
   High: Husband in next room; female neighbour in kitchen
   Low: Alone in house.

5.2 were plotted in Figure 4.1. This cognitive network is consistent with many of the informal impressions to be gained from Table 5.1 and supports some of the hypotheses pursued in the design of Table 5.2. Much stronger conclusions could be drawn if another set of tests gave a very similar cognitive network for this respondent.

These bivariate relationships can be highly illuminating and represent a considerable step towards objectivity in formalizing the interpretation of interview records. Nevertheless, they represent quite weak theoretical understanding of what is going on in the respondent's mind or, more strictly, in the interchange between interviewee and interviewer as made public in the partial regressions network. Undoubtedly many of the actual mental processes that influence food choice (and their communicated expression) interact in other ways than pairwise around a network.

Furthermore, two or more processes jointly acting on another process do not necessarily add together. Yet this is assumed by the multiple regressions that are calculated to give the partial regressions providing evidence for the network. For instance, disparate processes are more likely to combine in a Euclidean space of discriminable differences (Chapter 1).

In addition, some of the effects of features on choice may not be mediated by processes represented by the terms used in the experimental interview. Rather, these terms may reflect superordinate or even epiphenomenal processes. They may be monitoring or rationalizing other processes that have more direct influence on the overt response. Such processes may in some cases operate straight through from the sensed situation to the response in one mediating process, rather than the succession of mediating processes suggested by the network of partials. Latent causal processes may have quite different characteristics from the manifest variables. They may not be readily available to attention, let alone for simple description.

Hence, to improve theoretical understanding as well as practical efficiency, it is important to move on from the preliminary and possibly superficial evidence in the personal cognitive net. Hypotheses must be developed as to the processes of mental interaction and combination of apparently important features of foods and eating or purchasing situations into the decisions to ingest or buy. Some examples are given below of evidence for determinate cognitive integration formulae for material features of foods and drink and also for readily identified conceptual features.

In short then, a personally structured test of a marketable concept or physical product can measure the determinants of that individual's preferences in a familiar sort of situation. Individualized multi-dimensional testing requires a piece of software (on floppy disc) that has only just been developed in pilot form and so this technique of designing foods cannot yet be brought into routine use. In any case, this more scientific approach to product development requires empirical theorizing about what goes on in people's minds. That is an orientation and collection of skills that psychology students have to spend some years acquiring. As well as the approach of a behavioural scientist, however, effective food designing depends on understanding the relevant technology and marketing operations. The psychology, natural science and business grasp have to be properly coordinated before cognitive hypotheses can be realistic and testable economically.

The truly individualized approach to consumer research is also achievable by the use of recently developed software for the less integrated technique of multi-dimensional conjoint analysis. The consumer is run through a series of trade-offs between pairs of product features and the microcomputer estimates their relative effects on preference. Measurement (linearity of performance) is not necessary for this approach but the multiple non-metric trade-offs still need coordinating into a specification of how the individual would respond to different particular whole products.

The Sweet Feature

The features of a foodstuff that have to be designed into an appropriate combination are of course manifold. A food having high eating quality will have to have all its sensed characteristics at close to the levels preferred by the eater in the context of other foods in the meal. Extrinsic attributes may have to be adjusted to individual preference as well, such as the self-concept of a vegetarian or a person having religious principles about food preparation or contents or concerns about food safety or long-term health effects.

As yet, there has been very little direct investigation of how individuals put together the inherent features with the extrinsic attributes either controlled by the food supplier or brought to the eating occasion by the customer. A high proportion of the limited number of studies of cognitive integration of inherent and contextual features into preferences for foods and drinks that have been carried out to date involve the effects of sweetness. So this is now taken as a theme to illustrate the principles of a cognitive approach to food design. Some of the findings also provide important examples of facts about the psychology of eating and drinking.

Optimum Food Sweetnesses

It has been suggested that there is a most liked concentration of sugar on the tongue of about 10 per cent, regardless of context (Frijters, 1987). This is implausible if the most preferred level of sweetness in a food or drink is learned from experience of using that particular stuff. There is a peak intake of glucose solutions at about 10 per cent when they are presented to rats one solution at a time. This pattern is presumably innate. The peaked curve is sometimes called a 'single-stimulus preference function'. However, the peak occurs because the increase in innate preference as sweetness goes up is countered by an innate suppression of all preferences (satiety), induced by osmotic effects of the higher concentrations of glucose in the intestine (McCleary, 1953), which occur also in people (Cabanac and Fantino, 1979; see Chapter 3).

When discriminations of sugar concentrations from the most preferred sweetness in familiar foods and drinks are measured individual by individual, the distributions of personally ideal sugar levels differ greatly between fluids such as a fruit drink and a vegetable soup, as well as between the fruit drink and a solid based in large part on sugar, namely chocolate (Figure 5.1). The preferred sugar level on the tongue therefore depends on the food.

Various factors operating by a variety of routes may explain this dependency. Other tastes affect the sweetness delivered by a particular sugar concentration. The innate dislike of bitterness and sourness may drive up the traditionally used level of sugar because that encourages sampling and repeated use of the material by those to whom it is new, until the bitterness or sourness in that combination with sweetness and other qualities becomes highly attractive in itself (Chapter 2). The other items or the sequence in a meal in which the food is used may also influence the sugar level that is regarded as suitable and has become liked.

As well as those three foodstuffs differing in the average level of sugar that people prefer in them, individuals differ in the sugar levels they prefer averaged across the three foods (Conner *et al.*, 1988b). Indeed, there was a statistical interaction effect between foods and people in analysis of variance. This meant for example that some of the assessors preferred the lime drink sweeter than the tomato soup but other assessors had the reverse preference. When choices between sweet and non-sweet alternatives were included with the preferred sweetness levels in correlational analyses, two types of people emerged (Conner and Booth, 1988). One sort of person preferred sweetness in desserts and confectionery (both sometimes called 'sweets') and in snackfoods and drinks. They might be said to have a 'snacking sweet tooth'. Another sort of person still had some sort of sweet tooth but it was confined to foods and drinks based primarily on vegetables and fruit. The obvious interpretation is that both sorts of people are used to eating the items they like sweet between meals or as a course within a meal but some go for confections and fizzy drinks whereas the others are in the habit of selecting fruit, fruit juices, raw carrot and the like.

Preference Functions, Popularity Functions and Average Scores

The relationship between an individual's disposition to choose a sample of an item and the amount of a feature in that sample is a quantitative function describing the cognitive process by which the feature affects that person's preference for that sort of item in the tested context. A symmetrical preference function (an appetite triangle: Chapter 1) measures the strength of liking for that feature in that item, in terms of the fineness in difference between feature levels that make a difference to choice (the tolerance discrimination ratio or the Weber fraction for preference). It also measures the level of the feature that the individual most prefers in that item in the tested context, the ideal point.

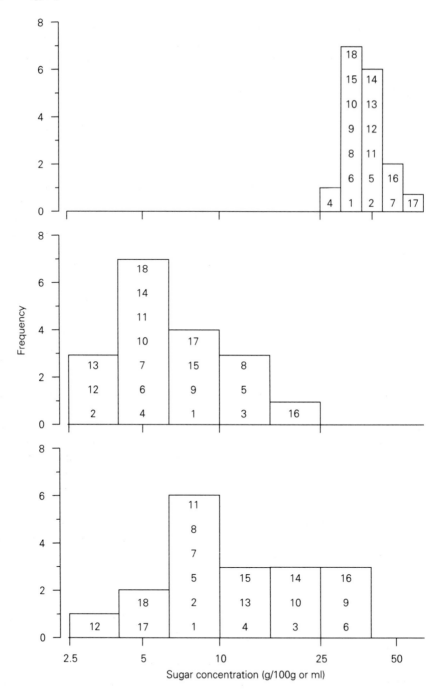

Figure 5.1 Distributions of individuals' most preferred levels of sugar in chocolate (top), limeade (middle) and tomato soup (bottom) (after Conner *et al.*, 1988). The numbers in the columns are codes for each of the 18 individuals tested.

These two measures of preference can be combined to estimate a range of feature levels around the ideal point over which the individual would tolerate the difference from ideal. Whether or not they could describe a difference towards the extremes of this ideal range, they would be less than halfway towards certainly regarding that sample as departing from ideal in that feature.

The ideal range can be used as a characteristic of the individual assessor's preference performance that could be combined with the same measure of other representative assessors' tolerance to provide a means of estimating how the market that the assessors represent would respond to any particular level of the feature in that item presented in the assessed context.

For example, we might measure sugar preference functions in coffee drinks in people who had just come to the coffee machine for a cup of coffee with sugar. The necessary data can be collected in a few minutes by taking a couple of sips from each of four to six samples of coffee at drinking temperature with different levels of sugar in them, carefully chosen to bracket the individual's ideal point and to stay within the range between unacceptably low or high levels. Ideal points for sugar in a particular food or drink have been found in a good number of studies to be close to normally distributed across the sample. The extremes of ideal ranges also appear to be normal. This means that we can cumulate the frequencies of ideal points or the bottoms or tops of ideal ranges along the sugar level dimension and get straight lines (Figure 5.2). Hence it becomes very simple and accurate to interpolate the frequency of ideal responses from the sample to any sugar level, using an equation based on all the individualized analyses of all the data collected.

This exercise was actually carried out for sugar in a particular brand of vended coffee. It was found that 75 per cent of the sugar currently placed in the coffee cups would not go below the ideal range for any more of the sampled consumers than the very high proportion for whom the current level was within their ideal ranges. The brand manager reduced the sugar level with no complaints from consumers and, even for an ingedient as relatively inexpensive as sugar, saved enough money within the first year to pay for the preference measurement project several times over.

The cost of this research in time and materials was no greater than that of a standard product preference test on the same number of consumers but the results provided much more detail, precision and hence confidence in the consequent decision making. In other words, the individualized cognitive approach enables better design of foods and improved cost-effectiveness.

The established procedure would use a fixed set of perhaps four or six samples containing different amounts of sugar given to every consumer and ask each assessor to rank them in order of preference (or possibly to provide some sort of rating on a subjective category such as liking or pleasantness). A function might then be drawn of the frequencies with the sample of assessors ranked each tested sugar level as top preferred, or perhaps some combination of the preference scores from all the assessors. (There has been a practice of averaging hedonic scores but this is rightly criticized for burying evidence of popularity, i.e. the frequency with which a sample is most preferred, in the variation in ways in which individuals use the scoring system.)

The answers from the standard approach depend on the particular samples tested. If 100 per cent and 75 per cent sugar had happened to be tested and had turned out to be about equally often most preferred, then the same redesign decision could have been taken. However, there is no exact equation for interpolating and so this approach lacks a way of determining whether 75 per cent is above or even

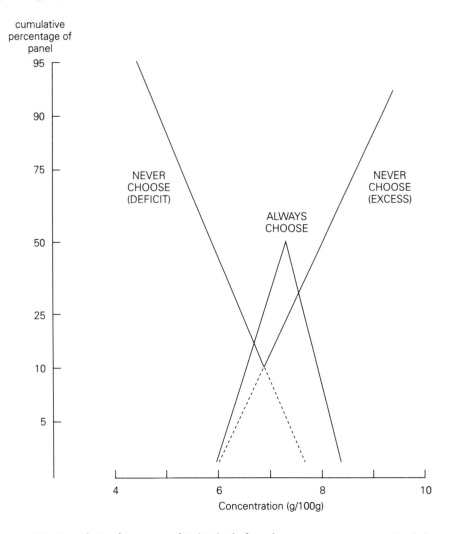

Figure 5.2 Cumulative frequency of individuals for whom a sugar concentration is just high enough (left-hand line) and just low enough (right-hand line) to be within one just tolerable difference from the ideal point for each person.

a bit below the level reduction without risk to sales. In other words, whether or not the test had hit on 75 per cent, such data do not provide the quantitative guidance that aggregation of individuals' cognitive performance characteristics can deliver.

Sweetness and Physical Context

Sweet Food Flavours

Many foods have a sweet taste, including a number that are not regarded as 'sweet foods'. This includes plant foods before any sugar is added, for example not only fruit but also some vegetables such as carrots and maize. This is because plants sometimes store energy as sugars rather than as starch. A meat soup can be sweet too, not just a vegetable soup. The sweetness in animal foods comes mainly from the free amino acids, especially when salt is not added to the inherently low level.

The addition of salt to the meat or indeed the acids in a sour piece of fruit do not just distract from the sweetness. They also appear to mask it. This is what the psychophysicists call 'mixture suppression': the rated sweetness of a given concentration of sugar goes down as the concentration of salt or acid (or bitter substance) with which it is mixed goes up. Unfortunately, psychophysics has been stuck in a subjective quagmire of trying to read the mind from numbers produced by assessors. The tradition has been to assume without the further evidence needed that ratings of, say, sweetness directly measure or scale the strength of experienced sensations of sweetness or even of the activation of neural pathways from a category of receptors on the tongue. Very little analysis has been carried out of the processes actually involved in the performance of such intensity judgments. Indeed, the obsession with isolated stimuli has made it virtually impossible to collect data that could resolve issues about the relationships between responses and stimuli generated by the assessor. It is not logically possible to carry out economical cognitive analysis without studying multiple responses to mixtures (Chapter 1).

Recently, Anderson's (1981) information-integration approach has been applied to taste mixtures (McBride and Finlay, 1990). Even this relatively coarse analysis of grouped responses from unrealistically pure solutions of sugars and citric acid provided some evidence that more was going on in the judgments of taste strength than sensations of sweetness and sourness.

Individuals' judgments of departures from the appropriate sweetness, sourness and fruity taste of an orange drink of reasonable quality can be subjected to multidimensional discrimination analysis. It then emerges that, when the mixtures and ratings permit, assessors operate with a memory of the integral pattern of stimulation by the sugar and acid concentrations that is familiar in oranges and products from them (Figure 5.3). They recognize departures from expected orangeyness of the taste of a drink, both in amount of orange and in realism of sweet–sour balance. The same discriminations in two dimensions are used to decide the degree to which each tested drink mixture is liked.

This shows that quantitative descriptive analysis or sensory profiling of foods need not, should not and psychologically cannot be separated from tests of consumer preference and their objective determinants, as has been the tradition in industrial applications of psychophysics (Booth *et al.*, 1983, 1987; Conner and Booth, 1992).

It also points to the possibility that mixture suppression is an illusion generated by data analyses founded on the assumption that ratings measure the named sensations. Psychophysicists have not realized that they are imposing on the assessor an often difficult struggle to make sense of the pattern of stimulation in terms of remembered experiences to which the words and numbers can be fitted. Not only is performance on familiar complex stimuli more relevant to practical needs; it is also more precise and differentiated and therefore much more powerful at discriminating between hypotheses about scales, shapes of psychophysical functions and integration of features into object recognition (Lockwood, 1992).

Flavour is not just taste. The right balance of tastants may be crucial to a good flavour but most of the differentiation among flavours depends on their aromas, colours and visual and tactile textures. So sweetness and other tastes interact with

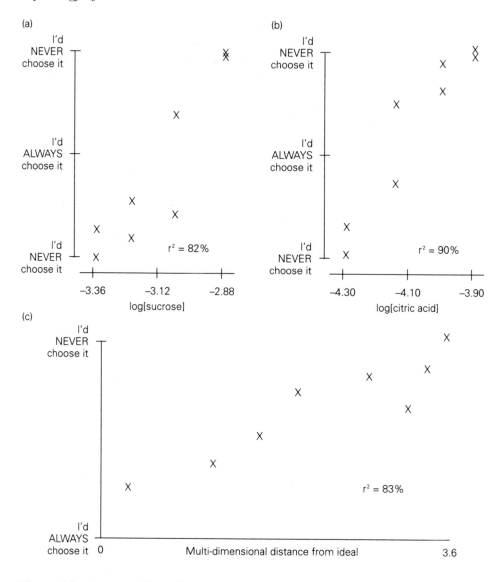

Figure 5.3 Separate effects of sugar levels and acid levels on an individual's liking (rated from always to never choose) for samples of an orange drink (upper panels) and the two-dimensional combination of sugar and acid discrimination distances from ideal for that person (lower panel).

other sensory modalities. However, again, the understanding of these interactions has been limited by the approach of seeking pattern in grouped ratings of a fixed set of unfamiliar mixtures. For example, there are reports that fruit colours and aromas increase sweetness and vice versa. However, when levels of both sugar and almond were varied in a set of realistic mixtures, there was no effect of sugar level on almondiness or of almond level on sweetness relative to the individually most preferred level (Marie, 1986). This is despite the fact that the smell of almond has a sweetish note that might have been expected to maximize the chance of an interaction.

Another indication that conventional approaches are inadequate to study sensory interactions is that the questions asked determine the direction of an effect of context on sweetness (Frank *et al.*, 1993). Nevertheless, intermodal suppression or augmentation may be more than an illusion of data analysis and artificiality of procedure. Appropriate colour has been reported to intensify fruit aroma (Zellner and Kautz, 1990). When the effect of colour on aroma strength relative to normal was measured, in some individuals there appeared to be an effect that could not be attributed to biased sampling of the integration of colour and aroma into judgments of departure from realism (R. Wigfull and D.A. Booth, BSc Project, 1992).

Such lack of understanding of how sensed constituents of foods interact in the mind to result in recognition of food quality is expensive for the industry as well as creating consumer dissatisfaction. Mixtures of sugars and/or synthetic sweeteners can be used to economize on ingredients (and, in the case of the artificial sweeteners, to keep within food regulations). Yet empirical rules based on judgments of pure solutions are unreliable and no theory has been used to build a general equation for the optimum composition of a particular food in a given use.

Sweet and Creamy

Creaminess means a flavour as much as a feel. Without an aroma and a taste similar to that usual in milk or cream, an emulsion of dairy fat in water seems 'empty' and unreal. The natural taste comes from the milk sugar (lactose) dissolved in the whey, plus some salts (mostly sodium chloride) filtered through from the cow's circulation. So, when the appropriate concentrations of lactose and sodium chloride are added to water-diluted cream, it tastes something like milk again.

Lactose is not particularly sweet. However, low concentrations of sodium chloride have a sweetish taste. Also, when we eat cream, it is often with something sweet like fruit or jam. Indeed, in some countries, sugar is added to the cream that is put in cakes or provided at the table for addition to desserts. Ice cream is of course a concoction based on sugar, milk and water. Indeed, fruit-flavoured dairy products of all sorts often include additional sugar, such as extra lactose (as in some yogurts), the sugars inherent in added fruit or added sucrose (table sugar). Considerable numbers of people have acquired the habit of adding sugar (or an artificial sweetener) and milk or cream to their hot drinks, such as coffee, tea or chocolate and much prefer the drink milky or creamy as well as sweet.

Thus, most people are used to eating and/or drinking combinations of sugar solution and fat emulsion at various strengths. They can therefore try to say which levels of sweetness and creaminess they prefer in plain mixtures of sucrose and dairy fat, presumably by analogy with the filling in a cream cake or the topping on a piece of apple pie. Use of such a technique has provided evidence that obese people may differ from those whose weight is in the range recommended for health in the average preferred levels of sugar and fat, or at least for the fat in those sweet materials (Drewnowski *et al.*, 1991). Ratings of pleasantness of sweetness by itself, presumably evoking the innate reflex as well as memories of poor-quality still lemonade, do not consistently vary with body weight, as initially claimed. Indeed, when preferred sweetness levels are assessed discriminatively in real foods, associations with age and gender explain a slight difference with body mass index (Conner and

Booth, 1988). Drewnowski (1987) and Halmi and Sunday (1992) have also found some differences between sufferers from different types of eating disorder with sugar/cream mixtures.

Associations between body weight and preferred high levels of sweetness or creaminess in foods do not of course in themselves indicate whether causation is one way or the other, due to a third factor or even non-existent and the limited and variable observations are coincidental and will prove unreliable. Nevertheless, if there is some association, the most plausible explanation on other grounds (Chapter 6) is that a habit of consuming sweet and creamy foods and drinks can contribute to weight gain and at the same time induces liking for creamy, sweet materials, which as a consequence will be commoner among fatter people.

Sweet Uses and Users

We saw in earlier chapters how individual learning history is likely to have determined a person's requirements on a food for top eating quality in a given context of use. We are considering examples when these requirements include a particular level of sweetness. We shall now focus on the way in which patterns of use of sweet foods tend to generate types of user of sweetness in food. You become what you eat.

In addition to recognizing the foodstuff's immediate impact on the senses, people may also expect certain effects from eating it.

Just above, we touched on the possibility that it is fattening to consume sugar and fat, at least if in sufficient amounts in certain circumstances by some people. Clearly, many people are aware of this possibility, indeed believe its certitude. This can create anxiety and guilt about eating sweet and fatty foods which can put people off the taste and feel or go on to create a frisson of self-indulgence ('naughty but nice').

Sugars and fats may be regarded as good at quickly damping down hunger pangs or satisfying a craving for something delicious. For example, a minority of drinkers of coffee with sugar and milk say that they sometimes have a cup to ward off or suppress hunger (Booth and Blair, 1988).

Glucose drinks and tablets have the reputation (justified or not: Chapter 8) of providing a boost to physical vigour and mental concentration; if similar effects could be attributed to sugar, it might be added more to the corn flakes on a busy morning, ladled more into the coffee sustaining the rush for a deadline on a piece of writing or sought among the canned drinks from a vending machine at the sports club.

On the other hand, the sensations or the satisfaction from sugar may be regarded as so addictive that, like alcohol for a member of Alcoholics Anonymous, they motivate total abstention. A woman who takes her first drink and food of the day at home as coffee and biscuits in the late morning said in an initial open-ended interview that she tries to postpone that drink as long as possible because she fears she would not be able to stop nibbling all day once she started. In a subsequent experimentally designed correlational mapping of her morning snack choices in her own words, this anxiety was certainly related to some of her evaluations of the common situations described back to her, although it did not appear to be a simple determinant of her reactions to the timing of the decision to take a drink (Figure 4.1).

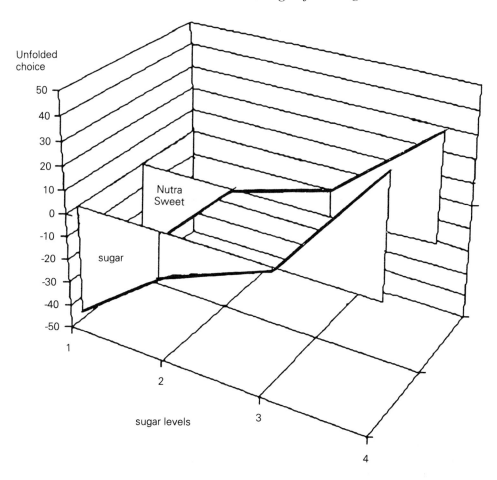

Figure 5.4 Effects on a person's disposition to choose test variants of an orange drink (0 = ideal; ±50 = never choose) of varying the amount of sweetener in the drink and changing the sweetener-calorie level indicated by the label on each test drink.

Cognitive Integration of Sweetness and Calorie Information

There may therefore be different types of consumer, distinguished by what they expect from sugar and therefore how they use it and in what quantities they like it in those circumstances. Someone who uses a soft drink to quell hunger or boost energy might have come to like the more sugary drinks. Such a person would prefer higher levels of sweetness in sugar sodas or fruit juices and would not be as strongly attracted to any level of sweetness in a drink containing a low-calorie sweetener. On the other hand, a dieter may like sweetness when it is free of energy but want less when it comes from sugar (Figure 5.4).

These two sorts of reaction combine the strength of the taste with the information on the label about the calorific nature of the sweetener in different ways. We can plot the strength of an individual's preference for a drink sample vertically and the level of sweetener and labelled sweetener calories horizontally in units of the

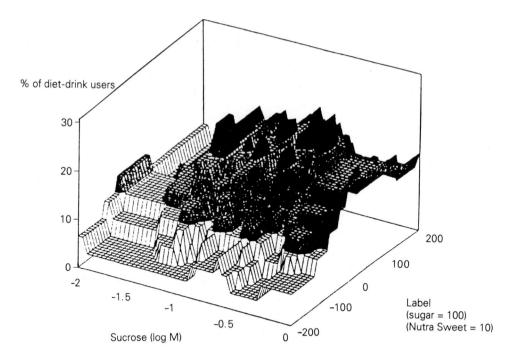

% of diet-drink users

Figure 5.5 Combined ideal ranges of sweetness (in sugar equivalents) and sweetener calories for diet-drink users.

difference thresholds (Weber's discrimination ratio: Chapter 1). The result is a personal response surface, shaped like part of a cone, from which the disposition to accept a particular combination of sweetness and label can be read off directly, for example whether it lies within one Weber ratio of ideal (the ideal range). The number of consumers whose ideal ranges include a combination can then be totted up (Figure 5.5). Consumer response surfaces are commonly used in food design but they are derived from grouped data not using discrimination measurement and so are not precisely predictive of take-up in the market.

The peak of the choice discrimination surface for an individual who is concerned to avoid any fattening effects of consuming sugar in drinks taken by themselves is liable to be diagonally displaced from the most preferred combination for a hunger-suppressor or boost-seeker. Studies currently being completed provide support for this prediction. In that case, designers of low-calorie versions of popular drinks might be advised not to match their sweetness to the sugared version.

There are, however, additional factors to be taken into account as well in such decisions. As indicated in Chapters 1 and 2, the innate preference for sweetness creates methodological problems for the usual testing of a fixed array of samples on people whose data are analysed as a group: if the test formulations are unfamiliar and the array of sweetnesses ranges high, the peak of the grouped response surface may be artefactually high in sweetener level.

There may also be an interaction between long-term marketing objectives and health policy (Chapter 6): a habit of consuming sugar between meals is a risk to the teeth and may be particularly fattening and so it may be desirable for all consumers to adapt to lower levels of sweetness in drinks and foods commonly used at such times. This would also save money on sugar and artificial sweeteners. The choice discrimination surfaces (or multi-dimensional spaces) from a representative sample of individuals predict which lowering (or indeed raising) of levels of different sweeteners would stay within the ideal range for the greatest proportion of users of existing marketed levels (as in the one-dimensional case illustrated earlier in this chapter). If supported by public opinion and declared on the products, competitors could benefit their corporate and sector images by collaborating in a co-ordinated stepwise reduction without prejudicing total sales or a particular company's development of distinctive strategies within the trend.

One common marketing strategy to increase competitive advantage while widening choice for consumers is to differentiate products. The development of diet sodas as well as sugar sodas is an example. Another conceivable example would be, say, 'fresh' and traditional versions of fruit-flavoured drinks, where the 'fresh' version is lower in inherent and/or added sugars while total flavour strength is maintained at a widely liked level by, for example, not reducing the content of acids in proportion and maintaining high-quality texture, colour and aroma.

It has been recognized from analysis of conventional group preference curves that the sales of a medium–low version and medium–high version together may be greater than those of a single intermediate version. Such differentiation could be more soundly based on individual cognitive analysis of food design requirements. Individualized choice discrimination analysis becomes indispensable when there are interactions between features and these interactions differ between uses or users. Then the whole design of both the sensed composition and the attached information and advertising can be optimized for the qualitatively different targets.

Consumer Typologies not Specific to Food

Mass marketing is passé. Even for staple foods like bread, potatoes and milk and mass-produced food products such as biscuits and orange juice, there are now sufficiently large minorities of consumers prepared to buy something different from one standard version, such as the large medium-sliced white loaf.

This has brought product development to the centre of the food business. The market share of a long-established brand may need protecting or the company may try to expand sales, whether by creating more interest in that sort of product or by taking a share of sales from competing brands. Then consumers' opinions may be sought about the brand and its competitors and the results used to redesign the packaging, distribution or advertising or even to fine-tune the composition of the food itself in the attempt to reach and please a higher proportion of customers or at least to have a balance of costs, pricing and sales that provides a good return to the organizations in the food supply chain.

New Product Development

There is however only a limited amount that can be done about an established brand. A company might think that there is a gap in the market for a type of food that cannot be filled by any existing variation on it. It seems that enough consumers already want another version or would try the new item and might be satisfied with it if it were available. Hence, the food manufacturers and increasingly now the producers of fresh foods and the supermarket chains have put a lot of effort into new product development.

Some new food products have been great successes. However, most new introductions by the food industry have been failures by commercial criteria.

The successes often grow from new things that eaters are doing or can do. For example, when everybody in the family is at work or school all day during the week, meals that take a minimum of preparation time become very attractive. Meals that are ready to heat and eat will sell better as more microwave ovens are installed, saving the time taken to bake, grill or boil – so long as the traditional cooked surface is not sacrificed.

Yogurts became a staple item once most households had a refrigerator. Those fridges then made soft spreads highly desirable: during the summer at least, traditional butter and margarine were too hard because it came straight from the cold, where it had to be put to stop it going nasty and runny. That soft spreads could be sold as high in polyunsaturates or low in total fat was a bonus.

Successful marketing, however, depends on far more than designing a product that prospective purchasers like. Sales may not pick up as hoped. Many things can go wrong. A competitor promptly introduces a similar product and mops up too much of the interest. The supermarkets have some difficulty with the new brand and so do not display it as prominently or consistently as anticipated and so too few people try it. As the distribution expands from a regional to a national or even international basis, production has difficulty keeping up or alternatively stock turns over more slowly than expected, which is especially serious for a perishable food.

Adequate financial management of a company that has introduced a new product requires some rate of return on the investment in development and initial promotion. Otherwise, drastic action may have to be taken to cut ongoing costs and/or to improve sales. It is therefore important to be able to predict and monitor the rate of take-up of a new product and be able to diagnose and act on factors that may be slowing sales or their growth. For this purpose, models have been constructed of the lifecycle of a brand of a repeatedly purchased product such as a food.

One of the simplest approaches is economic rather than psychological. Market shares and purchases tracked in a sample of consumers are often compatible with each purchaser having a particular disposition to buy an often purchased brand, given some reasonable statistical assumptions (Ehrenberg, 1972). In fact, this tendency to repurchase the item probably changes with experience in some consumers, even in a stable marketing situation; such changes cannot be modelled so easily because they depend on the psychology of interactions between product and user. Nonetheless, the model can be used to monitor the effects of advertising, repricing or other marketing efforts to reinforce the disposition to purchase the brand. Furthermore, such models can be used to interpret development in the brand's market share, by measuring changes in awareness of and access to a new product shortly after it has been introduced onto the market. Growth in share may slow down before expected and then action on awareness or repurchase can be considered. If market share starts to decline from asymptote later, the reasons can be investigated. In either situation, the current psychology of brand uses can be crucial.

Consumer Segmentation and Product Positioning

Such economic models of markets and brand life-cycles sometimes handle sales data and consumer panel data sufficiently well for it to be arguable that consumers do not differ qualitatively in their motivation to buy. Nevertheless, attempts to modify a product or to introduce a new one would be unwise to rely on presumption of a null effect that may be hard for aggregated analyses to refute.

With foods specifically, there is notoriously no accounting for taste. Consumers may differ in their uses and preferences, both along continua and also quite possibly discontinuously, for example with distinct combinations of features being required for disparate uses.

Thus, purchasers in segments of the market identifiable on demographic or psychological criteria may as individuals behave differently to a type of food or even towards the characteristics of a particular brand. Such situations provide opportunities to adjust the physical characteristics of the brand, the policy for distributing it or the content and channels of advertising, in order to position the brand to suit the target segment of consumers.

One possibility is particularly important for new products. Some people might be highly disposed to try a brand of food just because it is new. They then would be disproportionately represented among purchasers when the brand first appears on the shelves. Rogers (1962) in fact called the very first people to buy a new product the 'innovators' and the subsequent small minority 'early adopters'. How important this distinction is, or indeed that between these sets of people and the great majority who make their first purchase later after the introduction, will depend on their behaviour, in two respects. First, are innovators mediating an actual social diffusion of purchasing? That is, are the earlier purchasers bringing in the later ones? To the extent that they are 'change agents', how do they do it? Do they offer the new product to their guests or do they merely recommend it verbally to their friends? There is some evidence that early adopters are gregarious and so likely to share samples and also that 'word of mouth' contributes to brand expansion. However, a good deal of the growth in sales need not be diffusion. It may arise from additional consumers coming across the product in displays for the first time and the more frequent purchasers of that type of product buying a second item of the new brand.

Secondly, is there something about innovators or early adopters that disposes them to try new products as soon as they come on the market? They might be intensely curious about new things or attracted more than others by novelty or variety. They might be actively searching for change, whether out of the joy of exploration or because of dissatisfaction with what has been available thus far. If it is to explain their early purchase, innovators have to be alert to products as they come onto the market for the first time, not merely stumbling on them while scanning the shelves in the usual way.

The concept of a consumer trait of innovativeness has indeed been developed, partly from psychological constructs such as risk-taking and sensation-seeking (Foxall and Bhate, 1993). It has been found to have some validity in purchasing behaviour, particularly for more radical innovations. The innovator might get along to a new ethnic restaurant in the first week or a new type of fast-food outlet on its first day. Such people are well in touch with what is going on. However, they may be somewhat eccentric and cannot be relied on to be effective in creating interest among others.

For new versions of existing types of product, the first purchasers for one category of product tend to be different people from innovators for other categories. Their innovativeness is related to their major interests. For example, an enthusiastic or desperate slimmer is more liable to be among the first to try the latest diet product. Parents who sit their young children in front of television for several hours a day are most likely to be asked to bring home the latest new snackfood to be advertised at those times.

Another approach to the brand development cycle has been widely used for other purposes also in marketing circles. This is based on Maslow's (1970) categorization of what people want out of life – namely survival, protection, belonging, esteem and fulfilment. Someone who is chronically starving feels only the need to survive and in any case is not being offered a choice between brands. In affluent countries though, those below the poverty line are liable to go for the cheapest traditional foods and are least likely to try anything new. A sense of security is more relevant to food choice in affluent societies, given the levels of public concern about dietary risks of chronic disease and hazards from contamination of foodstuffs. A brand that offered assurance of health or safety might attract customers worried about such things, such as oats to reduce cholesterol or organically grown vegetables free of pesticide residues. Yet the need for personal fulfilment and motivation by ultimate values could equally support a self-concept as a vegetarian or organicist and hence produce early adoption of the same healthy and safe foods. Belonging and esteem might motivate the majority. It might be suggested that earlier adoption of a new brand might give a boost to esteem, while conformity might delay adoption; but the logic is not overwhleming and the evidence is negligible.

These are not stable personal temperaments but behavioural styles for managing one's long-term economic situation and current interpersonal relationships. Maslow, who originally developed this view, himself regarded the person's circumstances as predominant in which needs would be active at any given time. He claimed that needs formed a hierarchy, with personal growth being released as the more basic motives were satisfied (Maslow, 1970). The evidence for such ordering however is poor. Furthermore, many of us have several of the needs much of the time. There is therefore precious little guidance in this to the food developer or advertiser where to pitch the appeal.

Strategy and Tactics in Food Design

Too much has been expected of the search for purchasing-predictive traits, as of any research on personality or general motives and attitudes. Such traits are extracted from answers to questions or other estimates of behaviour across a wide variety of situations. The wider the range of situations sampled to estimate differences in trait strength between people is, the smaller necessarily is the variation in behaviour that the trait can explain in any one situation, such as diverse consumers' purchasing of a particular food product for a certain use.

Nonetheless, psychologists in marketing are expected to identify such styles or types of consumer, or at least needs or motives that we may all share to different degrees in different contexts. Typologies are easy to present as cameos and pull in funds for product development or advertising campaigns. They may provide some broad guidance in business strategy development, perhaps by challenging other assumptions or by providing an interim framework for discussion. All the same, they have little relevance when it comes to concrete decisions that have to be made between alternative physical and conceptual formulations of a redeveloped or new brand.

Nevertheless, it is obvious that global impressions of social trends, databases on brand life cycles and a thorough understanding of the industry's handling of the product are insufficient for successful development of foods and markets for them. It is essential to test what look like the best options, by at least an exemplary small amount of detailed behavioural and perceptual research into their suitability to growing uses for foods of that type. Even if other sorts of data are used to plan the timetable and financial strategy, research at the individual level into uses of the new product will expose faults in early designs, diagnose the diversity of most attractive functional qualities and illustrate the relevance and impact of the concepts used in the image that can be put over by, for example, the brand name, the packaging, pricing and advertising themes. Useful qualitative information can also be gained about the diffusion processes, both by communications among consumers and by distribution and advertising to consumers.

Further Reading

This chapter expounds an approach to sensory evaluation of foods and perceptual psychology, integrated with attitudes to food. This is a new cognitive approach to the well-established area of consumer behaviour, which endeavours to apply psychology and sociology to market research carried out with potential customers. Background to these research areas is provided in the following books, as indicated by their titles.

Consumer Behaviour

EAST, R. (1990) *Changing consumer behaviour*, London, Cassell.
Gives a brief introduction in the British context to consumer research for marketing.

ENGEL, J.F., KOLLAT, D. and BLACKWELL, R.D. (1968) *Consumer behavior*, New York, Holt, Rinehart & Winston.
This 'bible' of consumer behaviour remains valuable as a source of research classics, although it overelaborated the early information-processing approach (deemphasized by Engel, Blackwell and co. in Editions from 1982).

ROBERTSON, T.S., ZIELINSKI, J. and WARD, S. (1984) *Consumer behavior*, Glenview, IL, Scott, Foresman & Co.
Perhaps the textbook of consumer behaviour that is strongest in its psychological bases. Preferably use the latest Edition.

WILKIE, W.L. (1990) *Consumer behavior* 2nd Edn, New York, John Wiley & Sons.
A lively introduction to the theory and practice of consumer research in marketing. Plenty of classic and current examples briefly presented, with extensive follow-up references.

Sensory Evaluation

MOSKOWITZ, H.R. (1983) *Product testing and sensory evaluation of foods: Marketing and R&D approaches*, Westport CT, Food & Nutrition Press.
Empirical analyses of descriptive ratings to aid the design of products such as foods and drinks.

STONE, H. and SIDEL, J.L. (1985) *Sensory evaluation practices*, New York, Academic Press.
Exponents of the dominant tradition of difference testing and descriptive profiling separately from assessing degrees of liking and preferred choices, as procedures for gathering and analysing data rather than usefully distinguishing between hypotheses as to how consumers perceive and prefer products.

Psychophysics and Perceptual Measurement

ANDERSON, N.H. (1981) *Methods of information integration*, New York, Academic Press.
Attempts to distinguish additive from multiplicative interaction formulae by ANOVA of grouped data from a very wide variety of situations (motivational as well as perceptual).

LAMING, D. (1986) *Sensory analysis*, New York, Academic Press.
An advanced treatment of perceptual performance in various sensory modalities.

MACMILLAN, N.A. and CREELMAN, C.D. (1991) *Detection theory: a user's guide*, Cambridge, Cambridge University Press.
Includes recent work on multidimensional detection and recognition.

POULTON, E.C. (1989) *Bias in quantifying judgments*, Hove, Erlbaum.
Systematizes evidence on distortions introduced into psychophysical functions by various designs of stimulus-response relations.

Chapter 6

The Heart and the Diet

The Psychology of Healthy Eating

Many leading medical statisticians and some clinical scientists are convinced that people's diets in westernized societies contribute to the high prevalence of long-term illnesses. These common chronic conditions include heart disease and other degenerative disorders such as stroke and some forms of diabetes and of cancer. Despite modern treatments, these diseases can still often be fatal. They are becoming even more important causes of death as life expectancy increases in general and such diseases have time to reach fatal extremes. Moreover, heart attacks and breast cancer kill substantial numbers of people in only their middle age. In addition, if such diseases could be made less prevalent, some of the expense of complicated surgery and new drugs to treat them would be saved.

There is an obvious response from psychology to such concerns. This is first to find out what people recognize they are doing with food and drink and to distinguish habits that contribute to heart attacks or other chronic disease from feasible alternative eating practices. Given those popular descriptions of the habits and their implications for the design of foods and eating facilities, those at risk can be told which are the less risky uses of food and as many of them as possible provided with the means to switch to healthier eating.

The obvious difficulty in this research strategy (as any other directed at long-term health) is that people often cannot tell until late on whether or not they have heart or circulatory disease, diabetes or cancer. Many of the signs of liability to a chronic disorder or that the disease is developing can only be detected by chemical analysis of blood samples or other medical investigations.

Nevertheless, some risk factors for these diseases can be worked out by people for themselves. Heart attacks, strokes or high blood pressure in one's family make it more worthwhile doing something to reduce one's own possible risk. Getting badly out of breath after moderate exercise (like walking up several flights of stairs) is a sign of potentially dangerous unfitness of the heart and artery muscles.

Anyone can see even more easily whether they are fat around the middle or beginning to spread out there. Men who are bigger around the waist than around the hips and women having a waistline more than four-fifths of their hip measurement are statistically more liable to develop one or more of these killer diseases (Vague, 1953, 1991). Body weight is quite strongly associated with blood pressure, increasing the risk particularly of stroke. Abdominal fatness is associated with the circulating forms of fats that help to clog the blood vessels and with the strain on the insulin system that induces diabetes in adulthood. Obesity may also result from the high fat intake that may contribute to bowel and breast cancers as well as cardiovascular degeneration.

So there are questions about healthy eating that can be investigated purely by psychological methods.

Weight-control Eating Psychology

What uses do people living in a particular way make of food and drink that tend to make them fat around the waist? What alternative eating habits and indeed exercise are available to them that avoid unhealthy weight gain or cardiovascular unfitness? Wherever we had answers to such questions, they would provide information to guide communicators to the public and the providers of foods and opportunities to eat and to take exercise how best the prevalence of obesity might be reduced and health improved as a result.

Yet the extraordinary fact is that neither psychologists nor nutritionists have pursued this obvious line of research. The clinical psychologists have assumed that all that is needed is standard techniques of behaviour modification with some general advice on healthy food choices. The applied nutritionists have assumed that all that is needed is translation of the recommended levels of nutrient intake into healthy menus and recipes.

The first study that did seek out which self-reported practices were more or less fattening (Lewis and Booth, 1986) was limited by a focus on habits described by the investigators in terms of nutrient intakes, i.e. fat, starch, sugar, fibre. This was perhaps not too inappropriate, considering that much health education was couched in terms of nutrients rather than eating behaviour and that the respondents were selected to be professing dieters and hence were presumably well-briefed in nutritional messages. Only the effort to cut back on fat intake was associated with success at keeping reportedly lost weight off (Figure 6.1). Slimmers' meal replacements were not popular but their use was associated with ending up if anything fatter than at the start! Cutting back on snacks did not seem to have any effect. The term 'snack', however, is highly ambiguous. A snack can be a quick or small meal or a few items of food eaten when only a drink was needed. Similar results were obtained in an American study where people were also asked questions in investigator-determined categories (Kayman *et al.*, 1990).

A subsequent English study assessed a larger number of habits in a wider range of people interested in weight control, and described the sorts of behaviour in terms that others in the same population had come up with spontaneously (Blair *et al.*, 1989). Nutrients still figured strongly in what people said but nutrient-oriented strategies were often illustrated by types of food. Also, the timing of eating was quite often mentioned, particularly whether it was between meals or at meals.

The results indicated that avoiding all sources of energy between meals or substantial snacks was one of the most successful ways of keeping lost weight off (Figure 6.2). It was reasonable therefore to suggest that, in England at least, the consumption of calories in and with drinks between meals is one of the most fattening habits. That had also been predicted on theoretical grounds (Booth, 1988a). Determinants of calorie-free drinking occasions next need to be identified if that habit is to be supported effectively.

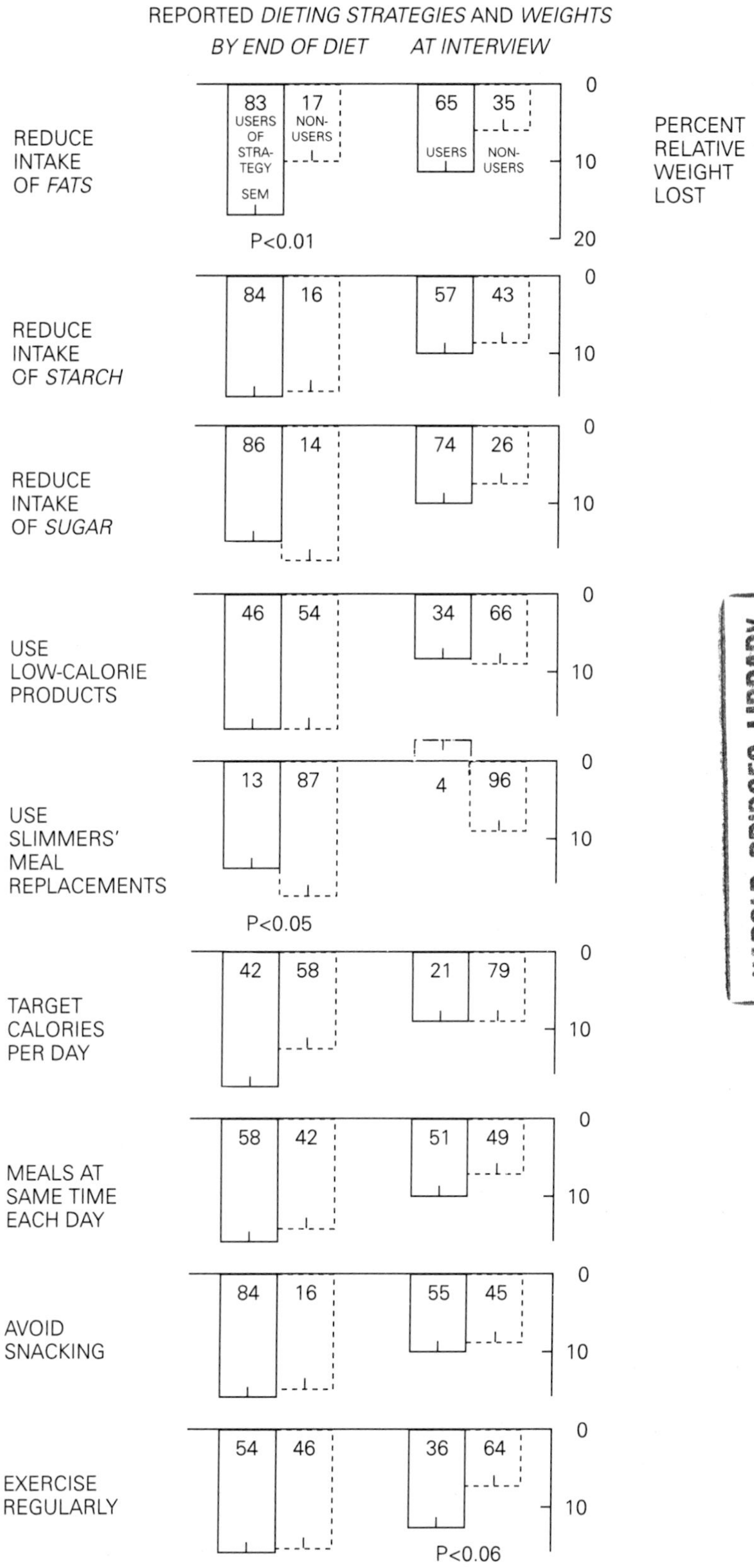

REPORTED *DIETING STRATEGIES* AND *WEIGHTS*
BY END OF DIET   AT INTERVIEW

REDUCE INTAKE OF *FATS*

83 USERS OF STRATEGY	17 NON-USERS		65 USERS	35 NON-USERS

SEM

P<0.01

0 — 10 — 20

PERCENT RELATIVE WEIGHT LOST

REDUCE INTAKE OF *STARCH*

84 | 16   57 | 43

0 — 10

REDUCE INTAKE OF *SUGAR*

86 | 14   74 | 26

0 — 10

USE LOW-CALORIE PRODUCTS

46 | 54   34 | 66

0 — 10

USE SLIMMERS' MEAL REPLACEMENTS

13 | 87   4 | 96

0 — 10

P<0.05

TARGET CALORIES PER DAY

42 | 58   21 | 79

0 — 10

MEALS AT SAME TIME EACH DAY

58 | 42   51 | 49

0 — 10

AVOID SNACKING

84 | 16   55 | 45

0 — 10

EXERCISE REGULARLY

54 | 46   36 | 64

0 — 10

P<0.06

Figure 6.1 Mean loss in reported weight during or without reported effort to follow a dietary strategy before and after 'going on a diet', in 100 women (mean 18% above ideal

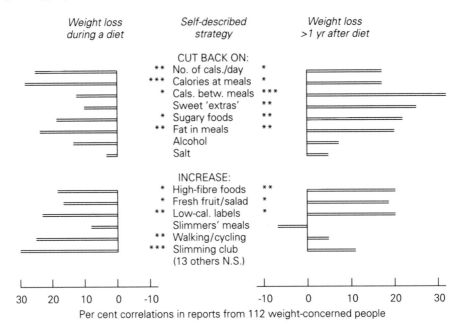

Figure 6.2 Correlation between reported use of a dietary strategy and loss in reported weight during a period of dieting (left-hand side) and (right-hand side) for a year or more after a period of dieting (***$P<0.001$, **$P<0.01$, *$P<0.05$, N.S. = not statistically significant).

On this basis, it is unhelpfully confusing to call a nutritionally rounded light meal a snack and to give the same name to a cola and a bag of crisps or a chocolate-coated bar, coffee with cream and sugar or tea and biscuits. It does not help to call packet items that are used in snacks in a mixture of types of foods and also contribute to calories-between-meals habits by the one term 'snackfoods'. It is also unfortunate to have terms like 'diet' and 'slim' in the brand names for fizzy drinks without sugar: unsweetened black coffee and tea are not sold with the implication that they cut into fat. It would be more accurate to give names instead to the original cola drinks and other sodas that included the term 'sugar' or implied calorie content.

Heart-protective Eating Psychology

A similar approach to identifying health-risking and health-promoting eating habits and indeed the factors supporting them should in principle be able to identify causes and preventive strategies for heart disease, diet-dependent cancers and so on. However, nutritional epidemiology has been based on international comparisons of various nations' figures for food production and disease prevalence. The nearest that the research base for guidelines on healthy eating has got to individual behaviour within a given culture and gene pool are surveys attempting to estimate average daily nutrient intakes or clinical trials of the prescription of dietary changes such as more low-fat or high-fibre foods. There is no database of cognitive anthropology of food choices and determinants of their diversity in groups having different prevalences of disease.

So for the rest of this chapter we have to abandon psychological theory and methods. We shall examine how food policy makers and nutrition educators have tried to identify and promote healthy eating.

Safe Foods and Healthy Diets

Even though eating and drinking are essential to life, they can also be physically risky activities. Food and drink can be great fun but they can also be dangerous. Two broad categories of danger can be distinguished.

Unsafe Foods

One sort of risk to the eater arises from a substance or organism in a piece of food or a particular drink. The risk may be acute or chronic, i.e. the harm can be done promptly after consumption or it may be a long-term after-effect, perhaps cumulative over repeated ingestion of the unsafe food.

For example, a bacterium or some other microorganism may contaminate the food material and produce a toxin during storage or multiply in the gut after ingestion. The result is commonly termed 'food poisoning'. This is particularly likely after unhygienic preparation of food. It can also arise from a bacterially infected source, such as salmonella in laying chickens or listeria in cheese. Catering outlets, for example, are therefore subject to strict regulations, enforced by food safety inspectors.

A historical example is a fungus in stored grain that produced psychoactive and poisonous alkaloids chemically related to the hallucinogenic drug LSD, causing outbreaks of a syndrome called ergotism (hence that drug's name ly*serg*ic acid diethylamide).

Viruses in meat might grow in human tissue. However, many viruses infect only one species. So it is unlikely that 'mad cow's disease' is a danger to human meat eaters. Nevertheless, the risk is not worth taking while we are not absolutely sure and so the law is that infected cattle are destroyed. This is not just a theoretical danger. Another virus that multiplies relatively slowly and attacks the brain was found to be the cause of outbreaks of a madness called *kuru* among some New Guinea cannibals who ate the brains of their defeated enemies.

Toxic substances occur naturally in a number of ordinary plant foods. They are usually dissolved out or destroyed by heat during cooking, such as the solanins in potatoes or the cyanide in cassava. Some of these natural toxins might have a cumulative effect after habitual ingestion. For example, both spinach and rhubarb are rich in oxalic acid; in large enough quantities, this might promote kidney stones even if it did not produce acute upset; so the frequent choice of both that vegetable and that dessert on the same menu might be unwise.

Residues of insecticides sprayed on fruit or vegetable or of growth-promoting hormones fed to animals might get carried through to the food we eat. In the quantities that could get though to the shops even if safety regulations had been breached, these substances are unlikely to induce acute illness but some of them might have a cumulative effect, such as promoting cancer.

Some substances are added to food products during manufacture, to help preserve them (and reduce the risk of food poisoning) or to make them look, feel or taste better. These additives may be extracted from natural materials that are not foods or they may be synthesized (which is often cheaper and may conserve natural resources). However, both natural and artificial additives (and synthetic compounds that are identical to natural substances) may have chronic effects on health if consumed in sufficient quantity for long enough. These may be beneficial, as in the cases of the preservative ascorbic acid (which is vitamin C) and the colouring agent beta-carotene (which is a precursor for vitamin A). They may be harmful, though, such as some of the colourings originally derived from coal tar which were found by toxicologists to promote or induce cancers in susceptible experimental animals.

Residues and additives for which experts in toxicology judge there is clear evidence for potential risk of disease in human consumers are banned from the food supply by law. Where the toxicological evidence is unclear and use of the substance has benefits that cannot be achieved economically in another way, then limits are imposed by legal regulations on the quantities that may be included in foods and drinks. The lowest dose for which there is clear evidence (usually from animal tests) of toxicity is taken as the basis for defining an upper limit on acceptable daily intake, such as that which would give no more than five per cent of the population one-hundredth of that minimally risky dose having regard to the range of current daily intakes of the foods and drinks in which that substance is included. Such a safety standard is a compromise between degrees of protection and expense to the consumer within the bounds of existing science and technology. That is, the criterion is not a purely statistical decision from scientific expertise; it has an ethical dimension and the general level of safety margins and even its application to a particular case are matters for informed political debate and decision.

The risk from an additive or residue might be greatest in a susceptible minority of the population. A well-known case is the sweetener aspartame which contains the common protein amino acid phenylalanine. Some babies are born without the gene for metabolizing phenylalanine properly and the resulting products from the proteins in ordinary foods damage the brain badly and come out in the urine: this condition is therefore called phenylketonuria (PKU). The diagnosis of PKU can be made at birth in families at risk. The intelligence and indeed the lifespan of a sufferer can be protected only by many years of eating special foods from which as much phenylalanine as possible has been removed. It is therefore important that these children do not consume lots of those drinks that are sweetened with aspartame and they are labelled accordingly for safety.

Well developed systems of toxicological evaluation and safety regulation are in place in industrialized countries. They provide considerable protection for the general public and susceptible minorities from dangers to physical health from substances and organisms in foods and drinks, including those that might be introduced by novel processes such as sterilization by irradiation or fermentation by genetically engineered yeasts. Is there then any place for psychology in food safety? The answer is yes, in two ways.

First, some of the risks may not be of physical disease but of physically mediated distress or psychological dysfunction. Measuring this sort of harm and indeed any countervailing subjective benefits is a task for psychologists. Do some food or drink constituents affect intellectual or emotional functioning, and when is it for better and when for worse? Examples of such concerns have included suspicions that substances in food products contribute to so-called hyperactivity in children and various supposed addictions such as caffeinism and 'chocoholism'. The undoubtedly serious problems with some uses of alcohol also fall into this category, as well as the physical damage it can cause.

Secondly, the relative values of safety and expense of consumer protection from a possibly hazardous substance, particularly if it has potential for some useful function, is a political matter. As such, it has psychological dimensions. Food risk management must take account of the perceptions of risk by the members of the public. How far are public fears of irradiated foods based on confusions with contamination by radioactive fallout? Could irradiated foods be labelled in a way that avoids such confusion? Is provision of alternatives to irradiated items the only way of dealing with outrage or ethical qualms? How far are these fears based on lack of trust in governmental regulation and enforcement of rules intended to prevent risky level of by-products from irradiation? Are the safety factors currently in use sufficiently in tune with perceptions of how much it is worth paying for various degrees of risk reduction? All these questions could be addressed by cognitive measurement of the interactions of labelling, pricing and perceived food composition or processing in choices between food items or food shops.

Unhealthy Diets

All safe foods can be part of a healthy diet. That is, there are no unhealthy foods, literally speaking. The only legitimate sense that might be given to the term 'an unhealthy food' is if normal use in the context of common diets generally puts health at risk. This is hard to argue even for items high in substances whose excessive intake is thought to be unhealthy, such as biscuits (high in fat and also sometimes sugar and/or salt) and chocolate confectionery (high in fat and sugar). A solid answer would only be possible when we know how healthy or unhealthy different uses are and measure the prevalences of the different uses among the market volume of that type of product.

Nonetheless, medical activists and food businesses have often been in confrontation over the implications of dietary guidelines for food marketing. The UK's now-defunct National Advisory Council on Nutrition Education constructed quantitative recommendations for the British diet on the basis of expert committees' reviews of the medical evidence on diet and disease. When the NACNE Report was published in 1983, it was widely interpreted in the Food Policies constructed by District Health Authorities as a simple message that British people eat too much fat, sugar and salt and not enough fibre and therefore should eat low-fat, high-fibre meals and never eat sugary or salty foods. There had been a delay in release of the NACNE Report that some attributed to governmental reservations about the implications of fat-intake reduction for dairy and cattle farmers and meat-product and baked goods manufacturers. Low-fat and low-salt versions of familiar foods are inedible. A food like a wholemeal biscuit containing a lot of bran (insoluble wheat fibre) tastes like cardboard unless the levels of salt and/or sugar are raised far above those in the white flour product.

Latterly, the Government, food retail chains and consumer organizations in the UK have developed a *modus vivendi* but still based on a literal translation of recommendations on the national average diet in terms of nutrient intakes into the nutrient compositions of foods for individuals to choose amongst. Packet foods have to provide information on their nutrient composition (e.g. grammes of fat per 100 g of the food) as well as listing their ingredients. If foods traditionally high in fat are offered with sufficiently less fat, they are allowed to claim themselves to be 'reduced' or 'low' fat. On the assumption that people have learnt that too much fat is bad for them, this amounts to a health claim. The UK governmental advisory Committee on Medical Aspects of Food Policy (COMA) reporting on diet and cardiovascular disease in 1984 relied on education and food labelling to reduce the high fat intake that they, like all other recent committees looking at the same evidence, concluded contributes to these diseases. The national Health Education Authority has cooperated with supermarkets to promote low-fat foods. Some retailers, like some manufacturers, have adopted nutrition policies or healthy eating programmes which regulate the nutrient composition of their products and attempt to enlarge the market for products making such health claims. As low- and reduced-fat products have become widely available, with the flavour and texture differences masked to some degree, purchases have increased greatly. Europe has exported its butter mountain (presumably to contribute to ill-health elsewhere) and milk quotas have been imposed on dairy farmers while the subsidy for high-fat milk is maintained.

However, it remains to be seen whether this coordination of medical advice and market development actually does improve dietary health. The effect on average fat intake has been small so far. Also, although less fatty diets reduce blood cholesterol levels and this reduces deaths from heart attacks, it remains to be shown that nations can reduce their prevalence of cardiovascular disease by lowering average fat intake. Cholesterol screening and lowering may lose as many lives from suicide and the like as it saves from cardiovascular disease. It has become evident from recent clinical research that only some saturated fats raise cholesterol levels. Monounsaturates do not and certain polyunsaturates are protective. Thus a reduction in total intake of fat, even with an increase in the proportion of polyunsaturates, may not be entirely the right aim. Also, labelling may not be an effective means of implementation.

The 'low fat' health claim for a food, as currently regulated, may be interpreted in consumers in a way that is quite counterproductive. Manufacturers generally replace the fat in a low-fat food product by sugars or starch products and/or increase the contents of the packet so that the customer gets as many calories. Presumably they fear that the low-fat version will be unsatisfying if it is low in energy content, although no good evidence for that has been published (see Chapter 3). Thus the low-fat packet is generally the same or even slightly higher than the conventional product in energy content and so does not offer any benefit to someone seeking to control weight. Yet, when consumers judge the calorie contents of such pairs of products, they consistently regard the low-fat product as lower in energy and hence less fattening (Table 6.1).

Risky Behaviour with Food Substances

Can we escape the trap of national statistics and clinical investigations on nutrient intakes averaged across days and totalled from the whole diet? Consideration of

Table 6.1 English shoppers' judgments of the energy contents of cartons of yogurt as sold, correctly labelled 'low fat' or 'whole milk' but with nutrition information not visible.

Yogurt label	1982 study		1991 study	
	Actual energy (kcal)	Judged calories (rank[1])	Actual energy (kcal)	Judged calories (kcal[2])
Low fat	128	3.9	140	105
Whole milk	127	6.8	120	139

[1] Rank out of 10 food portions presented, with larger-number rank for higher calories.
[2] Scaled on kilocalorie contents given by the interviewer for portions of two common foods not tested.

some of the physiological mechanisms by which eating may be having its impact on health can point to additional or even different conceptions of dietary factors in chronic disease. These risk factors are also behavioural (how one eats) rather than chemical (what one eats).

Sugars

White cane sugar and beet sugar, sold as table sugar and incorporated in many food products like biscuits and soft drinks, are pure sucrose. This is a simple carbohydrate and purely a source of energy (calories). Brown sugar, treacle and molasses are less refined forms of cane sugar but the only nutrient in them is also sucrose.

Sucrose is a disaccharide, a compound of the two monosaccharides glucose and fructose, into a mixture of which sucrose slowly breaks down under acidic conditions such as in colas and other fizzy drinks. Honey is mainly a similar mixture of glucose and fructose. The sugars in ripe fruit are dominated by fructose (fruit sugar). The sugar in milk is lactose, which is a disaccharide of glucose and galactose. Glucose can also be produced by breaking starch down with acids or enzymes to produce what the industry calls glucose syrups. If the strings of glucose molecules in starch, a polymer made by plants, are not broken right down to free glucose, then a highly soluble mixture of short-chain polysaccharides (oligosaccharides) is formed, known as maltodextrin. Maltodextrin is less sweet than glucose (or maltose, the disaccharide composed of two glucose moieties) and also forms a thicker solution than the equivalent weight of sucrose, making it useful in savoury pie fillings, for example.

Lactose is hardly sweet at all. Bacteria in the mouth do not convert it to acids either, unlike the other sugars and so unsweetened milk by itself is not a risk to the teeth as repeated challenges by the acid from sucrose and glucose can be. Weight for weight, fructose is at least as sweet as sucrose at the concentrations used in soft drinks and considerably sweeter than glucose. Since glucose is an isomer of fructose, glucose syrups can be converted industrially into high-fructose syrups which are widely used in the USA as a sweetener instead of sucrose.

All digestible starch is converted into maltose in the small intestine. This maltose, like sucrose and lactose, is digested into its component monosaccharides by enzymes in the wall of the small intestine. The glucose, fructose and galactose then pass into the blood supply to the liver which takes up various proportions of them and the rest circulates to the heart and then around the lungs and the rest of the body. Glucose is the sugar sustained by the liver in the blood and used by all the tissues for energy. The liver can convert fructose and galactose from the diet into glucose, although mostly they are metabolized for energy in their own ways.

Thus sugars in the diet are a readily assimilated form of energy that is ready to use. However, not only can oral bacteria use them to the deteriment of the teeth but also the liver converts sugar and other fuels in excess of current energy expenditure into fats. Thus, table sugar and all the other sugars, like every other dietary source of energy, can and will contribute to obesity if habitual energy intake is in total greater than habitual energy expenditure.

Because of this, many people assume that the more sugar you eat, the fatter you will be. A somewhat more sophisticated idea is that high sugar intake will be correlated with high intake of packet foods which are fatty and starchy as well, and sugar and all those sources of energy will make you fat. In fact, major studies of the sugar intake and body weight within samples from urban populations consistently show an inverse relationship. Now there is no reason to think that sugar makes you slim! There is on the other hand every reason to think that, because of the assumption that sugar is fattening, being aware of overweight makes you avoid sugar to some extent, for example by substituting noncalorific or low-calorie sweeteners. Sure enough, in studies carried out when energy-free saccharin was the main artificial sweetener, sweetener intake was directly related to weight. By the same token, this is no reason to suspect that saccharin is fattening, as some have wished to argue.

So we are left with the problem of identifying eating habits that are particularly fattening and determining whether sugar has any particular role in those. As we saw earlier in this Chapter, habitual consumption of modest amounts of any energy source more than an hour or so before a meal or snack is one of the most fattening habits. Sugar in drinks and in biscuits or confectionery eaten with them between meals and also in desserts and in and with drinks after meals will make its contribution to obesity in this way, alongside starch and, even more, fats and alcohol.

Concentrated maltodextrins eaten in the early part of a meal induce a reduction in interest in the desserts that regular appear on the menu with that entree. Thus, readily digested carbohydrates, including sugar, could well have a positive role to play in reducing obesity, both by replacing fat in entrees (see below and Chapter 7) and by encouraging moderation in energy intake that otherwise is hard to regulate. When adequate amounts of complex carbohydrates are being consumed, sugar is a useful source of energy early in meals and can make a contribution to palatability, even for savoury items when the cuisine is developed to mix fruit flavours and other sweet principles with the natural part-sweetness of amino acids from some meats and root vegetables.

Some decades back, sugar was accused of being 'pure, white and deadly'. This was largely because of some calculations that gave a positive correlation between sugar intake and heart disease. However, when fat intake is also examined, this is found to be an artefact of an association between sugar and fat intakes and correlation between fat intake and heart disease (of which more below). High sugar intake has been expected to go with a low fibre intake which has been suspected to contribute to bowel cancer or even to heart disease, for example by permitting better absorption of fats. However, no such associations have been established epidemiologically.

On the other hand, high sugar intake has been associated with tooth decay and gum disease within populations, particularly in childhood. Such associations remain, albeit at a reduced level, when fluoride is introduced in the water supply or in toothpaste. However, dental research has clearly shown that it is not the total daily intake of sugar as such that causes tooth decay (dental caries): rather, it is a pattern of frequent bouts of sugar consumption, which of course normally goes with a higher total intake. When a second acidic challenge to the teeth occurs before the enamel softening effect of the previous attack has been reversed by the saliva, then the chances of a permanent hole developing in the enamel are increased. Hence the danger to the teeth from sugar is habitually short intervals between eating that ends with sucrose-containing deposits on the teeth, such as boiled sweets and biscuits (except cream crackers). If chewing and taste stimulate saliva which helps to neutralize the acid and sticky substances are wiped or washed away, such by a hot drink after breakfast cereals or toast and marmalade, and particularly if the next eating of anything sugary is delayed by a couple of hours or more, the risks are much reduced.

It is therefore misleading to the public and an unfortunate diversion of professional effort from important matters when dental action groups fly in the face of the physiological research by their own colleagues and campaign against any and every use of sucrose and for an indiscriminate reduction in total intake in the whole population, regardless of current level of intake or whether the pattern of use is liable to be cariogenic (or whether the eater has dentures).

A few dietary surveys have attempted to relate dental caries to reported patterns of eating. However, these have been relatively crude and potentially biased assessments such as rated frequency of 'snacks' or the estimated sugar contents of recorded eating occasions between mealtimes. Such data have been related to caries incidence in children but only weakly (Rugg-Gunn *et al.*, 1984).

More exact recording of sequences and timings of consumption of items on each occasion would be worth using to test the hypothesized pathophysiology of caries more directly. Information on the acid production by and location on the teeth of different sorts of food items is severely limited by technical difficulties (a tooth implant with pH electrodes is the only adequate measurement technique). Nevertheless, in cooperation with food technologists, it should be possible to construct a rank order for acidogenicity. Retention on the teeth, on their surfaces or in the crevices between them, appears to be more important than content of fermentable carbohydrate above a low minimum. Hence factors like stickiness after chewing, amount of chewing and strength of sour taste (generating neutralizing saliva) and mouth-clearing foods following should be entered into a qualitative model to predict observed rankings of items and to assess particular sequences of consumption at the ends of drinks, snacks and meals. Psychologists, economists and other social scientists are more used to qualitative modelling of ill-determined systems than are physiologists and so collaboration on this research problem at the forefront of a health promotion requirement could be highly productive.

Salts

The amount of common salt, sodium chloride, and other salts of sodium in the diet appears from qualitative and statistical comparisons between populations to be a major factor in the rise of resting blood pressure with age. Most of the people in Western societies found with high blood pressure have no other physical disorder that could be causative; that condition is therefore known medically as essential hypertension. It is associated with stroke (the breaking of a blood vessel in the brain) and other cardiovascular disease.

Correlations between sodium intake and blood pressure across individuals within populations are less convincing. That may be at least partly because only some people's blood pressure is sensitive to sodium intake and so a relationship should be sought only among those having the higher pressures (Booth *et al.*, 1987). Also, of course, hypertension is likely to have other contributory causes. Weight is closely related to resting blood pressure. Chronic stress, perhaps particularly an aggressively competitive attitude to life (Type A behaviour pattern), may also contribute. Other mineral ions, such as chloride and calcium, have been implicated. Such factors would have to be partialled out of an analysis for relationships between sodium intake and blood pressure before lack of association amounts to counter-evidence.

In any case, sufficient reductions in sodium intake for at least some weeks lower blood pressure in a proportion of hypertensive patients. (Those who do not respond to dietary advice can be treated with antihypertensive drugs, although the danger from high blood pressure should be substantial to justify the cost and inevitably little known risks of long-term pharmaceutical treatment.) Furthermore, a presumably sensitive minority respond to short-term challenges with salt (taken in capsules, and compared with placebo capsules to exclude effects of directly tasting the salt).

Cumulative or Phasic?

If only to construct effective advice on eating choices, but also to sort out better the causes of essential hypertension, the question must be asked what eating habits result in the sodium intake patterns that are most dangerous to those sensitive to their effect. As in the case of sugar intake and dental caries, this is in part a very clear question in physiology, albeit one to which as yet the clinical scientists or even the animal experimenters may not have very clear answers. By what mechanisms does persistent consumption of sodium salts in common amounts and patterns contribute to chronic rise in resting blood pressure? In particular, is the average daily total intake (and excretion) of sodium salts, on which the nutritionists have almost exclusively focused their measurements, the sole and immediate causal factor?

Hypertension develops from the efforts of systems in the body to deal with the effects of ingested sodium on osmotic pressure and the volume of blood in the circulation. The hormonal and neural controls may adapt to work more vigorously and the walls of the blood vessels may thicken and so raise background pressure and responsiveness. Adaptive systems in the body will have thresholds. They may also saturate – that is, respond less to further increases in challenge.

Hence there may be an amount (or concentration) of sodium in a meal or snack that is below the thresholds and yet is an appreciable part of daily intake. In those circumstances, only eating occasions that include enough salt will be contributing to the development or maintenance of hypertension. This rising phase of the curve may be largely linear. Yet it could be positively accelerating over the prevalent range of meal salt contents. Then, less frequent high-salt meals would be more hypertensive than more frequent medium-salt meals adding up to the same total intake. This could have major implications for dietary advice and the regulation of food labelling and design.

At the higher end of usual doses per meal, though, the curve might be decelerating, as the compensatory capacity of the body is being approached. In that case, very salty meals would be no worse than just obviously salty meals and the meal dose moderation policy might be best adjusted accordingly.

It is proving difficult enough to establish the qualitative relationship between sodium intake challenges and chronic hypertension. Defining a meal-dose response curve for the general population, for those with high blood pressure or stroke in the family or even for diagnosed hypertensives is liable to be a distant prospect. The issue is, therefore, whether these theoretical principles are robust enough to be worth pursuing in the absence of definite physiological quantities.

It may be premature to seek ways of focusing public attention on avoidance of high-salt eating occasions and industrial action on reduction of salt contents of the foods contributing to such occasions. What should not be neglected any longer is the measurement of individuals' distributions of their total salt intake across eating occasions.

The parameters of such salt dose patterns should then be related to clinical control of hypertension and to its epidemiology. This would provide evidence on the importance or otherwise of factors beyond total intake. It could bypass the difficulties of clinical investigation of the dose-response curve for repeated challenges or, better still, provide some guidance to the design of such studies that increases the chances of informative results.

Good data on meal patterns of salt consumption would increase the validity and precision of dietetic advice to patients and to caterers and food manufacturers.

Furthermore, specifically psychological research is needed into the determinants of habitual food choices that differ between high-dose and low-dose meals and how those choices are perceived by the eaters. Such data are indispensible to inform dietary advice in the clinic, public education and marketing and the regulation and development of food composition. Indeed, the evaluation of interventions should also be based on the behavioural research results.

Intake, Preference and Attitude

Thus far, research on food choices involving ingestion of salt has been weakened as much as nutritional epidemiology by attention only to total salt intake. This is partly because the simplest of the valid and precise measures of salt intake is total urinary salt excretion, i.e. a series of 24-hour collections. However, it is also because cognitive analysis of habitual acts of food choice has hardly been started.

Instead, most research has been limited to questionnaire or taste tests of liking for particular foods or model samples. Such numbers are too far from measures of the causal processes operating within meals and snacks involving salt. They are also quite unrepresentative of the series of choices cumulatively leading to total salt intake. There seems no reason for the widespread expectation that such preference measures would be predictive of intake. So indeed they prove not to be (Shepherd and Farleigh, 1989; Mattes, 1987).

Some work has addressed broader questions of influences on food choice. However, these questions have been addressed directly to eaters about the rationales they can provide for the choices they report, named in broad terms of different categories of foodstuff (bread, potato crisps, milk, etc.) or even of salty tasting foods. Unsurprisingly, numbers based on conventional reasoning to justify common behaviour are moderately well correlated with numbers based on reports of the behaviour (covariances up to 60–75 per cent). As pointed out in Chapters 4 and 5, such rational defensibility of described actions however may tell us little of major influences on the actual behaviour and is not likely to reveal the relative strengths and interactions of the real causal factors, reflected and missed in the attitude questionnaire data.

Salt-generated Influences on Sodium Dose on an Occasion

Salt can influence an individual's momentary eating behaviour in two ways, like any other food constituent.

It may be sensed, in this case primarily via gustation (but not always then via a sensation of saltiness) but also via effects of the salt on other sensory or postingestional effects of the food, such as on texture, aroma or other tastes or (via digestion) on satiety.

Salt in a food may also influence behaviour via reliable information, such as provided by the compositional or nutritional labelling of the item being chosen or brought to the situation from prior education. (Incorrect beliefs about salt content are not influences of salt because they result from factors such as misinformation, faulty thinking or the like, i.e. lack of control of cultural or cognitive processes by the actual salt.)

No research appears to have been done yet specifically on the effect of salt labelling on individuals' food choices. However, the strength of influence of tasted salt on the disposition to accept a foodstuff has been measured in a sample of individual consumers (Conner *et al.*, 1988a). The same technique has been used to measure the strengths of influence of salt and the other sensed constituents of a soup on the acceptabilities of various samples in a substantial sample of consumers (Booth and Conner, 1991). This multi-dimensional analysis could also be applied to interactions with labelled levels of salt, as was illustrated for sweeteners (Booth and Blair, 1988). These cognitive analyses give a range of concentrations of salt in a food that would make no difference to a person's liking for that food as tested. This ideal range is the most preferred level of salt plus and minus the just tolerable difference in salt level (50 per cent discriminable from ideal in the preference ratings). This individual measure could be cumulated over representative panels (Chapter 5) to redesign a food to support salt reduction better without affecting sales, with the salt content declared but no health claim introduced. Alternatively, the effect of the combined reduction in salt and some salient relabeling on different sorts of consumers could be determined in order to decide the commercially viable strategy that is the most supportive of a reduction in population-average salt intake.

Palatable Moderation of Salt Doses

The main cause of excessive salt intake is the levels of salt that we have become used to in foods bought ready to eat, particularly packet foods like cereals, biscuits and crisps. Therefore these perfectly acceptable reductions in salt content of such foods by perhaps 20 per cent could be carried out immediately using cognitive technology to ascertain quality maintenance (Conner *et al.*, 1988a). It might also be feasible to provide more taste per mouthful from less salt by keeping it on the surface of the foodstuff (Shepherd *et al.*, 1987).

Furthermore, the new level of salt would become familiar and as a result ideal points should shift to the new level. When they had done so, another reduction within most people's ideal range would be possible, and so on, perhaps down to salivary sodium levels (Schutz, 1991). Such successive shifts would require industry-wide coordination, though, to ensure that all consumers' ideal points are adapted.

Alternatively, an increasingly wide range of choices could be developed as large enough minorities of consumers adapted to each step down in salt concentration. It is a psychological mistake to offer 'low salt' foods that are many tolerable differences below the traditional level. Only the fanatics will endure that terrible taste and try to get used to it. Labelling even a 50 per cent reduced salt content is a pointless public health policy. Companies should be encouraged to market sub-brands with less salt, evident from the nutrition information on the pack, but initially only 15 per cent or even 10 per cent less. Such a marketing strategy has been all too effective against health in the marketing of reduced tar cigarettes to young women. It is used with the energy or fat contents of some so-called 'light' foods.

Fibre

Roughage, or insoluble fibre, undoubtedly helps to prevent constipation. However, this is no basis for feeding oneself or anybody else with spoonfuls of bran. Even white bread contains a substantial proportion of indigestible or non-starch polysaccharides (the latest scientific name for dietary fibre). Worse, fragments of plant cell walls are effectively cardboard and so, to make bran edible, the salt level has to be brought up to match that of saliva at least and enough extra taste added as sugar or salt or perhaps acid (in sour bread) to make the stuff recognizable as food. Wholemeal biscuits hence tend to be saltier than those made from white flour. This may even be one of the reasons that fibre intake has been associated with decreases in colonic cancer but increases in gastric cancer.

Soluble fibre comes in more palatable forms such as the bran from oats, which is softer than that from wheat, and the pectin in fresh fruit and the juices of fruit in desserts and drinks. Natural and artificial polysaccharides are widely used by the food industry as added thickeners too. The higher viscosity produced in the digestive tract slows the diffusion of digestion products into the wall of the intestine. This can lower the peak of absorption of sugars, readily digested starches and fats. Thus soluble fibre has been thought to be useful in preventing strain on the insulin system for disposal of glucose from the blood, hence reducing the risk of mature-onset diabetes. Similarly, slower absorption of fats may reduce the synthesis of cholesterol: thus, oat bran has been promoted as a treatment for hypercholesterolaemia, a serious risk to the heart.

It is increasingly recognized that the medical benefits of dietary fibre have been oversold (Rössner, 1993). Cancer-preventive effects, reduction of plasma cholesterol levels and prevention of non-insulin dependent diabetes are limited at best and require levels of fibre intake that are unrealistically high for the food technology available to serve general populations. High-fibre diets continue to be enthusiastically promoted for weight control by many nutritionists but there is no evidence that the fibre content of foods by itself does anything to reduce obesity or prevent weight regain.

Fats

Medical advisory committees over the last two decades have all given reduction of fat intake top priority among the dietary advice on reduction of risk of cardiovascular disease. Smoking and heavy drinking are worse risks and there are strong genetic components in susceptibility to heart disease. Some forms of behaviour in stress also have a role. The consensus is, however, that the ordinary diet, even of non-smokers and moderate alcohol consumers, is too fatty at an average of 40 per cent of energy intake and should be reduced to 30 per cent at most. As a practical measure, a reduction towards 35 per cent has been advocated in the UK.

Total Fats

These recommendations have been couched in terms of all types of fat in the diet, from plants or animals, saturated and unsaturated. To date, the medical advisors and the policy makers and implementers have considered that the way to reduce total fat intake is to inform consumers of the fat contents of particular food items and encourage the food industry to design and market reduced- or low-fat versions of traditional foods that are relatively high in fat.

Commonsense informed by some technical knowledge of what fats contribute to the nature of foods raises some immediate practical problems about low-fat products. We shall consider whether a specifically psychological view puts a different slant on any of these.

PALATABILITY

Fat-rich foods with the fat content markedly reduced (if still recognizable as that food) feel, taste and look very different from the genuine article. Hence they are much less acceptable in any of the usual contexts – in a word, unpalatable (or maybe downright inedible). As we have seen (Chapters 1 and 4), palatability is a treacherous term, however: it tends to be an unrealistically stereotypical attribution to a foodstuff that takes insufficient regard in the variations in sensed characteristics that are appropriate for different contexts, even in one person on a single eating occasion. Therefore we should treat the 'palatability' problems of low-fat foods as the need to sustain high sensory quality for particular uses of the food. A change in sensed characteristics from fat reduction or substitution may be far more tolerable in some circumstances. It might even be more popular than the traditional greasy stuff, especially as people become used to less fatty foods and milk drinks.

Major problems are created for sensory quality by the advice of medical committees to replace fats with complex carbohydrates when needed to provide energy. That means unrefined starchy foods, that contain bran (which helps avoid constipation), perhaps indigestible forms of starch (which may also act like fibre), and little or no sugars (which will rot the teeth if left sticking on them from biscuits or sweets). Such foods have a physicochemical structure very similar to that of cardboard – and they taste like it! Sugar and/or, ironically, salt has to be added to make low-fat starchy and fibrous foods anywhere near edible.

Also, slightly more subtly, many typical volatile compounds are held more in the fat than in the more water-attractant components of the foodstuff. So, even if taste is maintained, full flavour can be lost because the aroma is weak or wrong. Bulky, sweet and flavoursome fruit is added to make low-fat yogurt seem rich enough, thereby boosting the energy content. This also brings us to the after-effects of eating.

SATIETY

Usually, some of the energy obtained from fat is needed for fuel. This is especially important for young children: they grow fast and spend more energy in proportion to their weight. Also, manufacturers may be concerned that their product will become less acceptable if it is less satisfying and assume that the after-effects of eating fat contribute to an impression of satiating power of a food. As we have seen (Chapter Three), the effects of fats and other foods on the desire to eat in everyday life have yet to be investigated effectively. Different after-effects will be stimulated by different forms of fat and the effects on subsequent behaviour towards a particular food and foods in general will depend on how those after-effects interact with a person's eating pattern. There are at present no grounds for believing in general that fat is crucial to acceptable satisfaction with a food. Nevertheless, effective investigation may yet show that a popular use of a type of food depends on its fat content. More likely, replacement of fat by sugars and readily digested starch products induces some learned satisfaction not provided by the traditional version of the food. An important issue to pursue regarding weight control is whether the carbohydrate substitution needs to be equivalent in energy to gain this boost in acceptability.

Saturates

Most fats are acyl esters, which is to say that the major part of the molecule is fatty acids, combined with an alcohol. (The main exception is cholesterol, which is not an ester at all). The most common alcohol in plant and animal fats is glycerol, which has three hydroxy groups and so up to three acid molecules can esterify with one glycerol molecule. Hence the old name for this common sort of fat was triglycerides, although now the chemists prefer the term triacylglycerols. 'Acyl' means that the organic acid moiety (the carboxyl group) is attached to a chain of carbon atoms. When all the spare valencies on these carbon atoms are taken up with hydrogen atoms (as in paraffins, like gasoline), the fatty acid is saturated. If some of the carbon valencies are taken up by other carbon atoms, instead of hydrogen, then the acyl group or fatty acid is unsaturated to some degree. Fats made up principally of saturated fatty acids are known for brevity as saturates.

In plants and animal fats, most of the fatty acids have 16 or more carbon atoms in their chains, up to 22 or more: these are known as long-chain fatty acids. Some important metabolites and indeed minor dietary components are short-chain fatty acids, the most abundant being acetic acid which has no chain at all really (one carbon atom attached to the carboxyl): acetic acid predominates in vinegar. In fact, if the long-chain fatty acids in dietary fats are used by the body, this is by first breaking them down into shorter chains. The liver synthesizes cholesterol from acetic acid components from saturated fatty acids.

Dietary and synthesized cholesterol is attached to special transport proteins by the liver, together with various amounts of triacylglycerol to form lipoprotein globules ('lipo' meaning lipid, i.e. fat). These are then secreted into the circulation. Muscle, adipose tissue, the liver itself and other tissues using the fats break off the fatty acids and glycerol from the lipoproteins using enzymes called lipases. However, the blood vessels themselves may also pick up fats from the lipoproteins, including cholesterol, mainly by slight damage to the otherwise very smooth inner walls of the arteries snagging the whole lipoprotein globule; when this deposit accumulates it becomes a plaque and stiffens the otherwise very active muscular wall of the artery, causing atherosclerosis (which means artery-hardening). When the deposits become thick enough they reduce the artery's ability to expand when more blood is needed and also slow the flow of blood by reducing the inner diameter. When this happens in the 'crown' of arteries around the heart (coronary atherosclerosis), then even a slight crisis may not be met with the needed rush of oxygen in the blood to the heart muscle and a heart attack occurs: if oxygen does not get to the heart soon, that part of the muscle dies (a myocardial infarction).

One of the influences on how much cholesterol is synthesized by the liver and, even more important, what sort of lipoprotein is produced is how much of which saturated fatty acids are in the diet. Some lipoprotein contains a lot of fat and is easily deposited on artery walls: these are low (and very low) density lipoproteins (fat is lighter than water and protein and so these lipoproteins float to the top in a centrifuge tube). High-density lipoprotein contains less fat and is not so easily deposited; it may even scavenge incipient deposits in effect.

Saturated fatty acids vary in their cholesterol-raising potential. Stearic acid, for example, is a saturated fatty acid that is abundant in dairy fat but probably does not raise blood cholesterol at all. Longer-chain saturates are the main culprits, as in palm oil and coconut oil, two vegetable fats that used to be common in margarines amd are still used, for example, in coffee whitener, thereby making nonsense of the supposed rule that animal fats are more dangerous for the heart than are vegetable fats.

Although it has yet to be generally recognized, there may also be a behaviourally important distinction between the background levels of cholesterol synthesis and lipoprotein formation and the levels produced during absorption of a particular meal. The average daily intake of saturates will determine the baseline, which is what most research has been concerned with. However, the amount of saturates in a meal might have to be above some threshold before the atherosclerotic potential of the liver's activities is temporarily worsened. Hence, it might be the case that the cumulative effect of spreading a given intake of saturates evenly over the meals in a day is less than that of taking the saturates content of one meal, perhaps especially the evening meal, well over the threshold. This prediction is consistent with a recent finding that switching from three to six meals a day for four weeks reduced various blood measures of cholesterol (McGrath and Gibney, 1993).

If this threshold idea is true, it would have implications for the design of nutritional surveys for epidemiological research and health monitoring as well as for advice to the general public about healthy eating habits.

Unsaturates

The triacyl glycerols in fish oils and in plant oils, such as from olives, corn (maize), soya beans and sunflower seeds, are rich in unsaturated fatty acids. The double bonds produce kinks in the fatty carbon chains and stop the molecules from lining up with each other: that is why they are oils, not solid fats in which the saturated chains have lined up and effectively crystallized.

The unsaturates in olive oil and corn oil have a single double bond (in the *cis* configuration). Such monounsaturates do not raise plasma cholesterol levels.

Oily ocean fish such as mackerel and sardines contain fats that are rich in polyunsaturates. However, both mono- and polyunsaturates provide as much energy as any other fats when oxidized to fuel the tissues of the body. They are also deposited as readily in adipose tissue: indeed, the average fatty acid profile of a person's diet can be estimated from a biopsy of a fat depot. So, unsaturates are just as fattening as saturates are.

It should also be noted that it is incorrect to generalize that animal fats are bad and vegetable fats are good. Coconut oil is one of the most highly saturated fats in the food supply. The fats in lean meat are not as saturated as those in visible fat and milk fat is not as cholesterolaemic as lard. Fish are animals too, whatever the meat avoiders may feel.

Olive oil and sea fish are widely eaten in countries bordering on the Mediterranean Sea. Southern European countries have lower rates of heart disease than many parts of northern Europe. Therefore a so-called Mediterranean diet has been advocated as heart-protective. Like most healthy eating ideas, this suffers from more than one sort of *non sequitur*.

Genetic dispositions to heart disease presumably vary across Europe. However, the immigrant studies so important to identifying environmental factors in health in the USA have not been carried out on the smaller European migrations.

Urban Italians and Spaniards, for example, have long been eating a wide variety of diets including dairy fats instead of olive oil. Fish eating is more popular on the coast; inland, meat and cheese displace fish. There is much more distinctive to Mediterranean cuisine than olive oil. Pasta and/or bread is more common than fried potatoes are elsewhere in Europe. Tomatoes and other vegetables may play a larger role in the main cooked dishes. Garlic may have all sorts of health-promoting constituents to merit adapting to its odour! Wine has been the usual drink with meals, instead of beer, water or juice.

A physiological rationale might be found for eating more pasta, bread, fresh or even cooked vegetables and unsaturated cooking and dressing fats, washed down with a modicum of wine. Some north European diets have become much more interesting with pasta, pizza and pitta bread and all the dressings and fillings. It would be a bonus if there were a health spin-off.

Alcohol

We mostly drink alcohol rather than eat it. Also, the consumption of alcoholic beverages can affect safety as well as health, in the sense of that distinction drawn generally at the start of this chapter.

Nevertheless, alcohol is a substance that is a normal part of many people's diet. In addition, alcoholic drinks often contain substantial amounts of carbohydrate, minerals and sometimes vitamins, as well as the water and the ethanol, which is a very ready source of energy, albeit (like fatty acids) not convertible into glucose.

Furthermore, for a substantial proportion of users, alcohol is consumed as a part of meals (usually as wine). Unlike others (often drinkers of beer or spirits), some habitual users of wine with meals tend not to consume alcohol on separate occasions when ingestion is mainly confined to fluids.

Thus, even though ethanol also has pharmacological actions, it is not correct to treat it as an entirely anomalous substance in the diet, either theoretically in the estimation of nutrient intake or in practice during dietary advice about healthy meals.

Wine, beer and spirits producers operate as separate industries, distinct from the soft drinks industry, and entirely separately from the food manufacturers.

For commercial reasons rooted in legal regulation of retailing, alcohol outlets in some countries (Britain and the USA, for example) have until recently been quite separate (public houses and off-licence shops in the UK) from food shops and eating places. However, supermarkets now sell alcoholic drinks alongside all the other foods and drinks and the increasing availability of attractive (if expensive) soft drinks and food in bars has reduced the distinction from those eating places that provide wine or beer. Hence, the food business can no longer treat alcohol as anomalous either.

So it would seem that more attention to the existing scientific understanding of ordinary uses of alcohol could be of considerable help to nutritionists and food marketers alike. For the gravity of the personal, social and medical problems arising from excessive consumption of alcohol have led to a considerable volume of psychological and social research. This has included the study of ordinary uses of alcohol, whether because they might become problematic or because they are the culturally accepted background with which alcohol abuse contrasts. Although there is a good deal less of it, some useful work has also been done on the patterning of intake relevant to driving after drinking and its origins in youth.

The nutritional problems about common uses of alcohol bear some resemblance to those for sugar, especially insofar as their primary dietary contributions are both purely as energy sources. Hence, two concerns are possible contribution to obesity and possible displacement of nutrient-dense foodstuffs and hence inadequacy of some minerals or vitamins. The latter risk may be as unlikely as with sugar, except at the extremes of living off confectionery or spirits. (Deficiency of B vitamins has been thought to contribute to the brain damage caused by chronic alcohol abuse.)

That leaves obesity. 'Beer gut' is prevalent in regions where bars serve as social centres in the evenings, after a quick supper on getting home from work. Regions where per capita consumption of wine is high, and where it is more the custom to consume alcohol with slowly eaten meals, have not recognized a 'winebibber's belly'. Once again, as with sugar (and parallel to alcohol and road accidents), it may be the pattern of alcohol intake that has at least as much to do with obesity as the total consumption. The theory than energy consumed in modest enough amounts long enough before the next eating occasion is less efficient at moderating energy intake, developed from consideration of sugar's relation to obesity (above), would also predict that drinking after supper and at other times away from major meals would be particularly fattening. Some recent studies of individuals' patterning of intake may have provided some empirical support for that theory (Blair *et al.*, 1989; de Castro and Orozco, 1990; Foltin *et al.*, 1993).

The whole question of eating, drinking and obesity is taken up in detail in the next chapter.

Alcohol and Heart Disease

Before we leave specifically dietetic issues about alcohol, however, we must come back to heart disease. It has recently become apparent that common levels of consumption of alcohol, within the limits recommended, may be making a substantial contribution to the incidence of heart attacks. Higher levels are a substantial risk factor. This effect does not appear to be mediated by obesity. Effects on fat metabolism, blood pressure, chemistry and cells and blood vessels may be important. Until more is known about mediation, it is not possible to evaluate theoretically the relevance of pattern of intake relative to total intake, although the issue could and should perhaps be tackled empirically before that.

Even more interestingly, low levels of alcohol consumption may be protective to some degree against heart disease, relative to abstention as well as to higher consumption. A glass or so of wine a day is associated with the lowest prevalence, even when possibly confounding factors have been partialled out statistically.

The statistical evidence is more convincing than some other dietary epidemiology. Yet there is considerable reluctance to recommend a drink a day for the heart. This is understandable. A variety of groups have objections to alcohol on religious or moral principle. No one wants moreover to undermine the much more important message to avoid excessive alcohol intake and indeed to keep habitual intake well within the current limits.

However, these problems with communicating the implications to the public in part reflect the dearth of psychosocial research. If more was known of the influences over different patterns of alcohol consumption, then the cultural contexts for different uses associated with different intakes could be identified more clearly. This could illuminate the reasons for the U-shaped function. It would certainly help better attunement of the content of the messages to convey unambiguous meaning and to have appropriate effects on beliefs relative to personal values.

Foods Not Nutrients

Clearly, people are aware of eating foods. Even when they have been educated into thinking of foods as containing or (less accurately) being nutrients, their beliefs are often inaccurate. Indeed, the values for nutrient contents of foods used in research nutrition and dietetic practice are rough and ready and too complex to be handled other than by computer. So practical concepts of healthy eating have to be constructed in terms of food choices.

However, dietary epidemiology in affluent countries might be better advised to base data analysis on foodstuffs at least as systematically as it has traditionally been in terms of nutrients. When deficiencies of particular nutrients are the issue, then applied nutrition had better be nutrient centred. When however it is inappropriate combinations or proportions of more than adequate amounts of nutrients that are likely to be the health problem, the logically possible number of combinations of nutrient intakes will explode exponentially. We need to limit the possibilities by combinations occurring in foods and commonly eaten combinations of foodstuffs.

Even more to the point, the search for causes of ill-health in eating might be best based on food, menu and habits which are causal nexuses not reducible to combinations of nutrients.

Antioxidants and Cancer

A case in point is currently emerging strongly for fruit and vegetables, particularly green leaf vegetables. The fibre (roughage) in these has long been thought important in prevention of cancers. It now seems that they are highly beneficial components of the diet but because of non-nutritive pigments and protective phenols, as well as some of the vitamins. Certain compounds, called antioxidants, help to destroy free radicals that are formed by certain oxidation processes in the body and may set cells on the path towards cancer. These include beta-carotene, the colouring in carrots, and vitamins A, C and E. Such food constituents are likely to act in synergy against free radicals. This provides a clear example therefore of a scientific reason (not just an educational one) why nutritional recommendations should be made in terms of foods, not nutrients.

Daily Food and Nutrient Intakes

Nutritional research is not equipped to address questions about eating habits as perceived by the eaters. Even in countries where major health problems arise from the abundance of food, nutritionists are limited to an approach to 'dietary measurement' based on the historic success of their discipline in the biochemistry of nutrient deficiencies. The established methodology of applied human nutrition attempts to estimate the average daily intake of nutrients in all the foods and drinks consumed (although alcohol tends to be neglected as well as the carbohydrate, minerals and vitamins in alcoholic drinks).

This technique is utterly reliant on the cognitive processes of perception and control of eating behaviour to obtain records and recalls of materials and amounts consumed. Nevertheless, the psychology of this performance has not been investigated and indeed has yet to be recognized as relevant to this foundation of nutritional science and practice. Furthermore, the established method is to throw away the information on eating behaviour at the very start of analysis. The interest in the supposedly exhaustive record of eating and drinking occasions is only to tot up the day's accumulated intake of each nutrient or perhaps each 'type' of food. However, these categorizations of foodstuffs are by nutritional criteria, not in accord with eaters' concepts. Here, then, experimental cognitive psychology may have a role in improving nutritional research methods.

Further Reading

Background reading on the medical evidence and the efficacy of existing methods of intervention is given below.

Reports on Healthy Eating

COMA (COMMITTEE ON MEDICAL ASPECTS OF FOOD POLICY) (1984) *Diet and cardiovascular disease*, London, Her Majesty's Stationery Office.

GORMLEY, T.R., DOWNEY, G. and O'BEIRNE, D. (1987) *Food, health and the consumer*, London, Elsevier Applied Science.

VAN DER HEIJ, D.G., LOWIK, M.R.H. and OCKHUIZEN, T. (1993) *Food and nutrition policy in Europe*, Wageningen, Pudoc Scientific.

NATIONAL RESEARCH COUNCIL (USA) (1989) *Diet and health: implications for reducing chronic disease risk*, Washington, DC, National Academy Press.

Effects of Health Promotion on Eating Habits

BOOTH, D.A. (1989) 'Health-responsible food marketing', *British Food Journal* **91**, 6, pp. 7–14.

FEHILY, A., *et al.* (1989) 'The effect of dietary advice on nutrient intakes: Evidence from the diet and reinfarction trial', *Journal of Human Nutrition and Dietetics*, **2**, pp. 225–235.

KEMM, J.R. and BOOTH, D.A. (1992) *Promotion of healthier eating: How to collect and use information for planning, monitoring and evaluation*, London, Her Majesty's Stationery Office.

NUTBEAM, D., SMITH, C. and CATFORD, J. (1990) 'Evaluation in health education: A review of progress and possibilities', *Journal of Epidemiology and Community Health*, **44**, pp. 83–89.

WALTER, H.J., HOFMAN, A., VAUGHAN, R.D. and WYNDER, E.L. (1988) 'Modification of risk factors for coronary heart disease – five-year result of a school-based intervention trial', *New England Journal of Medicine*, **318**, pp. 1093–100.

Chapter 7

Dieting

This chapter sketches the cognitive psychology of uses of food that are conventionally regarded as appropriate to people who are too fat.

Body Shape and Eating

All food is potentially fattening. This is a fact of physics: any ingested calories that are not spent are stored. The body, like any other material object, abides by the law of conservation of energy and so what goes in and does not come out cannot disappear. If the body is not growing or recovering from damage and the muscles are not being built up, then once the liver has made enough glycogen, excess of energy intake over expenditure must go into the main storage form, which is fat. That is, larger amounts of triglyceride are deposited in cells in adipose tissue under the skin around the body and within the abdominal cavity.

The potential for fattening effects of eating is also a commonsense fact, well known in some form in every culture. Feeding up an animal, a child, a bride-to-be or an eminent personage may be regarded as the way to make them impressively big and beautiful, fertile or healthy, especially in a society where food is scarce.

The least sophisticated views of size and shape of the body do not distinguish between two different ways of getting bigger. Growth is the lengthening or thickening of bone and muscle, with proportionate increases in fat. Getting fatter, as distinct from growing, is an increase in adiposity, whether or not there are also changes in height or musculature. Adiposity is the proportion of fat tissue to the total body mass including lean tissue and fluid. Obesity is the medical categorization for a degree or pattern of adiposity that is clearly associated with risk to health (a definition that leaves room for argument over grades of obesity and degrees of risk).

What Used to be the Point of Getting Fat?

The laying down of fat from food has important biological benefits. There may be enough fat even in a normally shaped adult's body to keep that person alive for several weeks without eating. The emaciated look that results from starvation indicates, apart from the wasting of muscle, how much energy is stored in fat under the skin. The adult female human body typically contains a higher proportion of fat than does that of the male. This presumably promoted survival of the genes carried by the foetus when the pregnant woman and her family or tribe ran out of food.

Furthermore, the subcutaneous fat deposits of the upper part of the leg do not get larger and smaller in the same way as fat depots elsewhere in the female body. They become rapidly mobilized only during lactation, providing the very rich supply of energy demanded by the fast growth and rapid heat-loss of a small infant. Thus, mature women tend to have fatter thighs and behinds than men and it is difficult to get rid of that female 'pear shape' by slimming.

Indeed, this aspect of the female figure appears to have been admired by men over the ages at least as much as the more distinctive apparatus from which the baby feeds! One can speculate whether reproductive advantage has selected into male brains some mechanism facilitating a desire to mate or to bond with someone having a pear-shaped figure. Any such attraction to broad hips or a well-padded bottom might be entirely acquired from experiences of being mothered as a toddler and/or intuitive estimates of childbearing prospects or reciprocation of sexual interest. Such controversies may be entertaining but it is doubtful whether they can ever be resolved on evidence.

Why Do We Now Not Like Being Fat?

Whatever the biological relevance, though, fatness in women has been regarded as a sign and symbol of fertility in many cultures. The ancient Venus of Willendorf is a stone figurine of a grossly obese woman. Moreover, prodigious size has in some places been prestigious in prominent citizens of either gender. Obesity can be a sign of wealth and power perhaps because it is taken to be the result of an abundant supply of rich food and lack of a need to be active.

Thus the stigma attached to obesity in the Western world during the twentieth century, far from being the natural part of human life that it probably seems to most readers, is in fact a strange phenomenon demanding an explanation. In large part, the reasons may be quite obvious. When attractive food is abundant and affordable in unlimited amount by a high proportion of the populace, as in contemporary affluent countries, then being noticeably fatter than average or than what the consensus regards as normal, is easily taken as a sign of culpable excess of intake over expenditure. In short, fat means greedy or lazy or both; indeed, the unwarranted assumption that a fat person must be gluttonous and idle is extended to stigmata of general ill-discipline and unreliability (Allon, 1976).

Unfortunately the medical science of obesity and even its psychological investigation has been built on subtle or not so subtle attributions of the same sort. The supposedly scientific theories have in effect been that fat people, for example, have personality defects like weakness of will, are too stupid to count calories correctly, are oversusceptible to temptations to eat, have deficits in their satiety mechanisms, or have emotional problems making them overeat. They are hypothesized to gobble their food or to be insufficiently disciplined to sit down and eat at the proper time and place. When clinicians try to treat obesity, they advise on ways to change these presumed habits. Practitioners and theorists are not discouraged from these lines of thought by the fat people whom they try to help or study, because social stereotypes tend to become internalized and so this is how people who feel fat tend to talk about themselves.

What Makes Us Fat?

When looked at objectively, however, the obese in general have been found to be no different from the lean in any of these ways. Furthermore, it is thermodynamically quite unnecessary to have a behavioural or mental abnormality to get very fat. A few mouthfuls a day of intake in excess of energy expenditure could put on several kilogrammes in a year. This is the result of an energy imbalance of around only two per cent. That is such a small difference between food energy content and the losses of energy from the body as barely to be measurable, even when a person spends some days in a calorimetric room in the laboratory. Considerably greater differences in intake between or within individual people in everyday life are impossible for scientists to measure reliably. Recent techniques using isotopic water can assess energy expenditure as people go about their daily lives but inaccuracies in the assumptions and measurements preclude detection of small imbalances in individuals.

So people can, and indeed often do, gain weight insidiously without they themselves or anyone else being able to see any excessive eating or deficient exercise. The only way to know whether you are eating a little too much or not taking enough exercise to keep your weight steady is by using accurate scales and showing an increase that is consistent over repeated weighings for at least a few weeks.

In short then, eating (and/or lack of exercise) is what makes people fat and yet the fattening eating habits need not be unusual in the slightest way.

Nevertheless, when people are fat, they blame their eating. And they are right, even if they are also right to curse their metabolism or the constraints on taking exercise. However, they are probably not right about what specifically it is in their eating that they think has helped to make them fat. If they actually knew that, would not more people than at present be able to avoid getting fat or to reverse the habits responsible and lose the fat?

The Pressures to Slim

In a culture where fatness is blamed on gluttony and laziness, people are more liable to be unhappy about being fat. A social trend could therefore develop to feel fat even when merely plump, or indeed just short or big-boned.

Female hormones dispose to greater fat deposition than male hormones, in places traditionally regarded as good-looking in a woman. Yet when plumpness is bad, then a normal female figure may become unattractive. Hence, in such a society, women are more likely than men to feel too fat. Even quite lean women will struggle with their eating habits.

The sociology of affluence brings further turns of the screw. Years in a productive workforce tend to bring higher income, less time to spare and fewer calls on physical effort. Work gets tied to the desk and the busier person gets the visit rather than making it. Hence, literally running around becomes less necessary and even less feasible. At the same time, opportunities may increase for feasting on the job! So the energy balance shifts and, even if lunches do not get longer, the eating habits of youth become fattening. Middle-age spread becomes common among those in employment. Women easily broaden out with childbearing too. The tendency is then for slimness to come to mean the freedom of youth.

Looking Young

Recent social developments led to decades in which the entertainment industries had large markets among young men and women. A large sector of the population could earn a living wage without the heavy financial commitments of building a new household. Their shapes were not fully mature, let alone beginning to fatten as a more sedentary lifestyle took hold. Hence, readily available and fashionable clothing went down in size. Also, as women's roles became more like men's, designs became less suited to mature female shapes. This trend fitted well with a requirement that always tends to be put on fashion models: they need to be super-slim in order to sell expensive clothes, because fine cloth hangs straight better than it wraps around lumps and bulges.

The clothing industry's own economics is reinforced by the dress of the models in advertising by other industries selling to the youth market. This includes canned and bottled drinks, snack foods and new eating places. Moreover, all sectors of the drinks and foods business have to find ways of fending off customers' well-founded fears of being fattened by their products, greatly intensified by the pressure to be as slim as an immature youth. Non-caloric drinks, foods with fewer calories and even calorific drinks and foods that can be consumed on the run can be marketed with brand names, catch phrases and visual images to make any of them seem plausible parts of a lean and vigorous lifestyle.

There is therefore an economically powerful and socially pervasive cult that has institutionalized an ideal of slimness which is beyond that attainable by the majority of adults. This worship of scrawniness supports and is supported by a diet industry and dieting myths, rituals, values and moods that are all the more seductive for their informality, discoordination and uselessness. To top all that, official medical campaigns help put chubby people as well as the grossly fat into fear for their health and their lives.

Dieting

Dieting then is a collection of practices centred on attempts to eat less in order to be thinner. Dieters feel that they are regarded as fat and so try to do things that seem suitable to helping them eat less and lose weight, even though they may not in fact get slimmer or keep off any weight that they do lose.

Thus there are two presuppositions to dieting. One is that there is a desirable leaner shape and/or a lower weight. The other is that there is an appropriate sort of eating to attain that shape or weight.

These conceptions give rise to endless discussion because they raise issues that have yet to be resolved to general satisfaction among those who are expected to have expertise in such matters. This is largely because both the assumptions behind dieting involve scientific matters to which the relevant research discipline has yet to be applied. Why people want to lose weight and the influences on whatever eating practices are conducive to effective weight control are psychological facts. Yet these facts seem intuitively obvious to members of the same culture – above all, to those with expertise in dietary health or in food design. Hence, even when psychology is seen as relevant to the motivation to lose weight and the determinants of food choice, it remains difficult to grasp the scientific requirements for finding out, first, how to motivate slimming selectively for health and, secondly, which food choices are least fattening.

As a result, several false starts down the road to reduction of obesity by eating less have been made by psychological scientists and practitioners as well as by educators, nutritionists, physicians and diet-product developers.

The Psychology of Obesity

At this point in history in more affluent countries, most fat people are liable also to be unsuccessful dieters. Psychological research into human obesity should therefore centre on dieting. The key job is to elucidate what maintains unhealthy adiposity that goes on in the mind of the dieter, in relation to the body and the culture.

Yet the basic physics, social medicine and mental processes of fatness, eating and physical activity have over the decades generally been neglected by the psychologists as well as the other scientists and practitioners concerned with obesity. This floundering in fundamental research has left us without valid professional advice and effective public action to avoid the miseries of striving for fashionable shape and the burgeoning prevalence of obesity with its associated risks of chronic disease and premature death.

The still almost universally neglected fact of physics is that, to gain 10 lb (4.5 kg) in a year, it is sufficient to eat only 50 calories (kcal) more each day than personally needed or to take a couple more rides daily instead of walking fast for half an hour or so. Yet psychologists have pursued research programmes and treatment regimens that stigmatize even moderately overweight people as overeaters.

The fact of social medicine whose implications have been neglected is that obesity is much more prevalent among the poorer paid in the city regions of industrialized countries (Goldblatt *et al.*, 1965; Knight, 1984; Gregory *et al.*, 1990). This may follow from the prestigiousness of leanness rather than fatness in those countries; because richer people have more access to extra tidbits of food, to transport and to labour-saving devices at work and home, they will be more motivated to avoid getting as fat as they might. Shame at the fat shape and a display of efforts to get rid of it should therefore be major features of the social psychology of obesity among the rich citizenry of affluent countries. Despite this sociological context for distinctive cognitive consequences of obesity, however, psychologists have more usually theorized about personal peculiarities that might cause obesity.

The cognitive processes of dieting have therefore been largely ignored in research on obesity, even by psychologists. Instead of seeking differences between successful and unsuccessful dieters in how they sustain changes in what they do with foods and drinks and their opportunities for exercise, experimental social psychologists have chased after stable characteristics of overweight people or dieters that are associated with dramatic effects on food intake. Research psychiatrists have looked for unstable personalities or symptoms of emotional disorder such as depression. The *sine qua non* for research into methods of weight control remains measurements of psychometric and physical traits that are predictive of weight loss.

No obese personality (Rodin, 1980) or eating style (Spitzer and Rodin, 1981) could be found. Fat people proved to be no more compulsive or melancholy than many with a healthy appetite who blame themselves for not restraining it enough. As a result, medical research on obesity gave up on psychology (MRC, 1976) and addressed the problem as purely metabolic differences, despite the far greater dependence of energy balance on variations in behaviour (Booth, 1980b).

Standard techniques of behaviour modification were aimed without validation (Mahoney, 1974) at presumed habits of overeating. Yet, while this approach is less liable to immediate regain of weight than other treatments for obesity, it too is ineffective in the long term (Bennett, 1986). Years of abdominal obesity is what matters for health (see Chapter 6), not a few months down in weight by several kilogrammes.

Externality

The most famous programme of research in this area was based on a piece of cognitive theory – Stanley Schachter's 'externality' mechanism of overeating. Highly ingenious tests of the theory were run on students in the laboratory and different sorts of people in their jobs and home life (Schachter, 1968, 1971; Schachter and Rodin, 1974). The basic idea was that obese people are overreactive to external stimuli, which include cues to eat. Sure enough, again and again, fatter people ate more when food was not hidden away or was brightly illuminated, when the food items were larger or more palatable or when the clock was run fast to bring the mealtime illusorily early.

However, the research designs applied a purely physical criterion, namely body weight, instead of addressing the psychology at issue, such as the sort of habit that puts weight on or keeps it off. Moreover, for experimental groups to be large enough, generally only mildly overweight people and those in the recommended range were compared. That led to the eventual downfall of a programme that purported to address obesity: although overweight groups usually appeared to be more 'external' on average than normal-weight groups, still heavier groups were not any more 'external' but rather, if anything, less so (Rodin, 1981).

A similarly odd biologism also developed in work on the mechanisms by which 'externality' might cause obesity. Obesity is associated with insensitivity (resistance) to the actions of insulin and a compensatory extra secretion of that hormone. Excessive secretion of insulin in response to food in the mouth has been proposed (Powley, 1977) to be important in the obesity of rats with damage in the hypothalamus (Chapter 8), with which human obesity was compared (Schachter and Rodin, 1974).

Insulin drives glucose from the blood into cells of adipose tissue and encourages its conversion to fatty acids in the liver and so increases the synthesis of storage fat. Considerable attention has therefore been paid to secretory responses to 'external' stimuli such as the sight and smell or the thought of delicious food, both of insulin and also of saliva.

It is physically unrealistic, however, to suppose that extra deposition of fat induced by oversecretion of insulin would result in weight gain. Larger fat deposits that contribute to higher body weight have to get the extra stored energy from somewhere. That is, the only way in which physiological overreactivity could contribute to weight gain would be to stimulate overeating. So the priority should be on examining the assumption that externality-induced eating causes weight gain. Purely cognitive mechanisms for such eating are obvious and, unless they were proved not to be operative, there is no call to seek a physiological loop for the eating or a less relevant objective measure than higher energy intake.

Undereating as a Cause of Overeating

Keeping strictly to issues in the psychology of weight control, however, there are serious problems with the theory that externality causes overeating. These were not addressed by the social psychologists who criticized the externality theory of obesity (Nisbett, 1972) and so remained as weaknesses in the idea of 'dietary restraint' that replaced externality (Herman and Mack, 1975; Herman and Polivy, 1980: 10–item questionnaire, DRQ).

Externality and restraint are both supposed to be stable differences between people or traits of personality or approach to life. Tests for externality and scores on the dietary restraint questionnaire of Herman and Polivy (1980) do indeed show considerable stability over months, even when weight changes. Furthermore, both scores predict overeating in experimental tests, as both lines of research repeatedly confirmed, and externality predicts weight gain in an environment where food is abundant (Rodin and Slochower, 1976). Nevertheless, stability over time in responses to questions or short-term tests is not sufficient to distinguish a trait from a temporary state that is being continuously reinstated. This leaves open the possibility in this case that the overeating in the tests for externality or restraint results from a current state that the moderately overweight person, the external or the dietarily restrained are likely to be in. That state could be induced by efforts earlier in the same day and perhaps the previous day to eat less at meals and/or to refuse opportunities to nibble or quench hunger pangs with a calorific drink.

In other words, as suggested by the Kaplans (1957), 'externality' may simply mean being in a chronic state of hunger, in contrast perhaps to being susceptible to the socioaffective triggers of emotional (over)eating. Similarly, the supposed trait of 'dietary restraint' may reflect habits among some who are therefore continuously disposed to start eating at any opportunity.

Indeed, the likelihood of undereating and the certainty of feeling self-deprived follow inevitably from the concept of restrained eating (Herman and Polivy, 1980). Moreover, recent undereating is the only usable aspect of the suggestion by Nisbett (1972) that gave rise to the concept of dietary restraint, namely that Schachter's supposedly externally overreactive people are below their physiological 'set point' for weight: the notion of a set point is vacuous even when a regulated variable and machinery for monitoring and restoring it to a reference value are specified (see Chapter 3) and so all that this can mean is that these people are not higher than their present weight because they have been in the practice of eating less than they would like to.

The technical construct of externality virtually presupposed food deprivation anyway. Schachter and Rodin (1974) operationalized high externality as a stronger reaction to strong stimuli. These stimuli were assumed to be in the external environment and to include food stimuli, because internal stimuli were assumed to be weak. Such assumptions seem arbitrary and liable to muddle the arousal, drive or excitation of general sensitivity and reactivity produced by caloric deficit with the specific bodily stimuli contributing to the appetite for food. States of mind (which may persist across time and situation as traits) are no more and no less than relationships across an individual between aspects of the stimulus situation and aspects of the response pattern. The causation of the larger food intake involves the deprivation-induced state of general arousal just as much as the strength of the food stimuli or indeed the vigour of the food-gathering movements that can be an aspect of its expression: these are not competing explanations but different aspects of one account of what is going on cognitively at that moment.

One argument against this basis in food deprivation has been that people do not have to be on a diet currently to show the breakdown effect. The weakness in that suggestion is that dieters who say that they are not currently dieting are generally still restraining their intake. Anyway, restraint breakdown is a group effect and there has been no attempt to match frequencies across high and low restraint-score groups of those who either have eaten less that day or feel that they have deprived themselves to some extent. Lots of people eat cautiously these days.

Information on the calorie content of the sweetener in a drink affects preference even in non-dieters (R.P.J. Freeman, D.A. Booth and J.A. McEwan, unpublished data 1993). Even though none of the participants professed to be dieters, the richness of an aroma augmented satiety in low DRQ scorers but attenuated it in high DRQs (S. Rawle and D.A. Booth, unpublished data). The effects of cognitive salience of food on snack intake was not predicted by DRQ score alone; however, when we added more ways of sampling emotional response, a combination of restraint, state anxiety and emotional responsiveness was predictive of intake (H. Leeming and D.A. Booth, unpublished BSc Project).

In short, strong responsiveness to food stimuli is being in a state of hunger, as also is strong responsiveness to food deficit signals and to cues from clocks, pictures and colleagues' invitation to lunch. Presentation of physically strong or attentionally salient stimuli that facilitate eating in the individual, whether from foods or the external or internal environments, constitutes a state of hunger: the stimuli only cause hunger in the sense that they are more appetizing than less strong stimuli (or than different sorts of stimuli that do not facilitate eating at all). It should be noted that stimulus 'strength' in the sense used in this context is quite different from the sense in which an aspect of a learned eating stimulus can be too strong, i.e. above ideal intensity. In the case of flavours or colours, for example, the distinction might be between smellability or visibility of the food and an intensity of aroma or hue that is repulsive for that food.

It was therefore unnecessary to revoke the concept of externality, understood as defined (namely, as drive), and incorrect to regard dietary restraint as a different concept of chronic mental state. Nevertheless, dietary restraint or, to phrase it more properly, being a dieter is a polymorphous concept, unlike drive (as defined by learning theorists). In consequence, it has led us into a theoretical quagmire. Like IQ and IQ tests, dietary restraint has in effect been reduced to a questionnaire score by its theoretical inchoateness. In fact, scores on the dietary restraint questionnaire do not even represent a quantitative trait; rather the median score of a sample from the general population serves as a qualitative criterion with which to categorize people into responders, and non-responders, to an intake test for breakdown of dietary restraint in response to external food stimuli (Heatherton *et al.*, 1988).

The lack of usable theory is apparent from the absence of a research programme of testing cognitive hypotheses of this restraint-breakdown effect. The initial ideas on the effect were ideas of emotional disinhibition by anxiety (Herman, 1978). Discussion moved later to rational release from constraint: 'What the hell!' (Polivy and Herman, 1985). Unoperationalized concepts of cognitive and physiological boundaries are deployed. Yet all satiety is cognitive – the issue is what the basis is for the person's loss of appetite following some eating. No amount of speculation can settle such an issue, only experimental analyses of cognitive processes and, if relevant, physiological states as well.

Tests for externality or restraint breakdown should be theoretically tight models of what people who try to eat less do, because they feel fat. The applicability of the model to a particular set of data should be monitorable. Then there will be a chance that the results will increase our understanding of what is going on in their minds and in their circumstances when they are stimulated to eat more than they otherwise would (whether or not that is overeating by any other criterion). Moreover, such a scientifically based test for propensity to overeat would give us better ideas of how to help individuals in general (and social groups) for whom dieting is problematic. A really good test would also be diagnostic and a guide to advice in a particular individual.

A psychological construct simply cannot be anchored on a physically specified test like the two-food intake test for dietary-restraint breakdown; there must be a theoretical specification of a design according to the monitored psychological mechanisms that it is supposed to recruit. This lack of theory is shown up by an increasing number of reports of failures to replicate the breakdown effects, under conditions which are hard to specify (Lowe, 1993).

Can There Be a Psychometrics of Dieting?

This theoretical vacuum is also evident in the unstable structure of responses to the original dietary restraint questionnaire (Drewnowski *et al.*, 1982; Ruderman, 1983) and the ambiguity of the scales that emerge when instruments are developed psychometrically (Stunkard and Messick, 1985; van Strien *et al.*, 1986). A questionnaire that assessed personal investment in the cult of dieting would assess all sorts of rationales, moods and activities and might well show no traitlike consistency (Figure 7.1). The original Dietary Restraint Questionnaire opens with the somewhat awkwardly worded item, 'How frequently are you dieting?'. The Dutch instrument makes a dozen separate questions out of this and responses to them hang together well in all sorts of groups. Stunkard and Messick went through elaborate psychometric procedures but purely empirically and then applied questionable labels to the factors that emerged, namely 'restraint', 'disinhibition' and 'hunger'. Restraint is the muddled

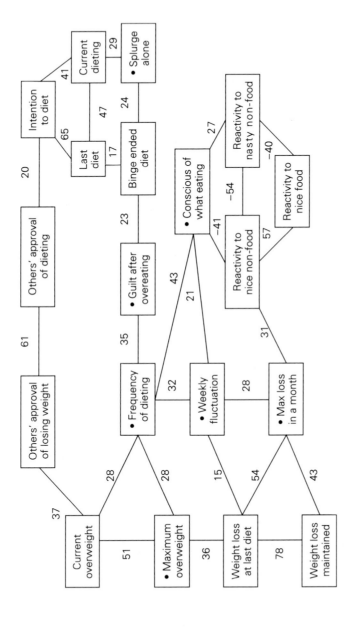

Figure 7.1 All the statistically significant percentage correlations between responses from 100 female dieters to questions about attitudes, emotionality and behaviour to do with dieting, including items (*) from Herman and Polivy's (1980) Dietary Restraint Questionnaire (Lewis and Booth, 1986).

concept we started with, which was meant to include disinhibition. Hunger is the name for any eating for eating's sake, again arguably part of the original concept of what results from self-deprivation like any other deprivation. None of these scales, disinhibition, hunger, cognitive restraint, has proved to be predictive of the intake effect in the original test for breakdown of restraint.

The Way Forward

Laboratory or questionnaire investigations of dieting and obesity are productive when they tell us something more about what is going in in the participant's mind when they are dealing with food. Experimental tests and questionnaire items are ways of making people attend to their appetite for food. The research challenge is to design them to reveal how people behave whose appetite is that day, and for a long time, raised above others. To be relevant to dieting, the tests should pick out those who attribute gluttony to themselves to account for what they regard as fatness and struggle to restrain that supposed overeating and so feel, and may well actually be, self-deprived of food. Many people who are not dieters find some foods attractive even when they have just had a meal at a regular mealtime. Anybody would tend to be made hungry easily when they are not feeling full. Someone who is not a dieter may not have eaten to fullness for some time for all sorts of other reasons.

What Dieters Think, Feel and Do

Dieting is an informal institution built up around the belief and fact that you have to eat less to become less fat. Since eating is so complex, there is a great variety of dieting practices. Different beliefs, values and emotions build up around these practices and their consequences. These attitudes and moods are mostly self-doubt and disappointment, since few people reach the shape or weight that they desire. Dieting is therefore a daunting challenge for cognitive research.

A lack of such research itself contributes to these doubts and disappointments with dieting. If the more successful strategies had been identified, they could be communicated to the public. Yet psychologists and others have hardly begun to sort out what people who feel fat think it is that they are doing with foods and drinks, and their physical activity too. This is a necessary step to ascertaining which strategies are more and less effective at getting weight off and keeping it off. That in turn could help specify how best to resist undue pressure to be slim and how the susceptible to unhealthy weight gain might avoid it.

Daily Food and Nutrient Intakes

When estimated daily intakes of nutrients and food types are compared between dieters and non-dieters, no clear differences emerge between groups (Tuschl *et al.*,

1990). This is hardly surprising in groups from the same parts of society, shopping in the same supermarkets, living in the same range of households and acculturated to widespread concern about healthy eating. In any case, as argued in the previous chapter, the standard nutritional research technique of estimating total intake over a day is not equipped to address questions about eating habits as perceived by the eaters.

INTAKE ESTIMATES AND WEIGHT LOSS

Potentially more relevant would be differences in estimated intakes between successful and unsuccessful dieters in terms of weight lost and held off for some years at least.

Estimates of energy intake have been compared between obese and normal-weight groups many times. Nevertheless, this is a highly questionable research strategy, for two simple reasons.

Psychologically, records from people who feel fat are unlikely to be accurate representations of what they normally eat. If any confirmation were needed of the higher prevalence of under-recording to be expected in groups at higher body weight, it has been provided by recent isotopic methods. However, no amount of objective measurement can improve the estimates from records until the sources of invalidity are identified psychologically.

The physical reason why it is questionable to study the energy intake of the obese is that a person's current energy intake is not the intake that made them fat. They may or may not have continued the eating pattern that contributed to their weight gain. The costs in energy of carrying around extra fat are small compared with the energy cost of laying the fat down.

Even if those two problems were overcome, the approach is doomed. The reason was mentioned at the start of this chapter. An unmeasurably small difference of intake at equal expenditures could be sufficient for the modest loss of weight that generally is maintained at best, as well as the insidious weight gain commonly seen.

Intake estimation might have something to contribute to the understanding of weight change if a less absolute approach were taken. Relative interpretations of estimated intakes could be useful if there were a nutrient (or food type) which was disproportionately more fattening than people thought it was and so tended to under-report. This condition may well be met by total dietary fat, especially fat relative to carbohydrate (starches and sugars). The reasons are as follows.

Much dietary fat is in the same form as that stored in the cells of adipose tissue, namely triglycerides. In these compounds, the three alcohol (-OH) groups on glycerol are linked to fatty acids, chains of carbon-hydrogen groups attached to the acidic pairing of a carbonyl group (-CO and -OH). One fatty acid (-COOH) combines with each glycerol -OH group with loss of a water molecule (HOH) to form an ester, a process therefore called esterification. The break-up of one of these ester links, taking up the water again, is called hydrolysis. Triglycerides can get from food into adipose tissue without undergoing any more profound transformation than some hydrolysis and re-esterification. (Thus, some of the fatty acids in your fat depots have the same chemical structure as those fatty acids in your food that your body cannot make, such as the polyunsaturated fatty acids in fish oils and some vegetable oils.) Starches and sugars, on the other hand (as also amino acids and alcohol) have to be broken down to two-carbon fragments and built up again into the carbon chains of the fatty acids before the carbohydrate energy can be stored as triglyceride in adipose tissue. As a result the energy values conventionally assigned to fats and carbohydrates underestimate their relative fattening potential. That is because the 9 kcal/g of fat and the 4 kcal/g of carbohydrate refer to the energy released in the tissues by complete oxidation to carbon dioxide. A lot more of that energy is spent merely storing energy when it comes from carbohydrate than when it comes from fat. So, when dietary energy is being stored, it would be more realistic to increase the 9:4 ratio for fat:carbohydrate, perhaps up to 10:4 or even 12:4. (The figure 4 may also be rather high, because it applies to oxidation of glucose from dietary starch and some forms of starch turn out to be resistant to digestion, as well as free sugars being 5 per cent less energy-dense than fully digested starches.)

It is increasingly realized that fat is rich in energy as well as a powerful source of temptation to eat. However, even if fat is thought to be twice as fattening as starch or sugar, weight for weight, that is still a major under-estimate. Also, dietary fat (in spreads, for example) is less often diluted by fibre, water or air than dietary starch (in bread, for example). Furthermore, starchy and sugary foods still have a strong fattening image in some people's minds, although nutritional opinion on that reversed, for starch at least, 10–20 years ago. Thus, the tendency to avoid and under-report fat intake relative to carbohydrate intake may still be low in proportion to the actual difference in fattening potential.

Intake assessments have recently supported this view. The most relevant study compared those who lost weight with those who did not after dietetic advice (Kayman *et al.*, 1990). Estimated fat intakes as proportion of energy were lower in the success-ful dieters. Another study prescribed diets that differed between groups in fat con-tent (Lissner *et al.*, 1987). The reported fat intakes (and total energy intakes) varied between groups in the rank order prescribed and weight changes also tracked the purported fat differences, with the high-fat group gaining most.

SNACKFOOD ADDICTION

It has nevertheless been claimed that obese people tend to show a 'craving for carbohydrate' and that this is a form of emotional overeating. This research did not rely on people recording their intake or on observing intake directly or unobtru-sively in laboratory tests. Instead, the participants obtained their food and drink around the clock from multi-channel dispensing machines and individuals' selec-tions were recorded automatically, an approximation to the accuracy of free intake measurement that can be obtained in a metabolic ward (e.g. Porikos and Van Itallie, 1984). The observed phenomenon was a tendency to take food from the dispenser after meals and to prefer packet foods (that tend to be high in fat, starch and/or sugar) to fresh foods such as ham sandwiches.

A 10-year prospective study in Copenhagen found that young adults tended to be fatter if, when they were children, their mothers professed not to know about their sweet-eating habits (Lissau *et al.*, 1993), presumably thereby allowing consid-erable consumption. Eating food between meals ('snacking', in one of the many senses of that word) is associated with chronic obesity among Parisian women (Basdevant *et al.*, 1993). Yet this is not an effect of frequent eating: rather, to the contrary, a larger number of meals is associated with less obesity and they resulted in a slightly lower daily intake in a field experiment with Dubliners (McGrath and Gibney, 1993). Obviously, therefore, it is important to conceptualize the pattern of eating correctly before we shall be able to relate it to effective weight control.

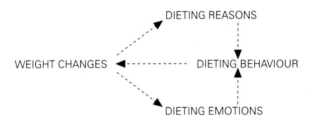

Figure 7.2 Skeleton of a causal model of the psychology of dieting, supported by the data in Figure 7.1.

Perceived Behaviour and Weight Loss

An initial attempt to distinguish between successful and unsuccessful dieters in what they said they were doing was carried out for the UK Health Education Council in the early 1980s (Lewis and Booth, 1986). The clearest result anticipated with the small set of measures used was support for the realization outlined above of the importance of fat intake in weight control (see Figure 6.1). Similar results were obtained by Kayman *et al.* (1989).

Towards a Theory of Dieting

A series of research projects on food choices in weight control (Lewis and Booth, 1986; Booth, 1987, 1988; Blair *et al.*, 1989) was started by an attempt to combine existing biological, social and psychological hypotheses about obesity, dietary restraint and weight control into a single theory of dieting. It was possible to construct a conceptual causal network (Figure 7.2) which was used to guide the design of laboratory and field experiments and questionnaire investigations. This network could be sketched in its crudest form as a statement that, within an individual's mind, the rational and emotional influences on eating behaviour affect weight which then feeds back into thinking and feeling.

The details in this cognitive-thermodynamic system illustrate the options within the socioeconomic system of dieting – a bewildering variety for participants no less than for investigators! In the first systematic questionnaire study, a hundred professed dieters were asked about the different beliefs and values (attitudes), emotional reactions, eating choices and weight changes. Their answers were subjected to multivariate correlational analysis to seek confirmation or otherwise of individual differences relating different pairs of variables in the hypothetical system. This path analysis confirmed the broad outline and much of the detail of the initially integrated conception (compare Figures 7.1 and 7.2).

It also revealed the wide but limited sampling of the options within dieting that are represented by the ten items on the Dietary Restraint Questionnaire. In professed dieters, when coupled with these other more differentiated questions, answers to different DRQ items seldom correlated appreciably with each other. This confirmed the doubts mentioned earlier in this chapter that the scores measured a quantitative characteristic of individuals that might be called 'dietary restraint'.

Keeping Weight Off and Prevention of Obesity

If we can identify the ways in which people living under current conditions can permanently reduce unhealthy overweight, this opens up the prospect of reducing the prevalence of obesity by preempting initial weight gain as well.

Values and Emotions

Many people are ready to recognize that they have a weight problem and most would probably want to to do something about it if they were confident that they could do so. There is however an under-acknowledged ethical problem which has consequences for more than moral integrity. Obesity is not just a risk to chronic disease. It is not just part of mental life that some mood-altering medicines can fix. One's physical appearance can be a central part of one's whole life and shape and weight a salient facet of appearance. Techniques for weight reduction and weight-gain prevention are as usable to reduce weight further, below the range desirable for health, as they are to attain it. The twist is that using weight reduction techniques purely to obtain a slim appearance can become an emotional and physiological trap, leading to the distress and risks to health of disordered eating and/or extremes of exercising.

The medical profession and other health service practitioners, including psychologists, are no better equipped to deal with this moral dilemma than many other agencies from whom people have a right to expect help. The family doctor has always been open to exploration of values. Nevertheless, balancing health with other considerations can hardly be left to health professionals. For some, religious ministers will have a role. Friends in local groupings and in the nuclear and wider family have their part in developing and supporting a person's whole balance of values.

Thus education and therapy for permanent weight control should begin with counselling in the moral considerations and social implications. This leads naturally to the problems of self-image that may need tackling before people can get the necessary control over their eating habits. Once the social pressures on women have been discussed, it is natural to consider the role of body size and shape in self-evaluation, the rationale for dissatisfaction with physical appearance and the emotional control achievable through assertiveness regarding comments about body shape or food choices. Even a written treatment of such issues can be used by those concerned about weight to become more relaxed about dieting and less emotional about eating (Blair *et al.*, 1990, 1992).

Confidence and Personally Effective Habits

A cool and controlled approach to weight control cannot help unless the person knows how to change their eating and exercise in a way that will sustain a reasonable weight loss indefinitely. Each person therefore needs to identify those habits that they are confident that they can change and that those changes would help to keep lost weight off. Desperation may motivate use of the latest unproven wheeze but each new trick inspires less confidence. Communication of research evidence as to the most effective habits at keeping weight off should both help in picking out the behaviour that matters and also boost the belief that the weight can be kept off by that strategy.

When people are told about the evidence favouring substituting starch for fat, cutting out calories between meals, taking opportunities for physical exertion and finding alternatives to emotional eating, they apply those principles for themselves when they decide to fight the flab around the waistline and so continue to lose weight after contact with the counselling professional has ceased (Lewis *et al.*, 1992).

Eating Disorders

For some people, the effort to control shape by constraining eating becomes so intense that it gets out of control. They acquire habits of playing with little pieces of food at the table or even elaborate cooking for the family, while not eating enough to sustain their weight. They may use laxatives a great deal or even acquire a trick of getting rid of any substantial meal immediately after it has been eaten, by vomitting. They may also be very active and perhaps make a hobby or start a career that involves vigorous athletics; this can have an additional slimming effect. In younger people, eating and absorbing less energy than is spent can prevent the rounding of the female figure and the thickening of the male musculature that is usually completed in the late teens and early twenties.

This may not be as much of a triumph of sheer will-power as ordinary eaters might imagine. The food-refusing habits are driven by a compulsion to avoid normal fleshiness and perhaps to achieve success in areas that do not implicate sexual maturity. The thinner body in any case needs less energy. Also, the digestive tract adapts to a very low intake by ekeing out what food it gets so that it takes longer to be absorbed; this may delay strong signals of hunger from the gut and liver.

Furthermore, the detailed business of food preparation may provide consider-able satisfaction without eating, once the self-starver has learned ways of diverting attention from and coping with hunger pangs and food cravings. Indeed, it may be possible to reinterpret the sensations as nausea or a sort of satiety and the desires as interest in others' appreciation of the food prepared or their acceptance of the preparer's own refusal to eat.

Nevertheless, at some level the self-starver still wants to eat: an appetite for food may be readily admitted. So 'anorexia' is a misnomer; 'hypophagia' would be more appropriate, if a Greek-based name is needed for self-starvation. Moreover, the undereating may not be as extreme as appears. A very energetic youngster who should be growing might be keeping weight at 75 per cent or 80 per cent below the normal average for age and sex while actually ingesting more energy than an over-weight adult who is trying hard to slim. Hence, since extreme underweight is a prime criterion for the medical diagnosis of anorexia nervosa, that would be a better basis on which to name the condition.

However, another prime diagnostic criterion is the intensity of the preoccupa-tion with avoiding any sign of what the afflicted interprets as fatness. It is less obvious than for weight and weight norms how to measure this psychological state objectively. Nevertheless, psychometric subscales of disgust at shape have been developed and might be worked up into diagnostic instruments at least for research purposes, as has been done with depression scales for example. Even then though, an accurate name along the lines of 'adipophobic self-starvation' is not likely to displace the odd term anorexia nervosa, since it is now a century old and everybody knows it is silly.

The term 'nervosa' can also be challenged but that view remains controversial. The issue is whether there is anything wrong with the nervous system in the origins of the disorder (Booth, 1987, 1989a). The argument is that, rather than the self-starvation being based on biological dysfunction, let alone neurological disease, the brain and body deal adaptively with behavioural practices and emotional turmoil that are a self-sustaining psychobiosocial syndrome, which a person may acquire on following a certain path through the dieting culture. Before briefly illustrating that approach, however, a little detail of the eating disorders should be introduced.

Starvation Disorders

Anorexia nervosa is most commonly diagnosed in late teenage girls. Nevertheless, plenty of sufferers come to the attention of psychiatrists in their early twenties and the problem can appear in the early teens, and also in a much lower proportion of male youths. There is a strong self-help movement, supporting self-starving youngsters and their parents, sometimes with an antipsychiatric slant and asserting the right to a lifestyle of extreme leanness.

The incidence of anorexia nervosa may have grown in recent decades. It can go in waves, too: the disorder shows signs of social contagion, the likelihood of its developing being increased by awareness of someone else having the condition. The fullblown diagnosis probably could only ever be given to one in several hundred of the female population.

The established view is that anorexia nervosa differs from hunger strikes by prisoners and religious fasts by monks, nuns and hermits. However, there are many similarities (Orbach, 1986). The only distinctive feature of the psychiatric diagnosis may be the extremity of the fear and loathing of fat on the body or even of an ordinary fleshiness. Other self-starvers may wish to mortify the body or be seen to be wasting away but the value judgment on their aims is that they are sane while the adipophobia is psychotic.

Food Bingeing Disorders

The psychiatric diagnosis of bulimia nervosa (Striegel-Moore *et al.*, 1986) has been developed out of the older diagnosis of anorexia nervosa over the last decade or so. The two syndromes that are thereby labelled as mental disorders have in common an intense preoccupation with bodily shape and specifically a loathing for an imagined degree of fatness. The diagnosis of bulimia nervosa can be applied to someone who is overweight or in the normal weight range, not just to the underweight. Nevertheless, someone who is mildly overweight may regard herself or himself as disgustingly fat, in as unrealistically exaggerated a fashion as an underweight person self-perceived as chubby.

The distinction between bulimic and anorexic diagnoses is in the eating pattern. Bulimia nervosa is characterized by frequent binges on food, whereas the diagnostic criteria for anorexia nervosa include persistent efforts to restrict food intake severely. Someone diagnosed as suffering from bulimia nervosa may attempt to restrict intake between binges or for periods of days or weeks but frequent bingeing recurs: this is the pattern of a 'restricting bulimic'. Others may binge unremittingly, bulimia nervosa without restriction.

Another feature shared by bulimic and anorexic syndromes is purging. In either disorder, there may be excessive use of laxatives. In bulimia nervosa, a binge is usually terminated or followed by intentional vomitting (usually very secretively). Thus the typical pattern for a diagnosis of bulimia nervosa is bingeing with vomitting several times a day, coupled with an intense fear of getting fat.

It is widely accepted from the clinical evidence that dieting invariably precedes the onset of a syndrome falling under the diagnosis of bulimia nervosa. However, it is usually argued that dieting is not a cause of bulimia nervosa because the vast majority of dieters do not develop that disorder. A substantial minority of dieters report what they regard as binges but only a very small percentage meet the criteria of frequency, purging and loathing of exaggeratedly perceived fatness. It should be noted that this does not show that dieting is not a cause. Nevertheless, it does show that, even if dieting is contributory, there must be one or more other predisposing factors in addition. Some sort of difficulty in managing the emotions is generally suggested, such as susceptibility to depression or poor control of impulses.

The clinical diagnoses of depression and bulimia nervosa are associated to a substantial degree (Hudson and Pope, 1990). It would hardly be surprising, however, if a loathing for one's shape was associated with an extremely low opinion of oneself and if being in the grip of a habit of bingeing and vomitting were allied to severe melancholy.

Biologically oriented psychiatrists seem to assume that some disorder of brain functioning predisposes some dieters to develop the syndrome of bulimia nervosa. A wide variety of chemicals have now been synthesized that have powerful effects on synapses between nerve cells and alter mood without obviously serious physical side-effects. Various drugs that are prescribed to sufferers from clinical depression and appear to help an elevation of mood have therefore been tested in the treatment of bulimia nervosa. The results have been variable and modest at best, although little has been done as yet to separate out depressed bulimics for this approach. Indeed, the benefits of taking such a drug when depressed for good reason (reactive) or not (endogenous) are not entirely clear.

Furthermore, any supposedly specific drug has side-effects and many antidepressants share effects such as on the autonomic nervous system. Thus, for example, most are anti-cholinergic or act on amine transmitters in ways that may slow the emptying of the stomach. This could augment the satiating effect of a meal and help a binger to resist the temptation to start on food when it becomes available between meals (Booth, 1985).

The bingeing–vomitting syndrome is quite conceivably a natural trap within the cognitive, physiological and cultural system of dieting. Following a path of cyclic dieting with certain attitudes and/or emotional propensities may lead one into the trap. On this view, bulimia should be more common among women while the pressures to be slim and even prepubertal in figure and to succeed in ways besides in acquiring a spouse and children remain part of both traditional and some of the recent more liberated conceptions of femininity and the incidence of chronic and repeated dieting is higher among women.

The trap may be that cyclic breaches of dieting could lead to snack-addictive conditioned desatiation and an emotionally and physiologically conditioned emotion-dependent eating (Blair *et al.*, 1990; Booth *et al.*, 1991). Then, once the binger begins to get rid of the food, a spiral can build up of emotionally conditioned emesis and emesis-conditioned desatiation.

Therapy

It follows from the approach taken in this chapter that therapies for weight control and for eating disorders are quite similar in principle. Sooner or later, the sufferer must tackle the problems with self-image, and the personal, social and even ethical implications. Even those who insist on being extremely thin need to eat substantial amounts in a healthy pattern to sustain themselves. The on–off dieting cycle and the binge–vomit–starve cycle differ largely in frequency, not in their nature. The antecedents of bingeing need to be tackled, much as those for emotional eating. With a more realistic self-image, a reduction in anxiety provoked by a normal meal should make it easier to avoid vomitting.

Further Reading

Other approaches to obesity and eating disorders are represented in the following books and review papers.

Psychology of Overeating

Bruch, H. (1973) *Eating disorders: obesity, anorexia nervosa and the person within*, New York, Basic Books.

Slochower, J.A. (1983) *Excessive eating: The role of emotions and environment*, New York, Human Sciences Press.

Psychology of Obesity

Rodin, J. and Schachter, S. (1974) *Obese humans and rats*, Washington DC, Erlbaum.

Stunkard, A.J. (1976) *The pain of obesity*, Bull Publishing.

Stunkard, A.J. (Ed.) (1980) *Obesity*, Philadelphia, PA, W.B. Saunders.

Psychology of Eating Disorders

CRISP, A.H. (1980) *Anorexia nervosa – Let me be*, London, Academic Press.

GILBERT, S. (1986) *Pathology of eating: Psychology and treatment*, London, Routledge.

PALMER, R.L. (1980) *Anorexia nervosa: A guide for sufferers and their families*, Harmondsworth, Penguin.

PIRKE, K.M., VANDEREYCKEN, W. and PLOOG, D. (Eds) (1988) *The psychobiology of bulimia nervosa*, Berlin, Springer-Verlag.

STRIEGEL-MOORE, R.H., SILBERSTEIN, L.R. and RODIN, J. (1986) 'Toward an understanding of risk factors for bulimia', *American Psychologist*, **41**, pp. 246–263.

Chapter 8

Neuroscience of Ingestive Appetite

An approach to research into brain mechanisms of human eating and drinking.

Food and the Brain

Is fish a good 'brain food'? If an inadequate supply of some vitamins or minerals does indeed slow the normal development of performance in tests of 'intelligence', by what actions in the brain might such a nutrient deficiency make learning more difficult?

Does chocolate stimulate pleasure centres in the brain better than any other foodstuff? Can the brain detect some good and bad things in our diet and so influence our choices among foods? Is feeling full simply the stomach telling the brain that it is holding a large volume?

Why does a heavy meal tend to make you sleepy? Do some depressed people crave carbohydrate because its effects on brain chemistry give them a 'lift'? Does alcohol dissolve worries by acting in the brain like an anti-anxiety drug? How does caffeine help concentration and does that help make us like to drink coffee, tea or cola?

Approach of This Chapter

Answers to these sorts of questions require careful psychological investigation, and sound nutritional and food sciences as well. In addition, though, we need to understand some basic principles of the functioning of the neural networks in the brain and the nerve cells connected to them around the body. This chapter briefly outlines some of issues that neuroscience now faces about the physical machinery underlying the desire for food and drink and the psychological effects of food substances. We shall consider first the brain mechanisms of ingestive appetite itself. Later in the chapter, we shall turn to effects of ingested substances on behaviour other than eating.

The viewpoint of the chapter is personal to a participant in current research, but this is a very new developing area of neuroscience and so no position is likely to command general assent. There are many exciting possibilities but at present virtually all of them remain very uncertain. The primary intention in this chapter is to encourage a constructively questioning approach to enthusiasm about a new finding and an informed and cautious position on often highly controversial suggestions that scientists discuss among themselves and which get put over to the general public.

Bases of Behaviour *versus* Influences on Behaviour

Within the neuroscience of eating and drinking, a clear distinction should be kept between, on the one hand, the basic mechanisms by which the nervous system organizes our thoughts, feelings, acts and reactions (e.g. towards food and drink) and, on the other hand, the influences on the brain and body that alter the operation of those neural bases of appetite or of other psychological phenomena.

Indeed, starting to think about this distinction can immediately make some of the ideas about food and the brain seem implausible in principle. At least, the sorts of mechanisms needed to make an idea work become clearer. The necessary mechanisms often begin to look remarkably special: in effect, magical properties are being attributed to the brain or some place or transmitter substance in it.

When such suspicions arise about a hypothesized psychological function of the brain, it is good scientific strategy to go back to the mind and society to check whether the phenomena could be accounted for by quite non-specific brain mechanisms, of learning for instance (Booth and Gibson, 1988; Booth, French and Gatherer, 1992). In other words, the specific causation for a so-called brain effect may well be psychosocial, established during individual development.

Brains are nothing like computers in detail but computers do illustrate the difference between the operations of the physical machinery and the performance of the machine – how it behaves. The chips and other 'hardware' put together by computer engineers are analogous to the nerve cells in the pint and a half of 'wetware' in our heads. The running of a computer program, with the keying in and printing out, correspond in a primitive way to thought and action. To that extent, the engineering provides the basis for the programming as the neurophysiology provides the basis for the behaviour. The point of this analogy in this context is to think now of what effects we could have on the running of programs by influencing the workings of the chips, discs, peripherals, etc. If something happens that does affect the running, it is very likely to be disastrous! Even if the computer hardware and software are robust enough to work when a part heats up or the power supply voltage is reduced, the effect may be quite crude, like slower or faster running. Calculations will not give different answers. The style of English printed out will not get better or worse.

To get a specific and functional change in a computer's behaviour, indeed, we have to key in a meaningful command or an alteration to the program. Similarly, a psychological influence is by far the most likely way to get a particular psychological effect. The action of a substance on brain circuitry is unlikely to have more than a very non-specific effect on behaviour. Even a very specific drug, that acts on only one sub-class of receptors, is liable to affect the synapses connecting the nerve cells of networks involved in quite different aspects of behaviour.

Therefore, probably the only way that a nutrient or other food substance could have a specific effect on food choices or other behaviour is if there were a 'key' for it (a specific receptor) that was exclusively connected in the appropriate way to the neural networks underlying that particular sort of performance. This general point has been illustrated in detail for the theory that the protein in a food affects subsequent selection of that food via effects of the protein's amino acids on a particular synaptic transmitter between neurones in the brain (Booth and Gibson, 1988), an idea further considered later in this chapter.

The Neurophysiology of Eating and Drinking

The core biological science of the brain is the integrative neurophysiology of connections among single neurones. This is the part of neuroscience that constructs theoretical systems in which sets of neurones interact with each other and with the senses, muscles and glands and tests these theories by recording the electrical activity of single cells. The part played by the recorded neurone in its neural system (or systems: a cell can operate in several) is worked out from the way its 'firing' varies with different patterns of input and output, cerebral or environmental, and the microscopic anatomical connections between neurones of that type in that region of the brain and other types of neurone.

Since ingestion is cognitively rich behaviour, much of its neurophysiology will rely on general resources in the brain, such as the different sensory systems, systems of learning and recognition, language systems, the control of oral and other movements and the autonomic nervous system modulating the viscera and metabolism. The first section of this chapter sketches the neural systems involved, with a strong slant towards those bits of evidence that implicate food and drink specifically. Afterwards we turn to possible effects of diet on the brain.

Sensory Inputs

An amazing limitation of ingestive neuroscience is that the neuroscientists lack usable ideas on how foods and drinks are recognized, despite the advanced state of visual neuroscience and the growing amount of electrophysiological data with complementing neuroanatomy for the chemical and tactile senses.

For example, it is known that the presence of water in the mouth is signalled to the base of the brain but, at least according to Norgren (1991), neurophysiologists do not yet understand the sensory basis of this information. Particular foods clearly can be recognized by sight and/or smell but again little coherent theory exists on the stimulation of the senses in the mouth by ordinary foodstuffs.

Part of the problem has been an unrealistic emphasis on taste, for a conjunction of scientifically strategic reasons. Tastes have dramatic effects on ingestion, even in pure aqueous solution; they also influence facial expressions in distinctive ways. Taste stimulus delivery can be controlled more easily than other sensory characteristics of food, except its visual appearance. Taste receptor types appear to be conveniently almost as few as colour pigments and so the same deceptively simple concepts of primaries, labelled lines and direct perception have seemed workable.

Oral Control

In fact, most of the actual process of eating or drinking is under tactile control of various sorts, some of it exquisitely subtle yet powerful and much of it subconscious.

One of the simplest is a reflex that stops us continually clashing our teeth together and even perhaps damaging them (or our gums with 'bullets' of food fragments when we crunch hard foodstuffs like ginger biscuits). The jaw muscles have to exert pressure, increasing rapidly to perhaps a very high level, to start crushing a piece of biscuit held between the molars. Once the biscuit fractures, though, the jaw-closing force must be shut off extremely rapidly. This is achieved by an exquisitely sensitive and rapid reflex from pressure receptors in the roots of the teeth.

One of the most complex tactile controls of eating is the textural appreciation of foods in the mouth (see Chapter 5). In the palatability of a foodstuff, mouthfeel is probably more important even than taste, let alone smell, colour or shape. Yet we know almost nothing of the patterns of pressure on the tongue, palate and other surfaces of the mouth that produce the sensations of the different crunches of corn flakes and raw apple, the distinct creamy feels of whole milk and soft cheese and the different chewinesses of gum, toffee and meats.

In the simpler cases like thickness of fluids and hardness of solids, the food scientists have found physical properties like viscosity and work of compression that predict people's ratings of the textural qualities quite well. However, in most cases, the physics of what is happening to the food in the mouth is almost impossibly hard to work out. The spatiotemporal patterns of force deforming the skin inside the mouth to which the different sorts of mechanoreceptor could be sensitive have hardly been thought about. Yet a theory of such receptor patterns is indispensible, not only to make progress with the tactile neurophysiology (LaMotte and Srinivasan, 1993; Hsaio *et al.*, 1993) but also to sort out the cognitive psychology of oral texture perception (Richardson and Booth, 1993).

For example, it has been suggested by the food physicist Kokini (1987) that the smoothness of dairy cream arises from its lubricating effect between the tongue and the palate. Yet it is not at all obvious how the mechanoreceptors in the skin could detect the small differences in these frictional forces because they are tangential to the surface and are unlikely to cause the microscopic deformations that stimulate the receptors. Roughness felt by the fingertips, for example, when it does not involve vibration from snagging, depends on the movement of millimetre-scale ups and downs across the skin (Johnson and Hsiao, 1992). Johansson and Westling (1987) suggested from neurophysiological evidence, nevertheless, that variations in pressure might stimulate certain receptors by interaction with irregularities in the skin down at the scale of micrometres (μm). It seems that μm-scale variations in the fat-globule sizes and spacings in milks can be detected by some people when making up their minds how similar a test sample is to a milk they know, such as the high-fat milk from Channel Island breeds of cow that is sold with a gold-coloured bottle closure in Britain (gold top) (Richardson *et al.*, 1993; Richardson and Booth, 1993).

Integrative Systems

The visual, tactile, gustatory, nociceptive (burn) and olfactory systems each first integrate their own information from a food in the primary relay regions of the cerebral cortex, usually in its back half (except for smell). The sensory modalities then have to be put together for food recognition and, sooner or later, related to other motivating influences such as linguistic and interpersonal meaning and also the internal signals from the digestive tract and liver and indeed from receptors in the brain itself.

The external senses to do with food recognition converge in association areas of the neocortex of the cerebrum – the much-folded surface mantle of the human brain. All sorts of visual information arriving right at the back of the hemispheres is integrated next door, in the back underside of the temporal lobes (deep in the head by the ears). Just under this infero-temporal cortex, the old limbic structure of the amygdala (so called because of its almond-kernel shape) picks up visceral effects of eating and uses them to tag sights as food (Sanghera *et al.*, 1979). These parts of the cortex are also closely connected to the frontal lobes, the lower parts of which are called orbitofrontal cortex because it lies just above the eye sockets. Both taste and smell information is relayed here and it converges to enable flavour recognition and also interacts with visual cues from food (Thorpe *et al.*, 1983; Rolls, 1989).

The internal senses probably converge in different places in different species of mammal. In rats, some behaviourally important integration is carried out in the brainstem and limbic system (Scott and Giza, 1993). The neocortical interactions are more important in primates (Rolls, 1993). Visceral and taste pathways run close to each other anatomically in the brainstem of all vertebrates but probably do not converge onto the same neurones lower than the forebrain, in sites like the amygdala where (as just stated) visual information is also involved. However, the places where the eyes and mouth talk to signals from the body about eating or rejecting the food are not clear. Probably at least some of this overall integration is done in frontal regions of neocortex, which are highly developed in human beings and critical to the control of action by sophisticated intentions and emotions (including sociality). More to the point than where these neuronal systems are, however, is that we have no idea of the mechanisms by which they carry out the sort of integration among dietary, visceral and social sources of information that we know people do and has been demonstrated in simple ways in animal behaviour too.

Such recognition of foods and of their appropriateness to context cannot of course be private: its neural bases must influence the neural bases of action. Frontal cortex is on the output side of the cerebrum. In cooperation with the cortical, sub-cortical and cerebellar systems controlling movement of the limbs and head, it will transfer information about the food and the internal and external context into the automatic routines of eating and drinking. In parallel, the more basic aversions and preferences, perhaps modulated by the state of the gut and metabolism, will be processed by the limbic system. Exchange of information between frontal and limbic systems is likely to pass through the brainstem as well as through the more reflexive sensory controls of movement and of the autonomic nervous system (ANS). Thus, the highest levels of the ANS, in the hypothalamus and limbic system, overlap anatomically with some of the more primitive influences on behaviour and may have some direct connections in those regions.

Hence virtually the whole of the forebrain, and possibly the cerebellum too, is involved in adults' selection of foods and drinks and how much of them to eat. Most of this information processing is distributed through networks involved in many of the other tasks and experiences of life.

However, before cortical control has reached the sophistication of later childhood, or in species which do not have the huge area of neocortex with which we are endowed, some of the learned integration of eating and drinking behaviour may funnel through anatomically discrete regions of the brainstem. Brain research has indeed picked up fragments of control of ingestive behaviour by different parts of the hypothalamus, particularly in rats but also in monkeys. A temptation that needs to be resisted is to assume that the bit of the hypothalamus where food or water intake can be affected is where the whole of the appetite for foods, water, salt, etc. or their satieties are organized. As we shall see, such 'hypothalamocentrism' has not helped us work out how the brain organizes eating and drinking.

One Neural Basis for Some Emotional Eating?

One of the alerting systems in the brainstem that projects to many regions of the brain has a tiny subset of synapses in a small region at the front of the hypothalamus (incidentally, well away from what were once thought to be the appetite and satiety centres). This little field of synapses is in or near the paraventricular hypothalamus (PVN) and their transmitter substance is the compound noradrenaline (NA–known as norepinephrine in the USA). When NA or an analogue is used to stimulate the PVN site in a rat, the animal will take a meal, even though it has eaten recently (Grossman, 1960). Also, if it is already eating, NA in the PVN will make it eat more (Ritter and Epstein, 1975). For this and other reasons, behavioural neuroscientists using PVN NA generally believe that it disrupts the satiating effects of food (Leibowitz, 1982).

Further analysis of the various processes controlling NA-elicited eating suggests a disruption particularly of the learned control of the size of a meal on a particular foodstuff, known as conditioned satiation (Matthews *et al.*, 1985; Booth, Gibson and Baker, 1986b). Hence, in the rat at least, activation of this part of the arousal system causes a minor binge on food (with water to wash it down if dry). If people have the same neural hook-up, some forms of emotional excitation might similarly interrupt habitual loss of appetite and make it harder to stop eating and perhaps easier to start.

Brain Mechanisms of Ingestion

Is noradrenaline therefore the (or an) 'appetite transmitter'? Obviously not. The noradrenergic projections have synapses in a great variety of regions of the brain, some possibly involved in functions as specific as conditioned satiation but many probably performing pervasive functions in memory, perception or action. Normal human eating and drinking rely greatly on memory, perceptual integration and high-level movement control. So it might with justice be considered absurd to claim to have identified the key type of synaptic receptor for appetite for food or for water, the appetizing or pleasurable effects of the sensory qualities of foods and drinks or the loss of interest in food as eating proceeds. Yet such claims have been made.

For example, amphetamine-like transmitters have been claimed to stimulate an appetite receptor and heroin-like receptors have been claimed to mediate the pleasures of eating. These two examples may be related, in that both of these drugs can be highly addictive (as food is – but we need that!). The former receptor might be a subtype of those on synapses using the major neurotransmitter dopamine, on which amphetamine acts strongly. Both some dopaminergic systems and the endorphin systems on which heroin acts have been implicated in a unitary neural system widely thought to be involved in sensual pleasures.

Indeed, low doses of specifically dopaminergic excitants like pipradol seem to increase the attractions of food in animal learning experiments (Robbins *et al.*, 1983) and amphetamine is a well-known appetite suppressant, probably having that effect largely via massive release of dopamine (Leibowitz and Rossakis, 1979). Furthermore, a modest dose of the opioid-blocking agent, naloxone, seems to reduce the attractions of palatable foodstuffs to people (Yeomans and Wright, 1991). There is therefore little doubt that that these two sorts of chemical transmission are necessary for the normal operation of our appetite for food.

That is a far cry, however, from attributing the neural organization of our eating behaviour and culinary experiences to the actions of those substances. That would be like trying to explain how an internal combustion engine works in terms solely of the bundle of wires connected to the positive side of the battery.

Moreover, such findings provide no basis for hopes of finding a drug that selectively suppresses or boosts appetite, without side effects that could be worse than the problem to which excessive or deficient appetite is meant to be contributing.

Brain Mechanisms of Satiety

Centrally active drugs have been used and continue to be proposed for the management of obesity, eating disorders and dietary symptoms of psychiatric disturbance. Effects of drugs on intakes of experimental diets has therefore been a major line of research on food and drink. Some results have generated much interest for their possible clinical implications more than for the insight they provide to the neural mechanisms of hunger and its satiation. This dichotomy is fallacious and therefore dangerous.

Serotonin and Satiety

For 15 years there has been a popular hypothesis that the neurotransmitter 5-hydroxytryptamine (5HT; serotonin) mediates satiety, those effects of eating that inhibit subsequent eating. This was initially proposed on the basis of a reduction in the size of the first meal after injection of the drug fenfluramine into starved rats. However, the rats have to work hard to stuff in all the chow they eat when food is first restored. The drug acts on 5HT synapses in the brainstem that could make the rats somewhat sleepy and also could interfere with the sensory control of the movements of the forepaws and mouth normally used in eating (Booth, Gibson and Baker, 1986a). So the drug may not be making the food any more satiating, whether by other actions in the brain or by acting on the 5HT synapses that are also influential in the gut wall. The drugged rats may simply be giving up sooner on the large meal. Indeed, subsequent meals are generally smaller, varying around the usual size for a freely fed rat (though they may be more frequent for a while after a period of starvation). These more modest meals do not differ in size between fenfluramine-treated and control rats.

It is a considerable experimental challenge to cognitive psychology to distinguish sedative and movement-disrupting effects from effects on sensory or visceral perception in the eating behaviour of rats or of people, or in what people say. Measurement of changes in visceral perception induced in the brain are rendered almost impossible if a drug also acts on the 5HT synapses in the gut wall that are involved in motility of the digestive tract. As a result, there remains no clear evidence that any subset of the myriad of 5HT synapses in the brain is specifically involved in the central processing of satiety.

Even if a single pathway through the brain did predominate in the inhibition of eating by eating, it would be unlikely to have either a single transmitter at all stages or to have any one transmitter that was unique to itself and not to other aspects of behaviour. (This point relates to the general argument made at the start of this chapter.) Consideration of the complexity of the behavior underlying general or food-selective satieties makes it inconceivable that the phenomena of satiation are mediated by a single circuit in any case. It would therefore be wise to recognize the futility of attempting to identify a satiety transmitter (or an anatomical centre in the brain or, indeed, a single physiological signal, subjective experience or objective measurement of satiety). A corollary is that we should not expect even the most receptor-specific drug to influence satiety or food selection without many side-effects. Therefore it is in principle unproductive to seek a drug to cure obesity or the eating disorders.

What drugs that affect eating or drinking could be useful for is to advance understanding of the brain mechanisms of satiety or other aspects of appetite. This requires their experimental administration to act on a specified synaptic field in a particular pathway in the brain or periphery, together with identification of the aspect of behaviour and/or physiology that is modulated by that localized action on a specific transmitter mechanism. This is a foundation for the future of research into how the brain works. Nevertheless it should be noted that, however exciting the fundamental implications of discovering a specific behavioural effect of a local specific receptor, that finding is most unlikely to have practical or theoretical interest for nutrition or food science, as distinct from its value in behavioural neuroscience.

The Hypothalamus in Satiety and Appetite

Many textbooks continue to promulgate the dual myths that the lateral regions on both sides of the hypothalamus (LH) are the appetite centre and the ventromedial nucleus (VMN) of cells on each side is the satiety centre. These ideas arose initially because tumours that disrupt the workings of the base of the hypothalamus (the ventral edge of its middle part, VMH) can cause complaints of voracious hunger and the patients get fat. The first experimental findings about the brain and eating intake (Brobeck *et al.*, 1943) were that destruction of the VMH region in rats, already known to make them very fat, caused a large increase in daily food intake. Shortly afterwards it was found that lesions in the lateral hypothalamus could stop the rats eating and drinking altogether (Anand and Brobeck, 1951). So it was suggested that hunger in the intact rat lies in the LH and satiety in the VMH (Stellar, 1954).

Such ideas encouraged Anand and others to seek evidence that the average level of electrical activity in these regions varied inversely, increasing in the LH after food deprivation and increasing in the VMH in fed rats. Grossman (1960) found that eating and drinking could be stimulated by different transmitter-like compounds injected into the hypothalamus. Coons (1965) found that, with care, rats could be induced to eat by electrical stimulation of the LH. Rats appear to find electrical self-stimulation of the hypothalamus more rewarding in some cases when they are hungry (Hoebel and Teitelbaum, 1962) and some of the individual neurones involved in this reinforcement also respond when the animal is given food (Rolls, 1976). Also there are neurones in the VMN whose firing rate depends on metabolism of glucose (which is not generally the case: cp. glucose and memory, below) and others in the LH that have receptors for glucose and other metabolites that alter their electrical activity. Even some current research papers still refer to the VMN or VMH as the satiety centre and the LH as the feeding centre.

That was all a big mistake, like the phrenologists' ideas that faculties of the mind lay under bumps on the skull. It says nothing about how the neurones organize behaviour (or about the mental processes themselves) to conclude that Broca's area of cortex is the speech production centre and Wernicke's the speech comprehension centre, however useful such ideas might be in neurological diagnosis.

The same mistake was made at the other end of behavioural complexity, in the neural control of breathing. Two regions in the medulla (the very bottom of the brain, next to the spinal cord) were reciprocally active during breathing in and breathing out. Lesions there stopped inbreaths and outbreaths respectively. Also, the corresponding respiratory efforts could be electrically stimulated from those sites. It was therefore concluded that these were the inspiratory and expiratory centres (Salmoiraghi and Burns, 1960). However, all these findings could merely reflect the passage of nerve fibres to the chest through those bits of medulla. Sure enough, subsequent recordings from single cells further up the brainstem showed that the breathing rhythm was in fact generated and controlled by quite complex networks reaching to the midbrain, that sent their output through the medullary 'centres' (Cohen, 1970).

Morgane (1961) pointed out that the hypothalamus had connections with many other parts of the brain. He provided some evidence that the LH lesions disrupted sensory control of movement quite generally, not specifically the motivation to eat. However, the fallacy was not widely recognized until Ungerstedt (1971) showed that LH lesions could stop eating by destroying fibres that had dopamine synapses in structures underneath cerebral cortex, called the basal ganglia, involved on the control of actions. Loss of these synapses inactivates the basal ganglia so that they cannot do their job – for example, enabling the appropriate next movement to be carried out. That is one of the main problems in Parkinson's Disease. The sufferer cannot carry out the intention to start some familiar activity (like walking or getting out of bed). The actions are still feasible if dopaminergic input can be restored or the need for it bypassed. Similarly, the rat with LH lesions still has its appetite: it will eat when there is some way to express the desire for food and drink, independently of the loss of this part of the background excitation on which all actions depend.

In any case, the electrical stimulation of eating and the single cells firing in response to presentation of food occur in different regions of the hypothalamus from the lesions that stop eating. Eating is stimulated chemically in rats from the front end of the hypothalamus, not from the LH (Booth, 1967). Food neurones are found in monkeys well above the hypothalamus as well as in it (Rolls, 1993).

Similarly, the obesity and even the overeating of the rat with VMH lesions does not imply that the brain mechanisms of satiety are affected in any way, let alone that they reside in that bit of the hypothalamus (Rabin, 1972). The high food intake need not depend on any behavioural abnormality at all: it could be caused by abnormalities in the way that food is processed after eating. The VMN and LH neurones (and similar ones in the medulla) that are stimulated by metabolites or affected by their own metabolism could be involved in control of the viscera via the autonomic nervous system and the pituitary gland (which is also strongly connected to hypothalamic neurones).

The simplest explanation of VMH obesity and the overeating (when it occurs, which depends on the diet) is that the stomach empties abnormally fast after the region has been destroyed (Toates and Booth, 1974; Duggan and Booth, 1986). The VMH normally transmits inhibition of gastric emptying through the autonomic nervous system (ANS). This inhibition is particularly strongly activated by the circadian clock nearby in the hypothalamus during daylight when the rat is naturally inactive and sleeps in its burrow. Hence the stomach starts emptying very slowly around daybreak and only speeds up again towards dusk, when it is time to forage again. In the laboratory, where food is available all the time, rats hardly eat at all in the morning unless they are disturbed by people. Food from the end of the night keeps the stomach fairly full for a while and certainly continues to be passed on for digestion and absorption for many hours, thus maintaining the satiety signals from the gut wall and from metabolism in the liver and the brain. So the rat takes fewer meals in the light than it does in the dark. When lesions are placed in the VMH, this rhythm of gastric emptying and meal frequency is lost. The VMH rat eats as frequently by day as the normal rat does by night. As a result, instead of living off its fat as it sleeps, the VMH rat gains weight night and day (Le Magnen *et al.*, 1973). Indeed, even some residual night-time inhibition of the stomach from the brain is lost and VMH rats eat more frequently than normal at night too.

This speeding of absorption by uninhibited gastric emptying will provoke extra insulin secretion to deal with the absorbed nutrients. This is how the extra food gets deposited as fat. However, the VMH normally inhibits the secretion of insulin as well as gastric emptying and has parallel effects on liver metabolism through other ANS projections. After lesions in the VMH, insulin secretion is chronically increased within a few meals at least, either or both in response to the faster absorption or/and from direct loss of inhibition. Hence the VMH rat gets fatter even if it is not eating more than a control rat (e.g. because an unappetizing diet is provided).

Arguably then, we have learnt more from the VMH syndrome about visceral mechanisms than we have about the brain mechanisms of eating. This might seem ironic. However, it should not be surprising that banging holes in the brain tells us nothing about how the destroyed pieces of tissue work, only about what the rest of the brain and body can do.

Another irony about the VMH syndrome in the history of the psychology of eating is that it diverted social psychologists into the biology of obesity away from the psychosocial dynamics of eating and exercise (Chapter 7). Schachter (1968) got inspiration for the 'externality' theory of human obesity from the emotionality of VMH obese rat (Schachter and Rodin, 1974). Nevertheless, Graff and Stellar (1962) showed that the emotional reactivity of VMH rats was not related to their obesity: the two symptoms arose from damage in different parts of the VMH area. Indeed, as we have seen, VMH rats overeat because their fast-emptying stomach makes them hungry again quickly and it turned out, as we saw in Chapter 7, that the arousal from such normal hunger contributes to the over-reactivity to food and other stimuli so ingeniously demonstrated by Schachter and colleagues to characterize mildly overweight people: overweight people are more likely than the normal-weight to be restraining their intake.

Brain Food

Some ideas about diets that are good for the brain persist from before we began to understand in the mid-twentieth century a little of how brain cells actually work. For example, chemists had discovered that the brain was rich in phosphorus a century earlier. Fish were found to be relatively rich in phosphorus. So it was assumed that eating fish would help the brain to work better. Such ideas make at least two major sorts of assumption that, on present knowledge, appear just to be silly.

First, the idea presupposes that the phosphorus in fish is in a form that would be useful to the brain when it got there, assuming also that it did reach the brain. Chemical elements, like phosphorus, generally occur in compounds with other elements. Compounds containing phosphorus in fish include phosphoproteins, phospholipids and nucleic acids. Sugars (mentioned later in this chapter) include glucose (blood sugar), fructose (fruit sugar) and sucrose (cane or beet sugar) and are all compounds of carbon, hydrogen and oxygen only (hence the name carbo-hydrate). All chemical compounds in food are liable to be transformed by digestion, absorption, circulation around the body and transport into and out of other tissues as well as the brain, before being put to use in the brain by further conversions within nerve cells. What the brain sees of and does with the phosphorus com-pounds in fish (or the carbon in sugars and other carbohydrates in many plant foods) is therefore totally unpredictable form the amounts of those chemical ele-ments in the diet.

The second highly implausible assumption is that the brain is nutritionally frail. This is not what a biologist should expect. Good functioning of the brain has pre-sumably been the most critical of requirements on the tissues for success of the species. Hence the brain can live off the rest of the body if the diet is lacking. Indeed, medical studies of volunteers fasting for many weeks showed how a basic supply of glucose for energy to the brain was maintained by other tissues, the liver and kidney converting amino acids released by muscles and glycerol released by mobilization of fat stored in adipose tissue. Moreover, subsequently it was found that the brain could adapt to using ketone bodies, breakdown products of the fatty acids separated from glycerol in fat mobilization. The brain is extremely efficient at taking up the glucose that it needs from the circulation; so, the concentration of glucose in the blood has to become much lower than the level maintained during starvation for the nerve cells to lack any of the fuel they require. The same is true of normal brains for all of the essential nutrients that have been studied, including vitamins and minerals, with the partial exception of the amino acid tryptophan, whose rate of brain uptake can limit the synthesis and activity of the transmitter 5-hydroxytryptamine (5HT, serotonin).

Thus, generally speaking, foods can only affect brain development and functioning when the diet is chronically deficient in a substance that the body does not make that is crucial to the working of enzymes in brain cells. For these reasons, very small amounts of mineral elements like magnesium and copper are essential nutrients (and too much of them is toxic). Compounds essential to metabolism in small amounts that must come from the diet are called vitamins and among these thiamine is particularly critical to carbohydrate utilization and hence to brain function.

Glucose and the Brain

One popularly supposed brain food is glucose. There is no doubt that glucose from the blood supply is normally the brain's sole source of energy, although during starvation it can adapt to using ketone bodies from partly metabolized body fat.

Nonetheless, little of the glucose used by the brain comes from free glucose or other sugars in the diet. Much of it comes from the starch in food, which is strings of glucose molecules; these are released by digestion and pass into the blood. A lot of this absorbed glucose is stored for a while by the liver, in other strings of glucose units called glycogen. Glycogen and glucose can also be made by the liver from the carbon chains of some amino acids ('glucogenic' ones) from dietary protein and from turnover of muscle protein and the lactic acid that muscles produce. Much of the time, the glucose circulating to the brain in the blood comes from liver glycogen or the liver's synthesis of glucose from lactic and amino acids (gluconeogenesis), not directly from the carbohydrates in food. Gluconeogenesis is under the control of hormones from the pancreas, like insulin and glucagon (not to be confused with glycogen), as well as being affected by stress hormones.

Also, the brain in effect competes with the muscles for blood glucose. So, because the brain uses glucose for energy at a constant high rate, unlike muscles (and the brain cannot use fat, as muscles can), it is extremely efficient at transporting glucose from the blood, even when blood sugar is very low (as in hypoglycaemia). Moreover, the brain does not depend on insulin for this transport in the way that muscles do.

Furthermore, there is no evidence that forcing extra glucose into neurones in general makes any difference to their electrical activity. The exception is a tiny proportion of specialized cells that serve as central detectors of the need for the autonomic nervous system to mobilize or shut down the supply of glucose from the liver.

Hence it would be very surprising if the glucose tablets that students may take with the intention of fuelling their brain cells during examinations do in fact boost brain glucose uptake, let alone alter nerve cell activity in what in any case would have to be a very specific way that enabled them to remember or reason better.

Recently, nevertheless, some experimenters have been administering doses of glucose to rats (and to elderly people) in the hope of improving memory. Some positive results have been reported from very modest amounts of glucose compared with that available from starches and sugars in the diet. However, these doses of glucose have been drunk or injected at high concentration. Strong solutions of glucose burn the throat and are nauseating because of osmotic effects in the upper intestine. When injected into the abdomen, even dilute glucose solutions swell up osmotically and stretch the abdominal cavity, because they attract body fluid faster than the glucose is taken up. Any of these effects could be enough to wake the subject up, whether by direct sensory activation (pain) or via the action of stress hormones on the brain or other parts of the body: there is indeed evidence that circulating adrenaline mediates some effects of glucose dosing. These alternatives to the administered glucose fuelling the brain remain to be tested.

One modest correlation between blood glucose level and memory performance after breakfast has been reported (Benton and Sargent, 1992). Any such observation needs to be reliably repeatable before its reality is assured. Then also, other factors that could affect both the glucose and the memory should be excluded before serious pursuit of what is so unlikely biochemically and neurophysiologically as an effect of dietary glucose on memory processes in the brain.

Abnormally low level of glucose in the blood, a so-called hypoglycaemic syndrome, has been blamed for aggressiveness and behavioural disturbances. However, such claims have not been substantiated: when blood glucose levels have been measured in cases of behavioural disruption attributed to the 'hypoglycaemic syndrome', they have often been found to be in the normal range. Even if the correlation sometimes occurred, the behaviour could arise from any number of environmental or personal factors that also contribute to the hypoglycaemia.

A mild overdose of insulin pushes glucose into muscles and can bring down the level of glucose in the blood faster than the liver can restore it. Yet generally the only symptoms of an unfamiliar episode of insulin-induced hypoglycaemia arise from activation of the autonomic nervous system (ANS), such as sweating and a woozy or faint feeling. Insulin-induced coma can result if the loss of glucose from the blood is so rapid that the level goes down to a small fraction of the concentration maintained during starvation. None of this can happen in a healthy person where insulin secretion is under tight control by blood glucose.

So let us now turn to scientifically understood actions of the diet on the brain.

Chronic Effects of Diet on the Brain

There are broadly speaking two ways in which constituents of the diet could have long-term psychological effects. They may affect the general physical growth or deterioration of the nervous system: this we consider first. Alternatively, diet might permanently affect the functioning of the brain, via short-term effects on changes within specific neural connections that have long-term psychological consequences; that is considered in the next section.

Brain Development

The nerve cells in the human brain have virtually all been formed by the time of birth. Considerable elaboration of interneuronal connections occurs postnatally, however. Maternal nutrition might therefore affect the development of psychological capacities in the foetus or the breastfed infant. Nevertheless, the brain is very effective at extracting essential nutrients from the blood supply and is not susceptible to over-development. Hence, there is reason to think that only metabolic disorder or extreme deficiency in the diet is liable to prejudice development of the brain.

In the rare inherited metabolic disorders, the accumulation of unusual catabolites damages the brain unless prevented by dietary or somagenetic engineering. As well as neurological disorders, more or less severe learning difficulties (mental handicaps) result.

Possibilities currently under study include psychological sequelae of neurological defects, prematurity or very low birth weight, to which maternal deficiency (such as in folic acid) might contribute. There is concern that some fatty acids in breast milk may be needed in infant milk formulae, at least in premature babies, in order for the brain to develop to full intellectual potential.

Energy-protein deficiency early in childhood is associated with slow intellectual development. It is difficult though to disentangle effects of malnutrition and disease on brain growth from functional handicaps arising from effects of economic and social disadvantage. Nutritional supplementation has a separate effect from psychosocial stimulation. Also, school failure in low income areas is associated with missing breakfast. However, if regular provision of supplements or breakfasts did produce improvements in academic performance, that could be because of the salient environmental changes, aside from physiological effects of the intervention.

Brain Damage

Nutritional factors have repeatedly been proposed for schizophrenic and other psychiatrically diagnosed disorders. None has yet been substantiated, however, when subjected to controlled investigation. Thiamine deficiency produces neurological symptoms and lack of this and other B vitamins is generally considered to contribute to certain encephalopathies that involve several memory defects, such as Korsakoff's syndrome following chronic abuse of alcohol. Therapeutic effects of supplementation remain to be established, however.

Toxic contaminants of the diet may damage the brain, with psychological sequelae. Nevertheless, long-term psychological effects of the prevalent dietary levels of residues, heavy metals, etc. have not been established to date. Ingestion of flakes of paint or contaminated dust can contribute to an accumulation of lead in the brain but this largely results from hands or objects being brought to the mouth, not from dietary consumption.

Short-Term Mediation of Long-Term Effects

Any long-term psychological effects of dietary constituents on children, such as on IQ, personality or behaviour disorder, are likely to be mediated by acute psychological effects of the daily diet. For example, if school performance were permanently improved by regular provision of breakfast, it could be because each meal facilitated learning that morning.

Additives and Hyperactivity

Feingold's initial hypothesis that intolerances to food additives such as colourings cause widespread behavioural problems in children was early narrowed to tartrazine and salicylates. Much subsequent investigation has established that physical evidence of intolerances for food additives has much lower incidence than the misbehaviour and distress attributed to them. Proven allergenic reactions to natural proteins in food occur in young children but they are not very common and in any case may not last for more than some months. Moreover, recent work has shown no systematic behavioural effect when a toxicological sensitivity has been provoked.

Any obvious change of diet in the home or in an institution is likely to provoke emotional, attitudinal and behavioural reactions and to promote or merely coincide with remission of digestive symptoms and malaise. Hence neither the behavioural reaction nor the dietary change should be a cause of anxiety or contention or become regarded as a permanent feature.

Vitamins and IQ

Several recent reports have provided data that were interpreted by the authors as support for the hypothesis that supplementation with one or more unspecified vitamins and/or minerals prevents a supposed slowing of the normal rise in non-verbal intelligence test scores (IQ) in schoolchildren whose diet is alleged to be deficient in those micronutrients.

There is as yet however no satisfactory evidence that those whose IQ scores appear to respond to supplements are deficient in micronutrients, because the only relevant dietary data are the children's dietary records and these are likely to be confounded by factors that influence scores in IQ tests. Furthermore, children who are estimated to be consuming less than recommended levels of a micronutrient often appear also to have inadequate energy intakes. They may therefore be chronically hungry or reacting to other sorts of deprivation. This might account at least in part for the fidgetiness and apparent lack of attention that has been reported in children having the poorer dietary records, which in turn could make for poor learning and hence slowed development of performance in some IQ tests.

On the other hand, some children who are not being provided with breakfast and sandwiches or a school lunch may well manage to fill up on packet foods and confectionery. These contain lots of fat. As a result, a high fat intake could become associated with better learning because of less distraction from hunger.

Another (not incompatible) hypothesis is that the high sugar intake of some children has acute sedative effects. This could result in difficulty in thinking clearly and so the child becomes restless when faced with an intellectual challenge.

No biochemically sound mechanism has yet been proposed by which moderate vitamin or mineral deficiency could affect non-verbal learning. Theory is hardly feasible in any case because, although some speculations have been offered, the neural bases of individual differences in human 'intelligence' are, as yet, unknown. Indeed, even defining the cognitive processes whose characteristics are assessed in IQ tests has proved an extremely complex problem.

All in all, a biological approach to effects of diet on behaviour is unlikely to be valid if that means presuming the existence of specific biological mechanisms. Attention should first be paid to cognitive development and cultural specification of any physically mediated psychological effect of the diet, which could be as broad as hunger-reduction or social reinforcement.

Short-Term Dietary Effects on Behaviour

The most productive strategy for research into food and the brain could well be to focus on short-term effects of diet on behaviour. One reason for thinking this is that the best way to identify a subtle causal process is to examine it directly while it is going on, rather than to rely on the summation of after-effects or on averaging across occasions when many other processes are going on that may be correlated and therefore confound the data. Secondly, as just argued, the longer-term effects that have been sought mostly in the past are likely to be the cumulative results of repeated short-term effects.

Design of the Test Foods, Situations and People

When the issue is whether or not food constituents act physically in the brain, the postingestional effects of the diet must be distinguished from its sensory effects. This is crucial in principle because a flavour or texture may suggest effects to the consumer from cultural stereotypes (e.g. filling, nutritious, junk food, luxury) that could confuse the search for physiologically mediated effects. The distinction has become demonstrably necessary in some cases, for example reduction of distress in infants: just the taste of sugar can quieten a baby and raise the pain threshold (Blass, 1987).

Hence, the absence and presence or differences in dose of the hypothesised active constituent must not be detectable by sight, smell, taste, texture or any other sense. If the agent cannot be swallowed in a capsule, demonstration of effective sensory matching or masking is necessary. Even if capsules are used, this blinding of the subject to the experimental comparison can be broken when the capsules are opened or chewed and, for example, a vitamin can be smelt or the fibre looks or feels rough.

For major constituents of the diet, these requirements for unambiguous research design may be so unusual or technologically difficult to achieve as to be impossible at reasonable expense. Experimental cognitive psychology can provide a way round, by measurements that pick out the effects of sensorily triggered expectations. However, this demands more sophisticated design and analysis than has been adopted in much psychology, let alone elsewhere. Also called for is a modicum of good luck in how the results turn out.

Individual eaters may vary from one another in physiological susceptibility to a dietary factor, perhaps for genetic reasons or because the body has adapted to high or low intakes of it. They will certainly differ in prior experiences with foods and drinks containing the component(s) of interest.

Where the psychological effect being studied is known to the public, and especially if it is commonly sought or avoided, the effectiveness of a study is likely to depend on designing and analysing it around the participants' uses of items and occasions for that purpose (Booth, French and Gatherer, 1992). This will not only help to accommodate differences in both physiology and experience. It can also enable differences to be exploited. For example, disguised variations of a constituent, around the level at which an individual normally consumes it with the expectation of a relevant psychological effect, are likely to be a more sensitive design than the same levels imposed on everyone tested, without regard to their normal expectations.

THE TEST TASKS AND SITUATIONS

A psychological effect may only be wanted in certain situations by a given consumer. Indeed, the effect may only occur in specific circumstances. That can be because the effect is part of conventional behaviour and experience in those circumstances or because the user personally discovered something that the item could do for mood or performance when the conditions were right. It may well be crucial therefore that the setting investigated and the state of mind of the research participant is suited to the mood or performance that is being studied and that the behavioural tests measure those particular benefits that each participant obtains during normal use of the dietary item.

Alcohol

Alcoholic beverages have been an important part of the diet in many cultures from time immemorial. The alcohol content is widely regarded as a source of good cheer on social occasions and as soothing or even emotionally anaesthetic at times of distress. However, incapacitating effects of alcohol are also well-known, as also is the risk of problems from its continuous heavy use.

Neurophysiological evidence suggests that ethanol has psychological effects by acting on the GABA (gamma-aminobutyric acid) receptor system at inhibitory synapses throughout the nervous system. Such neural inhibition is critical to the precision of information processing. So the postingestional psychological effects of ethanol are likely to be protean. Maybe all forms of fine control are rendered less competent, including precise physical movements (walking down the straight line), vigilance against subtle dangers (crossing in front of approaching traffic), and self-critical social performance (ethical inhibitions and fears for self-esteem). However, ethanol has been regarded in animal pharmacology as specifically anxiety-reducing at sub-sedative doses. The benzodiazepines (such as Valium), that also act on the GABA system, are used as anti-anxiety agents, as well as muscle-relaxants and sedatives.

So it is conceivable that the neural actions of ethanol are somewhat more effective at reducing tensions than at incapacitating generally, even if not specifically anxiolytic.

Many of the effects of normal levels of consumption of alcoholic beverages on mood and social behaviour appear to have at least as much to do with the drinking situation as with neural actions of ethanol. Merriment and perhaps sexual predation are what is expected at parties, personal aggressiveness and vandalism became a norm for soccer fans and gloom is natural for the lone(ly) drinker. All these effects have been seen in experimental studies, but there tend to be large 'placebo' or expectancy effects too. It seems that ethanol contributes some disinhibition or incapacitation but a participative spirit achieves the rest. Furthermore, it may be possible to get quite merry at a party on a fruit punch containing no alcohol.

Behavioural effects of ethanol in the diet are therefore complex to investigate. The sensory qualities of ethanol and the after-effects of its ingestion on bodily sensations and mental and physical abilities are well-known to experienced drinkers. This weakens the interpretation of sophisticated experiments on the behavioural effects of ethanol (as also for other familiar substances).

One example is the so-called 'balanced placebo' design. This has four conditions, two drinks with ethanol and two without, where one of each pair is stated by the investigator to contain alcohol and the other is said not to. The presence and absence of alcohol are supposed to be masked. Yet when the sensory disguise is checked, it is often found to have been ineffective. Furthermore, characteristic effects of ethanol are liable to be noticed some minutes after ingestion of the ethanol-spiked drink that was alleged to be an alcohol-free drink. This is likely to provoke an emotional reaction and to change the strategy in the task set by the experimenter. An experienced user not feeling the usual effects when the drink was falsely said to contain alcohol is also likely to react to that disparity but in a different way, perhaps more disappointed than angry. Thus the effects on behaviour of stated and actual alcohol contents cannot be separated out by analysis of this 2×2 design on an additive model. In other words, this is not a balanced placebo design: the crossover effects are not balanced and there is not placebo control of after-effects. (For the same reasons, the balanced placebo is generally impracticable for familiar psychoactive substances.) Instead, detailed evidence is needed from each individual separately on the cognitive processes after drinking more or less alcohol when the approximate amount is known, as it usually is.

Traditional dose-response studies of behavioural effects of alcohol are subject to similar problems, even when the variations in alcohol content are not detected during consumption and after-effects are hard to distinguish, as say within the lower range of doses. Sensitive tests of psychomotor performance can show deficits at low doses that are proportionate to those at higher doses, thus justifying by extrapolation an argument for a zero blood alcohol limit on drivers. However, the consumer of a known amount of alcohol before driving or working may pay closer attention to the task and put extra effort into control and decision, in proportion to the disruption noticed on a previous occasion. In some circumstances, such an effort might overcompensate for the detrimental effect of ethanol. By this process, a low dose of alcohol can produce an objectively better performance than that after no alcohol at all. Of course, such an effect should not be confused with the personal belief that a little alcohol has improved one's performance, since that is liable to be an illusion fostered by ethanol's disruption of self-critical abilities. Nevertheless, this phenomenon does illustrate how actively people use effects of food and drink. We are not affected by alcohol just passively or automatically.

Caffeine

Caffeine is thought to be able to act as a mild alerting agent by blocking synaptic receptors for endogenous adenosine, which is sedative. However, the experimental literature on human behaviour has been confused by the use of large doses relative to coffee, tea and cola drinking, by differences between people in responsiveness to caffeine and in the benefits to performance or mood habitually obtained from such drinks, and by unrealistic tests for such benefits.

Recently, though, by using normal doses, H.R. Lieberman and colleagues (Lieberman *et al.*, 1987) have shown quite strong and consistent effects of caffeine (at a dose as low as 32 mg) on tests of mental concentration (attentive and integrative thinking), effects which the participants themselves noticed in ratings of their state. Furthermore, in one study the participants rated themselves also to be more cheerful and less anxious, perhaps because they felt that they were doing better at the cognitive tests. Such conscious benefits may mediate some of the attractions of caffeinated drinks, over and above cultural norms and advertisers' implications.

A remaining weakness in even these studies is a lack of dose-response relationships. As recognized by physiologists, engineers and others, if an effect does not become stronger with increasing strength of an influence, that is a sign we are not looking at the actual mechanism. Grouped designs may sample a wide range of personal dose optima, depending on the benefits habitually gained from the use of caffeine in particular contexts by different individuals. Hence studies of behavioural effects of caffeine (and of other dietary constituents) should investigate individuals' habitual uses at test doses ranging around that which is usual for each person in that situation.

When this is done, dose-response relationships are observed in the effects of caffeine on mood in a large minority of regular users of caffeine in tea or coffee (Booth, French and Gatherer, 1992; French *et al.*, 1994). In some people, even their habitual dosage appears to be aversive. In others, however, doubling the usual dose intensifies an effect on a positive type of mood. Interestingly, in people who were drinking tea or coffee primarily on social occasions, rather than to aid deskwork, these effects were mostly on sociality, not on intellectual ability.

Dietary Effects on Monoamine Neurotransmitters

A meal on a high-carbohydrate, low-protein diet by a rat stimulates insulin secretion. The insulin facilitates uptake by muscle of circulating branched chain amino acids (BCAAs: leucine, isoleucine and valine). These amino acids compete with other large neutral amino acids (LNAAs) for transport from the blood into the brain. LNAAs include tryptophan, the precursor of the neurotransmitter 5-hydroxytryptamine (5HT, serotonin), and phenylalanine and tyrosine, precursors of the catecholamine transmitters dopamine and noradrenaline. The supply of precursor can limit the rate of synthesis of the transmitter, especially in the case of 5HT. Thus, reduced competition by BCAAs for brain tryptophan uptake is liable to increase the activity of serotonergic synapses (those using 5HT as transmitter).

Serotonergic neurones are important in the control of sleep. Oral administration of a substantial dose of tryptophan is sedative. This tryptophan supply effect on brain 5HT probably explains why a high-carbohydrate meal promotes postprandial sleep in the rat.

LNAAs are abundant in protein mixtures of high biological quality. So, although a high-protein, low-carbohydrate meal also provokes insulin secretion in the rat, plasma levels of BCAAs are kept high by absorption and are not reduced enough to have a substantial effect on competition with tryptophan for transport into the brain. Hence, the high-protein meal does not increase 5HT activity and induce sedation by that mechanism.

Relatively modest dietary levels of protein, e.g. 10–15 per cent in the rat, keep the ratio of tryptophan to other LNAAs in blood plasma low enough to have no effect on brain 5HT levels. However, as little as 4 per cent protein keeps the plasma ratio low in human subjects. Few eating occasions provide that little protein. Even chocolate and sugar confectionery may contain milk protein and/or grain protein. Hence it is unlikely that carbohydrate-rich foods induce sedation or other mood changes in people via the 5HT mechanism.

This is a difficulty for the suggestion that drugs and psychiatric disorders affecting serotonergic activity induce a craving for carbohydrate via the action of carbohydrate-rich foods on tryptophan uptake, 5HT and mood. Another difficulty is that many of these foods are sweet, an oral sensation that by itself apparently dampens distress via opioid mechanisms. Also, the high-carbohydrate foods reportedly 'craved' are high-fat foods and the creaminess or crispness, with or without sweetness, make them highly palatable. They can therefore be pleasurable and cheering to eat, independently of postingestional factors such as effects on 5HT.

Finally, in a further illustration of the need for psychosocial analyses of diet and behaviour, these craved foods are generally convenience products that are recognized as nutritionally less desirable ('junk foods'). Hence, they may be avoided and as a result become tempting and craved for. Their consumption could then have the powerful impact on mood, related to feeling of guilt about the unwise sensual indulgence ('naughty but nice'). In other words, snackfood cravings could arise by purely cognitive processes, with no particular neurotransmitter mediation.

Meals

A modest amount of food is widely regarded as mentally and physically energizing or refreshing. However, a heavy meal is expected to make one drowsy (while not necessarily promoting a good night's sleep). Recent behavioural research has provided some support for these conventional beliefs. The physiological mechanisms involved remain obscure, however.

There is a semicircadian rhythm of arousal, including a period of reduced performance in mid-afternoon as well as more profoundly in the small hours after midnight. A series of experiments by A.P. Smith and colleagues (Smith *et al.*, 1993) have shown that a substantial lunch tends to depress objective and subjective alertness further for a few hours. Going without lunch can therefore improve cognitive performance in mid-afternoon, although other consequences may not be desirable. Caffeine helps to counter the 'post-lunch dip' and alcohol makes it worse. Different aspects of attention are affected by different protein/carbohydrate ratios in the meal. There is as yet no clear basis for theory as to either the cognitive processes or the physiological actions of food involved in these effects.

Breakfast is reputed to improve performance at work, although the evidence has been largely correlational with accident rates or school reports. Such effects are likely to depend on the size and composition of the breakfast, the physiology, personality and attributions of the consumer and the activities and tasks that follow the meal. Obviously the effects of any alcohol or indeed caffeine in or shortly after the meal are likely to combine with those of the solid items and any other drinks.

Conclusion

Clearly we know almost nothing definite about specific relationships between food and the brain in healthy or ill people, What needs to be realized on all sides is the importance of design and interpretation of research that is fully informed about the cognitive processes involved in any experiment or observation and about all the potentially relevant biological and cultural bases for that psychological integration. The same could be said at the conclusion of every other chapter in this book.

Therefore, cognitive psychologists, biologists and social scientists need to educate each other in the basics of all three approaches as they bear on the causal processes in eating and drinking behaviour, as no doubt would also be valuable in other important areas of human life. This chapter, like the whole book, is intended to make some contribution to this interchange.

Further Reading

The neuroscience of eating and drinking is a vigorous field of research but often is not well covered in more general textbooks. So two groups of specialized books are listed below for the reader to select among, first on the brain mechanisms of ingestion and secondly on the effects on behaviour of the actions of food constituents on brain processes.

Brain Networks of Appetite

Booth, D.A. (Ed.) (1993) *Neurophysiology of Ingestion*, Oxford, Pergamon.

Le Magnen, J. (1985) *Hunger*, Cambridge, Cambridge University Press.

Le Magnen, J. (1992) *Neurobiology of Feeding and Nutrition*, San Diego, Academic Press.

Ramsay, D.J. and Booth, D.A. (Eds) (1991) *Thirst: physiological and psychological aspects*, London, Springer-Verlag, Chapters 5–16.

Rolls, E.T. (1975) *The Brain and Reward*, Pergamon, Oxford.

Stricker, E.M. (Ed.) (1990) *Neurobiology of Food and Water Intake*, New York, Plenum.

Effects of Diet on Behaviour

ADAMS, J.E. (1991) *Caffeine and Health*, New York, Academic.

BENDICH, A. and BUTTERWORTH, C.E. (Eds) (1991) *Micronutrients in Health and in Disease Prevention*, New York, Marcel Dekker.

BLANE, H.T. and LEONARD, K.E. (Eds) (1987) *Psychological Theories of Drinking and Alcoholism*, New York, Guilford Press.

DEWS, P.B. (Ed.) (1984) *Caffeine*, Berlin, Springer-Verlag.

HEUTHER, G. (Ed.) (1988) *Amino Acid Availability and Brain Function in Health and Disease*, Berlin, Springer-Verlag.

SHEPHERD, R. (Ed.) (1989) *Handbook of the Psychophysiology of Human Eating*, Chichester, Wiley.

THAYER, R.E. (1989) *The Biopsychology of Mood and Arousal*, New York, Oxford University Press.

Chapter 9

Psychology and the Sciences of Food and Health

This chapter places psychological science among the several different sciences and professions that deal with food, nutrition and eating behaviour.

Psychology of Eating and Drinking

Psychology is the science whose defining duty is the systematic empirical study of mental processes that inform the observable behaviour of individual human beings, and indeed of members of other species. Thus, eating and drinking and thoughts and feelings about foodstuffs and beverages should be one of the major areas of research, teaching and application in psychology.

Curiously, it is not. What we do overtly and in our heads about food and drink has occupied a far lower proportion of psychologists' time, historically and to the present, than the fraction of waking life that people generally spend doing those things. Worse, the research community that specializes in the study of ingestive behaviour has largely been cut off from the main areas of research into human psychology.

For example, fundamental and applied experimental psychology can be considered to be the core of the academic discipline. Commonly called cognitive psychology in recent years, this central mainstream has more than a 150-year history of accumulating research findings and constructing theory, albeit in fits and starts as characteristic of any science. Yet food materials and the concepts involved in their uses have seldom been used in cognitive psychologists' experiments on perception, memory or language. This is despite the familiarity, ready control and obvious structure of the physical objects and social interactions involved in eating and drinking, their range from the biologically natural to the technological artefact and hence their suitability for analysis of mental processes involved in intellectually rich and emotionally important behaviour.

As we shall see, there has been a strong tradition of experiments on food intake by social psychologists, particularly in connection with obesity and dieting. Yet the eaters' thoughts about the foods and the interpersonal situation and cultural meaning of the eating behaviour have seldom been considered systematically in that line of research.

Clinical psychologists also have addressed the role of eating in weight control. However, they have tended to transfer to eating on an intuitive basis their very

general strategies for behavioural and cognitive change. These particular applications of general therapeutic principles have seldom been evaluated or even fully rationalized. Less attention has been paid to the possibilities of distinctive influences in the case of eating than for phobias or drug uses, for instance.

Most of the psychologists in recent decades who have used food materials in their research have been interested in sorting out biological aspects of eating and drinking, using experimental animals more often than people. Most such investigations have been limited to measurements of the weights of materials that disappear down the throat, human as well as animal. Psychology's central mission of analysing 'the mental processing of information involved in behaviour seems typically to have been forgotten. The weight or volume and even the calories or separate nutrients of a food item are assumed to be sensed by the mouth or the body, and/or to be read off or remembered from nutritional labels and then calculated into the size of the portion or meal consumed or even the intakes accumulating over a day or longer. The real psychology of nutrition concerns rather what is actually sensed and thought, so determining the succession of eating choices that adds up into intakes of foods and nutrients.

As a result of this strange neglect of our commonest cognitively complex behaviour, investigations of eating and drinking and their applications are not a regular part of the programme at meetings in psychology and its branches nor a major interest of a substantial minority of the membership of the mainstream psychological societies. There is no tradition in psychology degrees of courses and textbooks that cover the appetite for food and drink. (Eating was included in 'Motivation' but that field of psychology fell apart two or three decades ago into the applied social psychology of interpersonal and organizational behaviour and a largely non-psychological approach to brain and body mechanisms of food and water intake.) The few monographs on this area that are written by psychologists are listed at the end of this chapter, together with some recent symposium volumes to which psychologists have made a major contribution. This book will have fulfilled one of its main purposes if it calls the attention of some psychologists outside the field of behaviour towards food to the potential for close links to the mainstream interests of academic and practitioner psychologists.

The Gulf Between Natural and Social Sciences

This under-representation of food research is not just a historical oddity about psychology. It creates serious problems for other sciences concerned with eating, food design and its impact on health. When research workers or practitioners on food technology, food marketing or nutrition realize that there is a psychological dimension to food choices, there is no body of adequately systematized knowledge or professional research expertise among the psychologists for them to refer to and seek to use as a basis for cooperation and joint development.

Psychologists' limited interest in food research is, however, only one side of a bigger problem. Nutrition and the food sciences necessarily include many aspects of biology. Unfortunately, though, modern science and education have so far developed in a way that has made the intellectual bases of the sciences and professions of nutrition and of the technical side of the food business exclusively biological and

chemical. Some food degrees have a 'sensory' course, some nutrition courses include a 'social' element and marketing picks up broad psychological ideas usually
after they have been found too slippery to use and dropped by practising psychologists. Scientific issues about behavioural and social nutrition and the design of food
items for retail purchase are generally bypassed by ingenious uses of many forms
of statistical modelling to relate food intake or preference data to measurements
from the biochemical and clinical laboratories.

Food scientists and nutritionists find truly psychological science difficult to
understand and to use because their training and work is all in the natural sciences.
Behavioural aspects of biology are now recognized as very important in the welfare
and efficiency of food-production animals. However, behavioural zoology does not
begin to address the complexities of human behaviour that cognitive psychologists
tackle. This book has been concerned with all those aspects of food science and
nutrition to which human behaviour is relevant and illustrates a cognitive approach
to that behaviour. The necessary behavioural, cognitive and social science was
introduced non-technically. Nevertheless, the real scientific issues about the mental
processes involved in eating and drinking were exposed as fully as practicable,
given limited space and as yet so little hard information to hand.

Natural Sciences of Food and Dietary Health

On the other hand, the psychology of eating and drinking is absolutely dependent
on the physics and chemistry of foodstuffs and the sensory signals that they generate
in the brain. This psychology depends no less on the visceral physiology and biochemistry of food utilization and its neural and humoural signalling to the brain.
Equally, the psychology of nutrition would be empty without the ecology, economics, sociology and anthropology of the technology and culture of food production
and consumption. Moreover, psychologists cannot make a very effective contribution to the understanding and promotion of dietary health without a basic grasp of
the relevant clinical nutrition and epidemiology.

This book is not intended to provide psychologists with even the elements of
these natural sciences of food and health. A bibliography of introductory texts is
appended to this chapter. Nevertheless, the immediately necessary facts or concepts
from food science and technology, nutritional physiology and epidemiology and
food socioeconomics were included in non-technical terms at the relevant points.
Readers who are specialists in one of these other disciplines may of course have to
tolerate some simplification in this context but the hope has been to avoid gross
error or distortion.

The Food Sciences

The laboratory study of food materials is well developed and continues to advance.
It involves plant and animal biochemistry, microbiology, and the chemistry and
physics of the fluids and solids that are processed and consumed. These basic
sciences are applied by food technology and engineering to the production,
processing, distribution and uses of food and drink.

Molecular genetics is currently the fastest developing part of the sciences of food and agriculture, in common with much of biology. Biotechnology will make an increasing contribution to growth, manufacture and storage of what consumers will buy. Nevertheless, advances in molecular engineering, like the genes themselves, are useless without a framework of longstanding science and technology and indeed, like the ecology of a species, the culture and economics of a society using the products of modern biology. The applied sciences of food will always need a deep understanding of the whole materials in production and use.

The experimental psychology of palatability, just like any other branch of perceptual science, cannot proceed effectively without a thorough understanding of the applied physics and chemistry of food materials and the engineering of their manufacture, distribution, cooking and mastication. The visual appearance, flavour and feel of a foodstuff is the perceiver's interpretation of patterns transmitted from the surface of the material to the relevant sensory receptors. The chemical composition and the physical constitution of a food is liable to create consistent patterning in its stimulation of sensory receptors. Small variations in the processes of plant or animal growth or factory production are also likely to generate recognizable features in the food's sensed characteristics. Hence the describable qualities of the food and the factors important in its palatability are quite likely to relate closely to chemically or physically controllable or measurable factors. The natural science does not determine the mental processes but a good first step to investigation of food perception is to understand how the food is made (see Chapter 3).

The Nutritional Sciences

The biochemistry of the involvement of ingested nutrients in normal physiological functioning of the body is also a thoroughly established field of natural science. That was achieved on the basis largely of the identifying of the particular chemical substances whose consumption in sufficient quantities is essential to health, e.g. vitamins, minerals and some of the macronutrients. This is generally considered by nutritionists to be the foundation of their science. Hence research and training in nutrition, like that in food science, is almost entirely biological. The chemical composition of the foods and drinks consumed, in total comprising the diet, is of course crucial and so nutritional science includes that aspect of food science as well as the physiological effects of the diet.

The nutrition of animals used for meat and dairy produce (and indeed of agricultural plants) is also important for the food supply. However, many nutritionists are primarily concerned with the effects of food consumption on human health. Nevertheless, studies of human biology have to be limited in scope because of ethical and technical considerations and so much fundamental research is done on other species. Crucial biological information on the role of diet in disease can also be obtained when invasive clinical investigation is required for effective treatment or sufficiently impoverished volunteers can be found and paid.

Beyond that, the applied human nutritionist is limited largely to surveys relating estimates of the average chemical composition of the diet of a population to the incidence of diagnoses of physical illnesses (such as cancers or heart attacks) or the prevalence of characteristics that may be useful to predict disease such as height,

weight, perhaps thickness of fat under skin or maybe the chemistry of a blood sample. It is of course very difficult to relate such correlations between dietary chemistry and disease statistics to the biological processes of health and disease. Both sets of evidence are scrappy because of the limitations on data collection. The correlational data from epidemiology and indeed clinical observations are open to a much greater variety of alternative explanations than are highly controlled experiments. This is no less the case when the nutritional epidemiology compares a social intervention on diet with a control community or the clinical study compares treatments. The control is exerted at the group level and so quantitative comparisons of effects are legitimate only among sets of groups; there may be few groups available to form such sets and the manipulation is likely to vary considerably among the groups in a set.

Nevertheless, a psychological approach to the effects of food on physical health can be strengthened by hypotheses about physiological mechanisms and cultural processes that point to the sorts of behaviour that might be relevant to risk of disease (Chapters 5 and 6). That is, health research psychologists need to be informed by nutritional biochemistry and psychological practitioners in the health service need to collaborate with dietitians (as well as vice versa in both cases).

Social and Behavioural Sciences of Food and Dietary Health

This brings us to consideration of the economics, politics, sociology, anthropology and psychology of food and nutrition.

Psychology belongs among the social sciences, as well as being a (or the) behavioural science (and belonging among the life sciences too). Social psychology in particular deals not only with how individuals deal with each other but also with how individuals and small groups relate to purely social processes, like the educational system, the mass media, commercial markets and the law, as well as informal culture. Nevertheless, all parts of psychology should operate in the context of the purely social sciences, such as anthropology, sociology and economics. However important the genes are, and the structure of the body and brain, we are still social animals. Our species has not only co-evolved with our biosphere but has also built up over the centuries an elaborate cultural environment. An adult person is made of human history as well as of human flesh. Hence, even the operations of our most impersonal cognitive machinery may have been programmed by our social upbringing: most or all of our verbal 'computation', even about physical and logical matters, could be contingent on our education into a particular linguistic community. Certainly all our actions, thoughts and feelings about food will be permeated with cultural meaning.

Anthropology and Sociology of Food

Past distinctions between sociology and anthropology are becoming less clear in some respects, especially for example in the social science of food and nutrition.

Psychology and the Sciences of Food and Health

The two main disciplines still have separate societies and journals but the study of food in society is becoming common ground, although differences in method and interest are still visible and remain important at least to some. A distinction can perhaps be drawn between social nutrition and nutritional sociology or anthropology, with the former operating more within a medical framework and the latter having more academic objectives.

Food is central to both biological (physical) and cultural (social) branches of anthropology. On the biological side of the study of humankind as a species, social hunting for animal food was arguably central to the development of human agility and intelligence and changes in diet permitted the characteristic structure of the lower half of the human face. The social end of anthropology was founded on the study of rural groups untouched by industrialization, often hunting, herding, gathering and cultivating at subsistence levels but nevertheless sometimes having elaborate systems of food use and meaning. These days of course few Third World villages remain unaffected by the regional or even international economy and food trade but anthropologists study the cultural changes. They also turn their skills of investigation and interpretation to urban groups and indeed poor and rich in First World economies.

Anthropology almost defines itself by the ethnographic approach – literally, writing out the ethnic view. Ethnography is the use of records from open-ended interviewing of respondents from a cultural group, together with observation (often participative) of everyday behaviour, to draw a verbal picture of the group's shared practices and beliefs. Respondents and observations should be sufficient in number and variety to give a reasonably complete sampling and stability in the consistencies and divergences in the record.

The ethnographer's report is 'qualitative' in the social-science sense of having no numerical assessments of weight of opinion or prevalence of practice. It also involves no psychological measurement of the relative influence of different factors on an individual member of the culture or how the beliefs and values fit together in a respondent's mind (although individuals' cognitive networks can be built from experimentally structured interviews based on the respondent's spontaneous account). The interpretation is disciplined by intuitive plausibility of what after close study of all the material seems to lie behind the whole group's activities, by consistency across respondents having different roles and by support from illustrative quotations (or incidents).

Some sociologists also use socially qualitative methods. They may be less concerned to map the communal culture, however, than to identify differing social processes. Also, a sociologist will often use the qualitative results as a basis for designing a survey to get socially quantitative data, i.e. the frequency with which an answer would be given in a population, as estimated from the answers by a sample of interviewees. Many sociologists have worked exclusively with such aggregate data from surveys and from social phenomena that can be recorded without talking to individuals, whether numerical (social and economic 'statistics') or non-numerical such as types of foods in different sorts of shops. Market research is largely applied sociology in the sense that it relies on survey data from more or less representative samples and on social interpretations of economic statistics like market share (proportion of sales achieved by a brand relative to its competitors of the same product type).

Some of the methods of data collection used by psychologists are identical to those of anthropologists and sociologists but the data analyses and focus of

interpretation tend to be different. A psychologist is primarily concerned with working out what the individual is doing and only secondarily with the cultural background or the representativeness of a set of individuals.

However, the disciplines share a major methodological difficulty in that the anthropologists and social and market research investigators assume that they can read the culture through interviews with a number of individuals or read individual citizens from data combined from many interviews. The psychologist and sociologist share problems with interpreting the frequencies of particular alternatives among the responses specified for a given question. These are socially quantitative data because they are obtained from fully structured interviews with individuals selected to represent a defined population's range of demographic characteristics (age, sex, income, household type, etc.). Frequencies of particular responses weigh the body of those specific verbal expressions of opinion in that population or in any demographic subset that can be separated out. However, the polled frequencies provide no evidence on the views of any member of the population or even on the co-ordinated view of a subgroup. They are therefore not psychologically quantitative data.

It is possible to see which other opinions go with the individuals in the sample or in a subset of it. Statistical techniques have been developed in psychometrics to account for such associations among opinions by additive variables that appear to underly the multiple responses. These techniques traditionally rely on correlating across respondents numerical scores that have been assigned to graded answers to the questions posed, rather than treating each sort of answer to one question as a discrete event whose frequency is totted up across the sample. This technique is neither truly psychological nor truly social: it uses the variations in quantitative response among individuals to construct a pattern out of the multiple responses that is presumed to be in common among individuals. People are put in different places in a response structure. There can be considerably fewer dimensions in this structure than the number of question items from which it is derived. Item response scores that correlate highly fall close to one dimension: these items' scores then form a psychometric scale. (Note that the scores for the grades of response to one question item should not be called a scale: whether such ratings fall on a dimension and the numerical scores do measure distance along that dimension is a matter which can only be ascertained by other scaling techniques.) However, the scaling of the answers to question items that have been aggregated across a set of people is no more capable in general of measuring what is going on in the minds of individuals than is the sociologist's or market researcher's cross-tabulations of response frequencies. These techniques for interpreting grouped data tell us something about any of the individuals only if there is a very strong consensus in their mental structuring of the situation in their responses. This requires a virtual unity of approach to the issues and how they interact, within which opinions vary only in the relative truth, goodness or importance of different factors. That is, psychometrics makes a very strong and implausible presupposition that the respondents all conform to one single cognitive, biological and cultural structure.

Socially quantitative and psychometric approaches share another unrealistic feature: they impose the same wordings of questions and answers on all respondents, thereby risking both misunderstanding and distortion of the thinking they are trying to investigate. Instead, the questioning can be in broad terms that suggest as few particular ideas or words as possible and the respondent's own choice of words

in response can be recorded for subsequent analysis and attempts at interpretation. This technique of open-ended interviewing or unstructured group discussion, focused only on a conceptual topic or physical object, is often rather misleadingly called qualitative research. There is usually no attempt to estimate population frequencies or individual differences from open-ended interviews but social quantuition and psychometric assessment is possible; it is technically more difficult than with preset questions and fixed alternatives for answers. The frequency of spontaneous mention of a particular word or concept in a representative sample prompted with a topic could well be an important measure. Statistical techniques have been developed (such as generalized Procrustes analysis) for extracting consensus correlational structures from multiple responses by individuals who use different words.

The ethnographer or a psychologist interviewing open-endedly has the advantage of being able to consider each interviewee's pattern of responses before seeking to infer the shared culture or similarities and differences in cognitive structure. However, interpretation of such interviews is an informal practice, lacking in operationally statable objective criteria. Ethnography and qualitative social and market research can appeal only to the logical coherence and human plausibility of the interpretation in the report, bolstered by selected quotations. The interviewer is collecting testimony that the law courts might regard as admissible in evidence but the anthropologist's published report would in law be mere hearsay. Without some technique for formalizing the evidence from an open-ended interview, the psychologist's and ethnographer's conclusions are intuitive. This is yet another sense of the term 'qualitative research'. Some even claim that interpretation of open-ended interviews is a fundamentally different form of investigation from the objective scientific approaches purported by psychology and sociology – internal, phenomenological and empathetic rather than allegedly external, physical and positivistic. I think that there is a confusion here between expression that claims no reference to reality and the successful communication of meaning which is an observable event within a cultural group living in a physical world. Hence, content analysis and particularly the identification of consistent relationships among words and acts is open to inter-subjective criticism and empirical checks. Such relationships among an individual's words could even be quantitated, as could their prevalence in a group. Psychologists have developed some techniques for analysing data from an individual respondent that bring out formal structure from the results. Sometimes it is possible to systematize an individual's behaviour correlationally, as in path analysis, or even to make a within-subject measurement such as a personal scale of a cognitive process.

Psychology and Other Social Sciences

Mental processes develop and survive only within the suprapersonal context of individuals interacting within a common culture. This essentially social basis of thought, emotion and individual action has been demonstrated philosophically for half a century, in general terms by the later work of Wittgenstein (1953) and within science in particular by philosophers such as Popper (1959), Kuhn (1962), Lakatos (Lakatos and Musgrave, 1975) and Bhaskar (1978). Hence the science of mental processes cannot be fully productive without integration with scientific investigation of cultural processes, beyond what goes on in any set of individuals' minds.

It is therefore most regrettable that an intellectual and professional stand-off developed between anthropology and psychology in mid-century. The social psychologists studied interpersonal interactions and seemed blind to the suprapersonal social processes, while the social anthropologists read the culture while seeming blind to the individual action and thought which sustains and reveals it. The attitude psychologist also became divorced from the opinion sociologist. Both are at least one stage removed from what anybody is actually doing, the social investigator by response frequencies from a representative sample and the psychometrician by individual differences within a diverse set of respondents. Nevertheless, clear mass or consensus effects provide cost-effective guidance to research into the actual cognitive processes and the diversity of individual behaviour. The food marketer has experience with the sales figures, attitude polls and psychographic maps from which a great number of empirical hypotheses have been developed in implicitly if not explicitly psychological form about similarities and differences among consumers of particular products. The training and experience of a caterer, home economist or dietitian can give breadth of awareness of cuisine or culinary culture that is hard for the 'amateur' shopper, cook and eater to match in designing and interpreting research.

The current boom in cognitive science is in danger of neglecting the interdependence of mind and culture because of its focus on simulating physical perception, writing and speech by computer programs that operate essentially as solo systems, each on its own desert island. Cognitive psychologists cannot afford to ignore the social roots of the development of even the most physical perceptual tasks, such as recognition of food materials.

Research Opportunities

The now rapidly growing interest in the behavioural and social sciences relevant to food and nutrition is restoring lines of communication among the social disciplines. This provides many types of opening for psychological research. Psychology can also play a prominent role in relating social realities to the natural sciences in this area as others.

Productive research will depend on non-psychologists getting to grips with the theoretical concepts and methods of investigation required for the scientific study of the human mind. These are not absolutely different from the ideas and procedures needed to study other complicated adaptive systems, as in physiology, ecology, electronics and economics. Nevertheless, human behaviour has an order of complexity and flexibility that has to be faced from the start.

The mature person is a system of systems, even a system for building systems as required. How the mind is working depends greatly on the current task(s) the person is tackling, as well as on the procedures that have been developed in the attempts to deal with past situations. Only a small amount of the mental processing is being attended to at any moment; much of it can never be brought to awareness. New processes and combinations of processes are acquired throughout life, representing reality with increasing accuracy and sophistication. Such learning subtly but profoundly alters the performance of the system. Thus, the analysis of behaviour into the mediating cognitive processes and their adaptation to the demands of

performance can seem totally different from investigation in any other science. It can seem a long and arduous task to acquire very basic psychological skills such as picking out something that has been learned or characterizing the way in which two thoughts interact.

One of the biggest barriers to effective cognitive-behavioural analysis (for some psychologists as well as for those from other backgrounds) is the introspectionist fallacy that is built into popular and academic Western culture. Most scientists and practitioners, including numbers of psychologists, still think that psychology is primarily concerned with the phenomena of consciousness. They take words like sweet, hungry, convenient to refer to events in a different world from that investigated by all the other (or real?) sciences. They think that psychology can only deal in words, scaling sensations, moods and other mental states regarded as private and subjective. In fact, mentalist language cannot refer primarily to a private world of which only the experiencer has knowledge. The words could not be used to communicate anything meaningful if they were purely reports on phenomena that other people had no way of knowing anything about. Hence it is logically necessary for expressions of private experience to be rooted in observable social and physical events.

It follows that rating of a sensation, motive or emotion can also be treated as an objective achievement of discrimination or actions. In other words, subjectivity and the contents of consciousness are a communicable viewpoint on public reality that we have acquired the skill of expressing. We can say how things appear to us personally but this is not by inspecting an inner world of sensation or intention but by recognizing similarities between our situation and certain other situations that are publicly definable in our culture. Similarly, we can say what we are intending to do but this is not expressing an inner world of the will but invoking similarities between our current activity and other activities recognized as having those purposes. Thus, ratings and other verbal data are no more subjective than behavioural data or even food intakes. A weight of food swallowed or the actions taken to obtain the food provide no objective psychological information until these results are related to their causes for the person being studied. Similarly, what people say becomes scientifically interpretable information about the mind if the verbal data are related to measured factors that influence them.

What is subjective, indeed unscientific, is to take the face meaning of the words to be a measure of some underlying event to which it refers, without demonstrating a consistency in the use of the words that could be a measure of anything, let alone identifying what that is a measure of by identifying its cause. 'I am having strong hunger pangs' is not a measure of a disposition to eat that has been caused by an empty digestive tract unless the use of that sentence by that person in those circumstances has been shown normally to be predictive of eating and to arise specifically from an empty stomach or upper intestine (not from awareness of time since the last meal, or from the sight or smell of highly palatable food).

Cognitive Approaches

Experimental psychologists of perception, memory and language tend to work on artificial stimulus arrays, letter or word lists and sentence items.

Drinks and manufactured foodstuffs provide natural stimuli that can be varied visually and to smell, taste and touch. Many of the features that are likely to be integrated into recognition of the material are obvious from the start. Some of them are readily manipulated and measured with considerable refinement. Shopping lists, recipes and menus are natural verbal materials. The labelling, advertising and uses of foods provide scripts, computational and logical tasks, demands on memory and many of the requirements for cognitive experiments. The results may challenge conclusions drawn from laboratory tasks.

Psychophysics lost contact with cognitive approaches largely because of a focus on pure stimuli. These left only very weak measurement paradigms and no challenge to introspectionist assumptions from contextual effects. Only in the last few years are the elements of a cognitive approach to taste mixtures emerging. An intramodal or crossmodal psychophysics of real drinks and foods can only operate with fullblown cognitive analysis and strong scaling techniques.

Social psychometrics and experimental social psychology have been impoverished by lack of interest in the implicit social environment in the mind of a solitary eater and the really varied circumstances of interactions within pairs or small groups around a physically and verbally tightly-specifiable meal table or drinks party.

The Social, Thinking Animal

Nutrition, behavioural physiology and biological psychology have focused on the amounts of food and drink consumed and indeed on the intakes of energy or nutrients. Intake accumulates as a result of a stream of ingestive behaviour under circumstances that vary within a meal and from one meal to the next. The eater's thoughts about food must be changing. Hence the preoccupation with intake cuts off contact with the cognitive approach to the mental life in everyday behaviour on which psychological science is centred.

Moreover, the focus on intake engenders blindness to the social content of behaviour towards foodstuffs and their nutrient compositions. The food on the menu is considered to be a constant and the only circumstance that is thought to change the response to the menu is the accumulation of food inside the eater. In fact, the perception, palatability and appropriateness of a food is likely to be changing for cultural reasons as the meal progresses. The social role of the food and the eater bears in on the emptying of the plate, the choice of dessert and the taking of second portions. Is the leaving of some food a sign of meritorious restraint or culpable wastage? Is the refusal of a second serving an insult to the host or an expression of satisfaction with the initial portions? Meal sizes and meal timings too may be a product of elaborate social thinking rather than the outcome of cogitation on physiological signals.

Nowhere is the need for a social cognitive psychology more evident than in the emotional aspects of eating. Food cravings such as in pregnancy are widely presumed to reflect nutrient deficits and yet symptoms of hormonal changes and knowledge of the growing foetus are highly liable to social construction. Substances in drinks are attributed effects on mood and behaviour when consumption of the beverage is part of the conventional social patterns that define those emotions and activities, whether it is the mental boost from tea or coffee or the noisy behaviour associated with alcohol consumption.

Citizenship and Government

HEALTH   DIET

Food regulation

FOODS   WEALTH

Nutritional science and practice

The novel sciences of NUTRITIONAL BEHAVIOUR

Food sciences and technology

Leisure and Education

Nutrition education

Commerce and Work

Food employment

Social science and human services

E A T I N G

HAPPINESS

Even the most prominent recent contribution to the theory of eating from social psychologists centres on an effect on food intake with unknown cognitive basis. The concept of dietary restraint is of a commitment to dieting, expressed by responses to a questionnaire that are validated on the amount of food eaten shortly after inveiglement into a snack. It was originally suggested that this 'breakdown of restraint' was emotional overeating, disinhibited by social guilt or anxiety about weight induced by the initial snack. More recently, the favoured explanation has been quite different: that the dieter abandons the strict rules of the diet. The complications of what actually goes on in dieters' minds during the restraint breakdown test, its basic psychology, remain to be systematically addressed.

Envoi

This book has tackled questions about what goes on in eaters' and drinkers' minds about the foods and beverages they are consuming, about the effects on their bodies and about the cultural meaning of the eating occasion. The way forward both for theoretical understanding and practical application is for nutritional psychology and the biological and social disciplines of nutrition to work together in teams and more and more within the minds of individual students, research workers and practitioners. The novel sciences of nutritional behaviour lie at the centre (Figure 9.1).

Further Reading

This chapter has shown how closely the cognitive psychology of food and drink consumption relates to many other natural and social sciences. Hence, whatever the reader's background,

it is important to sample texts specialized in other relevant areas. The following titles are classified into broad areas to provide convenient entries into unfamiliar material. Further suggestions for some of these areas follow the relevant preceding chapters.

Nutrition

BINGHAM, S. (1987) *Everyman companion to food and nutrition*, London, Dent.

GIBNEY, M.J. (1986) *Nutrition, diet and health*, Cambridge, Cambridge University Press.

GORMLEY, T.R., DOWNE, G. and O'BEIRNE, D. (1987) *Food, health and the consumer*, London, Elsevier Applied Science.

HAMILTON, E.M.N. and WHITNEY, E.N. (1982) *Nutrition: concepts and controversies*, St. Paul, West.

NATIONAL RESEARCH COUNCIL (USA) (1989) *Diet and health: implications for reducing chronic disease risk*, Washington, DC, National Academy Press.

PASSMORE, R., and EASTWOOD, M.A. (Eds) (1986) *Human nutrition and dietetics*, Edinburgh, Churchill Livingstone.

Food Science and Technology

BENDER, A.E. (1982) *Dictionary of nutrition and food technology*, Sevenoaks, Newnes.

BIRCH, G.G., SPENCER, M. and CAMERON, A.G. (1986) *Food science*, Oxford, Pergamon.

BLANSHARD, J.M.V. and LILLFORD, P. (Eds) (1987) *Food structure and behaviour*, London, Academic Press.

BOARD, R.G. (1983) *Modern introduction to food microbiology*, Oxford, Blackwell.

FOX, B.A. and CAMERON, A.G. (1989) *Food science, nutrition and health*, London, Edward Arnold.

MARIE, S. and PIGGOTT, J.R. (Eds) (1991) *Handbook of sweeteners*, Glasgow, Blackie.

Anthropology, History and Sociology of Food

ARNOTT, M. (Ed.) (1975) *Gastronomy: the anthropology of food and food habits*, The Hague, Mouton.

BARKER, L.M. (Ed.) (1982) *The psychobiology of human food selection*, Westport, CT, AVI.

BASS, M.A., WAKEFIELD, L.M. and KOLASSA, K.M. (1979) *Community nutrition and individual food behavior*, Minneapolis, Burgess.

FARB, P. and ARMELAGOS, G. (1980) *Consuming passions: the anthropology of eating*, Boston, Houghton Mifflin.

FIELDHOUSE, P. (1986) *Food & nutrition: customs & culture*, London, Croom Helm.

HARTLEY, D. (1956) *Food in England*, London, Macdonald.

MURCOTT, A. (Ed.) (1983) *The sociology of food and eating*, Cardiff, Gower Press.

RITSON, C., GOFTON, L. and McKENZIE, J. (Eds) (1986) *The food consumer*, Chichester, Wiley.

SANJUR, D. (1982) *Social and cultural perspectives on nutrition*, Englewood Cliffs NJ, Prentice-Hall.

TANNAHILL, R. (1988) *Food in history*, Harmondsworth, Penguin.

Behavioural Biology of Food and Fluid Intake

BOAKES, R.A., BURTON, M.J. and POPPLEWELL, D.A. (Eds) (1987) *Eating habits: food, physiology and learned behaviour*, Chichester, Wiley.

BOOTH, D.A. (Ed.) (1988) *Hunger models: computable theory of feeding control*, London, Academic Press.

BOOTH, D.A. (Ed.) (1993) *Neurophysiology of ingestion*, Oxford, Pergamon.

CAPALDI, E.D. and POWLEY, T.L. (Eds) (1990) *Taste, experience and feeding*, Washington DC, American Psychological Association.

CHIVERS, D.J., WOOD, B.A. and BILSBOROUGH, A. (Eds) (1984) *Food acquisition and processing in primates*, New York, Plenum Press.

DE CARO, G., EPSTEIN, A.N. and MASSI, M. (Eds) (1986) *The physiology of thirst and sodium appetite*, New York, Plenum Press.

DENTON, D.A. (1982) *The hunger for salt*, Berlin, Springer-Verlag.

FITZSIMONS, J.T. (1979) *The physiology of thirst and sodium appetite*, Cambridge, Cambridge University Press.

FRIEDMAN, M.I., TORDOFF, M.G. and KARE, M.R. (Eds) (1991) *Appetite and nutrition*, New York, Marcel Dekker.

LE MAGNEN, J. (1985) *Hunger*, Cambridge, Cambridge University Press.

RAMSAY, D.J. and BOOTH, D.A. (Eds) (1991) *Thirst: physiological and psychological aspects*, London, Springer-Verlag.

ROLLS, B.J. and ROLLS, E.T. (1983) *Thirst*, Cambridge, Cambridge University Press.

STRICKER, E.M. (Ed.) (1990) *Neurobiology of food and fluid intake*, New York, Plenum Press.

Psychology of Eating and Drinking

AXELSON, M.L. and BRINBERG, D. (1989) *A social-psychological perspective on food-related behavior*, New York, Springer-Verlag.

BARKER, L.M. (Ed.) *The psychobiology of human food selection*, Westport, CT, AVI.

BENNETT, G. (1988) *Eating matters. Why we eat what we eat*, London, Heineman Kingswood.

BOLLES, R.C. (Ed.) (1991) *The hedonics of taste*, Hillsdale NJ, Erlbaum.

DOBBING, J. (Ed.) (1987) *Sweetness*, London, Springer-Verlag.

GILBERT, S. (1986) *Pathology of eating: Psychology and treatment*, London, Routledge & Kegan Paul.

LOGUE, A.W. (1991) *The psychology of eating and drinking*, 2nd Edn. San Francisco, W.H. Freeman.

RAMSAY, D.J. and BOOTH, D.A. (Eds) (1991) *Thirst: physiological and psychological aspects*, London, Springer-Verlag.

PIRKE, K.M., VANDEREYCKEN, W. and PLOOG, D. (Eds) (1987) *The psychobiology of bulimia nervosa*, Heidelberg, Springer Verlag.

SHEPHERD, R. (Ed.) (1989) *Handbook of the psychophysiology of human eating*, Chichester, Wiley.

SOLMS, J., BOOTH, D.A., PANGBORN, R.M. and RAUNHARDT, O. (Eds) (1987) *Food acceptance and nutrition*, London, Academic Press.

References

Allon, N. (1976) The stigma of overweight in everyday life, in Bray, G.A. (Ed.), *Obesity in perspective*, Part 2, Washington, DC: US Government Printing Office, pp. 83–102.

Anand, B.K. and Brobeck, J.R. (1951) Localization of a feeding center in the hypothalamus of the rat, *Proceedings of Society for Experimental Biology and Medicine*, **77**, 323–24.

Anderson, N.H. (1981) *Methods of information integration*, New York: Academic Press.

Anscombe, G.E.M. (1960) *Intention*, Oxford: Blackwells.

Ashby, F.G. and Perrin, N. (1988) Towards a unified theory of similarity and recognition, *Psychological Review*, **95**, 124–50.

Axelson, M.L. and Brinberg, D. (1989) *A social-psychological perspective on food related behavior*, New York: Springer-Verlag.

Baker, B.J. and Booth, D.A. (1989) Preference conditioning by concurrent diets with delayed proportional reinforcement, *Physiology and Behavior*, **46**, 585–91.

Baker, B.J., Booth, D.A., Duggan, J.P. and Gibson, E.L. (1987) Protein appetite demonstrated: learned specificity of protein-cue preference to protein need in adult rats, *Nutrition Research*, **7**, 481–7.

Basdevant, A., Craplet, C. and Guy-Grand, B. (1993) Snacking patterns in obese French women, *Appetite*, **21**, 17–23.

Bass, M.A., Wakefield, L.M. and Kolassa, K.M. (1979) *Community nutrition and individual food behavior*, Minneapolis: Burgess.

Beauchamp, G.K. and Moran, M. (1984) Acceptance of sweet and salty tastes in 2-year-old children, *Appetite*, **5**, 291–305.

Beauchamp, G.K., Bertino, M., Burke, D. and Engelman, K. (1990) Experimental sodium depletion and salt taste in normal human volunteers, *American Journal of Clinical Nutrition*, **51**, 881–90.

Bem, D.J. (1972) Self-perception theory, in Berkowitz, L. (Ed.), *Advances in experimental social psychology*, Vol. 6, New York: Academic Press, pp. 183–200.

Bennett, G.A. (1986) Behavior therapy for obesity: a quantitative review of the effects of selected treatment characteristics on outcome, *Behavior Therapy*, **17**, 554–62.

Benton, D. and Sargent, J. (1992) Breakfast, blood glucose and memory, *Biological Psychology*, **33**, 207–10.

Beidler, L.M. (1962) Taste receptor stimulation, *Progress in Biophysics*, **12**, 109–151.

Bhaskar, R. (1978) *A realist theory of science*, 2nd Edn, New York: Humanities Press/ Hassocks: Harvester Press.

Birch, L.L. (1980) The relationship between children's food preferences and those of their parents, *Journal of Nutrition Education*, **12**, 14–18.

BIRCH, L.L. (1987) The acquisition of food acceptance patterns in children, in BOAKES, R.A., POPPLEWELL, D.A. and BURTON, M.J. (Eds), *Eating habits. Food, physiology and learned behaviour,* Chichester: Wiley, pp. 107–130.

BIRCH, L.L. (1990) The control of food intake by young children: the role of learning, in CAPALDI, E.D. and POWLEY, T.L. (Eds), *Taste, experience, and feeding,* Washington DC: American Psychological Association, pp. 116–35.

BIRCH, L.L., BILLMAN, J. and RICHARDS, S. (1984) Time of day affects food acceptability, *Appetite,* **5**, 109–112.

BIRCH, L.L., BIRCH, D., MARLIN, D. and KRAMER, L. (1982) Effects of instrumental eating on children's food preferences, *Appetite,* **3**, 125–34.

BIRCH, L.L., JOHNSON, S.L., ANDRESEN, G., PETERS, J.C. and SCHULTE, M.C. (1991) The variability of young children's energy intake, *New England Journal of Medicine,* **324**, 232–5.

BIRCH, L.L., McPHEE, L., SHOBA, B.C., STEINBERG, L. and KREHBIEL, R. (1987) 'Clean up your plate.' Effects of child feeding practices on the development of intake regulation, *Learning and Motivation,* **18**, 301–17.

BIRCH, L.L., McPHEE, L., STEINBERG, L. and SULLIVAN, S. (1990) Conditioned flavor preferences in young children, *Physiology and Behavior,* **47**, 501–05.

BIRCH, L.L., ZIMMERMAN, S. and HIND, H. (1980) The influence of social affective context on preschool children's food preferences, *Child Development,* **51**, 856–61.

BLAIR, A.J., LEWIS, V.J. and BOOTH, D.A. (1989) Behaviour therapy for obesity: the role of clinicians in the reduction of overweight, *Counselling Psychology Quarterly,* **2**(3), 289–301.

BLAIR, A.J., LEWIS, V.J. and BOOTH, D.A. (1990) Does emotional eating interfere with attempts at weight control in women?, *Appetite,* **15**, 151–7.

BLAIR, A.J., LEWIS, V.J. and BOOTH, D.A. (1992) Response to leaflets about eating and shape by women concerned about their weight, *Behavioural Psychotherapy,* **20**, 279–86.

BLASS, E.M. (1987) Opioids, sweets and a mechanism for positive affect, in DOBBING, J. (Ed.), *Sweetness,* London: Springer-Verlag, pp. 115–26.

BLASS, E.M. and HALL, W.G. (1976) Drinking termination: interactions among hydrational, orogastric and behavioral controls in rats, *Psychological Review,* **83**, 356–74.

BLOOR, D. (1983) *Wittgenstein. A social theory of knowledge,* London: Macmillan.

BOLIN, A. (1992) Flex appeal, food and fat: competitive bodybuilding, gender and diet, *Play and Culture,* **5**, 378–400.

BOOTH, D.A. (1967) Localization of the adrenergic feeding system in the rat diencephalon, *Science,* **158**, 515–17.

BOOTH, D.A. (1972a) Satiety and behavioral caloric compensation following intragastric glucose loads in the rat, *Journal of Comparative and Physiological Psychology,* **78**, 412–32.

BOOTH, D.A. (1972b) Postabsorptively induced suppression of appetite and the energostatic [cytodynamometric] control of feeding, *Physiology and Behavior,* **9**, 199–202.

BOOTH, D.A. (1972c) Conditioned satiety in the rat, *Journal of Comparative and Physiological Psychology,* **81**, 457–71.

BOOTH, D.A. (1976) Approaches to feeding control, in SILVERSTONE, T. (Ed.), *Appetite and food intake,* West Berlin: Abakon Verlagsgesellschaft/Dahlem Konferenzen, pp. 417–478.

BOOTH, D.A. (1977a) Appetite and satiety as metabolic expectancies, in KATSUKI, Y.,

S A T O, M., T A K A G I, S.F. and O O M U R A, Y. (Eds), *Food intake and chemical senses*, Tokyo: University of Tokyo Press, pp. 317–30.

B O O T H, D.A. (1977b) Satiety and appetite are conditioned reactions, *Psychosomatic Medicine*, **39**, 76–81.

B O O T H, D.A. (Ed.) (1978) *Hunger models: computable theory of feeding control*, London: Academic Press.

B O O T H, D.A. (1979a) Metabolism and the control of feeding in man and animals, in B R O W N, K. and C O O P E R, S.J. (Eds), *Chemical influences on behaviour*, London: Academic Press, pp. 79–134.

B O O T H, D.A. (1979b) Is thirst largely an acquired specific appetite?, *Behavioral and Brain Sciences*, **2**, 103–4.

B O O T H, D.A. (1980a) Conditioned reactions in motivation, in T O A T E S, F.M. and H A L L I D A Y, T.R. (Eds), *Analysis of motivational processes*, London: Academic Press, pp. 77–102.

B O O T H, D.A. (1980b) Acquired behavior controlling energy intake and output, in S T U N K A R D, A.J. (Ed.), *Obesity*, Philadelphia, PA: W.B. Saunders, pp. 101–43.

B O O T H, D.A. (1981) The physiology of appetite, *British Medical Bulletin*, **37**, 135–40.

B O O T H, D.A. (1985) Food-conditioned eating preferences and aversions with interoceptive elements: learned appetites and satieties, *Annals of New York Academy of Sciences*, **443**, 22–37.

B O O T H, D.A. (1987) Cognitive experimental psychology of appetite, in B O A K E S, R.A., B U R T O N, M.J. and P O P P L E W E L L, D.A. (Eds), *Eating habits*, Chichester: John Wiley, pp. 175–209.

B O O T H, D.A. (1988a) Mechanisms from models – actual effects from real life: the zero-calorie drink-break option, in B O O T H, D.A., R O D I N, J. and B L A C K B U R N, G.L. (Eds), *Sweeteners, appetite and obesity*, London: Academic Press, pp. 94–102.

B O O T H, D.A. (1989a) Mood- and nutrient-conditioned appetites. Cultural and physiological bases for eating disorders, *Annals of New York Academy of Sciences*, **575**, 122–35, 466–71.

B O O T H, D.A. (1991a) Influences on human fluid consumption, in R A M S A Y, D.J. and B O O T H, D.A. (Eds), *Thirst: physiological and psychological aspects*, London: Springer-Verlag, pp. 53–73.

B O O T H, D.A. (1991b) Learned ingestive motivation and the pleasures of the palate, in B O L L E S, R.C. (Ed.), *The hedonics of taste*, Hillsdale NJ: Erlbaum, pp. 29–58.

B O O T H, D.A. (1992) Towards scientific realism in eating research, *Appetite*, **19**, 56–60.

B O O T H, D.A. (1994) Individual mentation. [Review to be submitted.]

B O O T H, D.A. and B L A I R, A.J. (1988) Objective factors in the appeal of a brand during use by the individual consumer, in T H O M S O N, D.M.H. (Ed.), *Food acceptability*, London: Elsevier Applied Science, pp. 329–46.

B O O T H, D.A. and C O N N E R, M.T. (1991) Characterisation and measurement of influences on food acceptability by analysis of choice differences: theory and practice, *Food Quality and Preference*, **2**, 75–85.

B O O T H, D.A. and D A V I S, J.D. (1973) Gastrointestinal factors in the acquisition of oral sensory control of satiation, *Physiology and Behavior*, **11**, 23–9.

B O O T H, D.A. and G I B S O N, E.L. (1988) Control of eating behaviour by amino acid supply, in H E U T H E R, G. (Ed.), *Amino acid availability and brain function in health and disease*, Berlin: Springer-Verlag, pp. 259–66 & 311–14.

B O O T H, D.A. and G R I N K E R, J.A. (1993) Learned control of meal size in spontaneously obese and nonobese bonnet macaque monkeys, *Physiology and Behavior*, **53**, 51–7.

BOOTH, D.A. and JARMAN, S.P. (1976) Inhibition of food intake in the rat following complete absorption of glucose delivered into the stomach, intestine or liver, *Journal of Physiology*, **259**, 501–22.

BOOTH, D.A. and MATHER, P. (1978) Prototype model of human feeding, growth and obesity, in BOOTH, D.A. (Ed.), *Hunger models: computable theory of feeding control*, London: Academic Press, pp. 279–322.

BOOTH, D.A. and SIMSON, P.C. (1971) Food preferences acquired by association with variations in amino acid nutrition, *Quarterly Journal of Experimental Psychology*, **23**, 135–45.

BOOTH, D.A. and TOASE, A.-M. (1983) Conditioning of hunger/satiety signals as well as flavour cues in dieters, *Appetite*, **4**, 235–6.

BOOTH, D.A., CHASE, A. and CAMPBELL, A.T. (1970) Relative effectiveness of protein in the late stages of appetite suppression in man, *Physiology and Behavior*, **5**, 1299–302.

BOOTH, D.A., CONNER, M.T. and MARIE, S. (1987) Sweetness and food selection: measurement of sweeteners' effects on acceptance, in DOBBING, J. (Ed.), *Sweetness*, London: Springer-Verlag, pp. 143–60.

BOOTH, D.A., CONNER, M.T. and GIBSON, E.L. (1989) Measurement of food perception, food preference, and nutrient selection, *Annals of New York Academy of Sciences*, **561**, 226–42.

BOOTH, D.A., FRENCH, J.A. and GATHERER, A.J.H. (1992) Personal benefits from postingestional actions of dietary constituents, *Proceedings of Nutrition Society*, **51**, 335–41.

BOOTH, D.A., FULLER, J. and LEWIS, V.J. (1981) Human control of body weight: cognitive or physiological? Some energy-related perceptions and misperceptions, in CIOFFI, L.A., JAMES, W.P.T. and VAN ITALLIE, T.B. (Eds), *The body weight regulatory system: normal and disturbed aspects*, New York: Raven Press, pp. 305–14.

BOOTH, D.A., GIBSON, E.L. and BAKER, B.J. (1986a) Gastromotor mechanism of fenfluramine anorexia, in NICOLAIDIS, S. (Ed.), *Serotoninergic system, feeding and body weight regulation*, London: Academic Press, pp. 57–69.

BOOTH, D.A., GIBSON, E.L. and BAKER, B.J. (1986b) Behavioral dissection of the intake and dietary selection effects of injection of fenfluramine, amphetamine or PVN norepinephrine, *Society for Neuroscience Abstracts*, **15**, 593.

BOOTH, D.A., LEE, M. and McALEAVEY, C. (1976) Acquired sensory control of satiation in man, *British Journal of Psychology*, **67**, 137–47.

BOOTH, D.A., LEWIS, V.J. BLAIR, A.J. (1990) Dietary restraint and binge eating: pseudo-quantitative anthropology for a medicalised problem habit?, *Appetite*, **14**, 116–9.

BOOTH, D.A., LOVETT, D. and McSHERRY, G.M. (1972) Postingestive modulation of the sweetness preference gradient in the rat, *Journal of Comparative and Physiological Psychology*, **78**, 485–512.

BOOTH, D.A., MATHER, P. and FULLER, J. (1982) Starch content of ordinary foods associatively conditions human appetite and satiation, *Appetite*, **3**, 163–84.

BOOTH, D.A., STOLOFF, R. and NICHOLLS, J. (1974) Dietary flavor acceptance in infant rats established by association with effects of nutrient composition, *Physiological Psychology*, **2**, 313–9.

BOOTH, D.A., THOMPSON, A. and SHAHEDIAN, B. (1983) A robust, brief measure of an individual's most preferred level of salt in an ordinary foodstuff, *Appetite*, **4**, 301–12.

BOOTH, D.A., THOMPSON, A.L., SHEPHERD, R., LAND, D.G. and GRIFFITHS, R.P. (1987) Salt intake and blood pressure: the triangular hypothesis, *Medical Hypotheses*, **24**, 325–28.

BOOTH, D.A., TOASE, A.-M., GIBSON, E.L. and FREEMAN, R.P.J. (1994) Small objects of desire, in LEGG, C.R. and BOOTH, D.A. (Eds), *Human appetites and their neural bases*, Oxford: Oxford University Press.

BOOTH, D.A., TOATES, F.M. and PLATT, S.V. (1976) Control system for hunger and its implications in animals and man, in NOVIN, D., WYRWICKA, W. and BRAY, G.A. (Eds), *Hunger: basic mechanisms and clinical implications*, New York: Raven Press, pp. 127–42.

BROBECK, J.R. (1947/8) Food intake as a mechanism of temperature regulation, *Yale Journal of Biology and Medicine*, **20**, 545–52.

BROBECK, J.R., TEPPERMAN, J. and LONG, C.N.H. (1943) Experimental hypothalamic hyperphagia in the albino rat, *Yale Journal of Biology and Medicine*, **15**, 893–903.

BRUCH, H. (1969) Hunger and instinct, *Journal of Nervous and Mental Disease*, **149**, 91–114.

BURTON, M.J., ROLLS, E.T. and MORA, F. (1976) Effects of hunger on the responses of neurons in the lateral hypothalamus to the sight and taste of food, *Experimental Neurology*, **51**, 668–77.

CABANAC, M. (1971) Physiological role of pleasure, *Science*, **173**, 1103–7.

CABANAC, M. and FANTINO, M. (1979) Origin of olfacto-gustatory alliesthesia: intestinal sensitivity to carbohydrate concentration?, *Physiology and Behavior*, **18**, 1039–45.

CABANAC, M., MINAIRE, Y. and ADAIR, E.R. (1968) Influence of internal factors on the pleasantness of gustative sweet sensation, *Communications in Behavioral Biology* (Part A), **1**, 77–82.

CHIVA, M. (1985) *Le doux et l'amer. Sensation gustative, émotion et communication chez le jeune enfant*, Paris: Presses Universitaires de France.

COHEN, M.I. (1970) How respiratory rhythm originates: evidence from discharge patterns of brainstem respiratory neurones, in PORTER, R. (Ed.), *Breathing*, London: Churchill, pp. 125–35.

COLLIER, G. (1980) An ecological analysis of motivation, in TOATES, F.M. and HALLIDAY, T. (Eds), *Analysis of motivational processes*, London: Academic Press, pp. 125–51.

CONNER, M.T. and BOOTH, D.A. (1988) Preferred sweetness of a lime drink and preference for sweet over non-sweet foods, related to sex and reported age and body weight, *Appetite*, **10**, 25–35.

CONNER, M.T. and BOOTH, D.A. (1992) Combining measurement of food taste and consumer preference in the individual: reliability, precision and stability data, *Journal of Food Quality*, **15**, 1–17.

CONNER, M.T., BOOTH, D.A., CLIFTON, V.J. and GRIFFITHS, R.P. (1988a) Individualized optimization of the salt content of white bread for acceptability, *Journal of Food Science*, **53**, 549–54.

CONNER, M.T., HADDON, A.V., PICKERING, E.S. and BOOTH, D.A. (1988b) Sweet tooth demonstrated: individual differences in preference for both sweet foods and foods highly sweetened, *Journal of Applied Psychology*, **73**, 275–80.

COONS, E.E. (1965) Unpublished PhD Thesis, Yale University.

COULTER, J. (1979) *The social construction of emotion*, Oxford: Blackwells.

DAVIS, J.D. and CAMPBELL, C.S. (1973) Peripheral control of meal size in the rat: effect of sham feeding on meal size and drinking rate, *Journal of Comparative and Physiological Psychology*, **83**, 379–87.

DAVIS, J.D., COLLINS, B.J. and LEVINE, M.W. (1978) The interaction between gustatory stimulation and gut feedback in the control of ingestion of liquid diets, in BOOTH, D.A. (Ed.), *Hunger models*, London: Academic Press, pp. 109–42.

DAVIS, J.D. and SMITH, G.P. (1990) Learning to sham feed: behavioral adjustments to the absence of gastrointestinal stimulation, *American Journal of Physiology*, **259**, R1228–35.

DE CASTRO, J.M. and OROZCO, S. (1990) The effects of moderate alcohol intake on the spontaneous eating patterns of humans: evidence of unregulated supplementation, *American Journal of of Clinical Nutrition*, **52**, 246–53.

DE GRAAF, C. and FRIJTERS, J.E.R. (1988) Assessment of the taste interaction between two qualitatively similar taste substances: a comparison between comparison rules, *Journal of Experimental Psychology: Human Perception and Performance*, **14**, 526–38.

DE GRAAF, C., STAFLEU, A., STAAL, P. and WIJNE, M. (1992) Beliefs about the satiating effect of bread with spread varying in macronutrient content, *Appetite*, **18**, 121–28.

DEUTSCH, J.A. (1987) Signals determining meal size, in BOAKES, R.A., POPPLEWELL, D.A. and BURTON, M.J. (Eds), *Eating habits*, pp. 155–73.

DEUTSCH, J.A., MOORE, B.O. and HEINRICHS, S.C. (1989) Unlearned specific appetite for protein, *Physiology and Behavior*, **46**, 619–24.

DREWNOWSKI, A. (1987) Changes in mood after carbohydrate consumption, *American Journal of Clinical Nutrition*, **46**, 703.

DREWNOWSKI, A., HALMI, K.A., PIERCE, B., GIBBS, J. and SMITH, G.P. (1989) Taste and eating disorders, *American Journal of Clinical Nutrition*, **46**, 442–50.

DREWNOWSKI, A., KURTH, C.L. and RAHAIM, J.E. (1991) Taste preferences in human obesity: environmental and familial factors, *American Journal of Clinical Nutrition*, **54**, 635–41.

DREWNOWSKI, A., RISKEY, D. and DESOR, J.A. (1982) Feeling fat yet unconcerned: self-reported overweight and the restraint scale, *Appetite*, **3**, pp. 273–279.

DUCLAUX, R., FEISTHAUER, J. and CABANAC, M. (1973) Effets du repas sur l'agrément d'odeurs alimentaires et nonalimentaires chez l'homme, *Physiology and Behavior*, **10**, 1029–34.

DUGGAN, J.P. and BOOTH, D.A. (1986) Obesity, overeating and rapid gastric emptying in rats with ventromedial hypothalamic lesions, *Science*, **231**, 609–11.

EHMAN, G.K., ALBERT, D.J. and JAMIESON, J.L. (1971) Injections into the duodenum and the induction of satiety in the rat, *Canadian Journal of Psychology*, **25**, 147–66.

EHRENBERG, A.S.C. (1972) *Repeat buying*, Amsterdam: North-Holland.

ERICSSON, K.A. and SIMON, H.A. (1980) Verbal reports as data, *Psychological Review*, **87**, 215–51.

EYSENCK, H.J. and EAVES, L.J. (1980) *The causes and effects of smoking*, London: Maurice Temple Smith.

FARR, R. and MOSCOVICI, S. (Eds) (1984) *Social representations*, Cambridge: Cambridge University Press.

FIELDHOUSE, P. (1985) *Food & nutrition: customs & culture*, London: Croom Helm.

FISHBEIN, M. and AJZEN, I. (1975) *Belief, attitude, intention and behavior*, Reading MA: Addison-Wesley.

FITZSIMONS, J.T. and LE MAGNEN, J. (1969) Eating as a regulatory control of drinking in the rat, *Journal of Comparative and Physiological Psychology*, **67**, 273–83.

FOLTIN, R.W., KELLY, T.H. and FISCHMAN, M.W. (1993) Ethanol as an energy source in humans: comparison with dextrose-containing beverages, *Appetite*, **20**, 95–110.

FOMON, S.J. (1974) *Infant nutrition*, 2nd Edn, Philadelphia: Saunders.

FORGAS, J.P. (1979) *Social episodes: the study of interaction routines*, London: Academic Press.

FOXALL, G.R. and BHATE, S. (1993) Cognitive style and personal involvement as explicators of innovative purchasing of 'healthy' food brands, *European Journal of Marketing*, **27**, 2, 5–16.

FRANK, R.A., VANDERKLAAUW, N.J. and SCHIFFERSTEIN, H.N.J. (1993) Both perceptual and conceptual factors influence taste-odor and taste-taste interactions, *Perception and Psychophysics*, **54**, 343–54.

FRASER, C. and GASKELL, G. (1990) *The social psychology of widespread beliefs*, Oxford, Oxford University Press.

FREEMAN, R.P.J. and BOOTH, D.A. (1994a) *Material, Semantic and Relational Recognition of Sugars and Acids*, MS in Preparation.

FREEMAN, R.P.J. and BOOTH, D.A. (1994b) *Individuals' Integration of Sensory and Semantic Features in Discriminal Object-recognition Space*, Working Paper presented to CSBBCS/EPS joint meeting, University of Toronto.

FREEMAN, R.P.J., RICHARDSON, N.J., KENDAL-REED, M. and BOOTH, D.A. (1993) Bases of a cognitive technology for food quality, *British Food Journal*, **95**, 9, pp. 37–44.

FRENCH, J.A., BLAIR, A.J. and BOOTH, D.A. (1994) Social situation and emotional state in eating and drinking, *British Food Journal*, in press.

FRENCH, J.A., WAINWRIGHT, C.J., BOOTH, D.A. and HAMILTON, J. (1992) Effects of meat species and particle size on postprandial satiety, *Proceedings of the Nutrition Society*, **51**, 57A.

FRENCH, S.J., READ, N.W., BOOTH, D.A. and ARKLEY, S. (1993) Satisfaction of hunger and thirst by foods and drinks, *British Food Journal*, **95**, 9, pp. 19–26.

FRIEDMAN, M.I. and STRICKER, E.M. (1976) The physiological psychology of hunger: a physiological perspective, *Psychological Review*, **83**, 409–31.

FRIJTERS, J.E.R. (1987) Sensory sweetness perception, its pleasantness, and attitudes to sweet foods, in DOBBING, J. (Ed.), *Sweetness*, London: Springer-Verlag, pp. 67–80.

FULLER, J. (1980) Unpublished Ph.D. Thesis, University of Birmingham (UK).

GARNER, D.M. and GARFINKEL, P.E. (1980) Socio-cultural factors in the development of anorexia nervosa, *Psychological Medicine*, **19**, 647–56.

GARROW, J.S. (1977) The regulation of energy expenditure in man, in BRAY, G.A. (Ed.), *Recent advances in obesity research II*, London: Newman, pp. 200–10.

GELIEBTER, A.A. (1979) Effects of equicaloric loads of protein, fat and carbohydrate on food intake in rat and man, *Physiology and Behavior*, **22**, 267–73.

GIBSON, E.L. and BOOTH, D.A. (1989) Dependence of carbohydrate-conditioned flavor preference on internal state in rats, *Learning and Motivation*, **20**, 36–47.

GIBSON, E.L. and BOOTH, D.A. (1992) Aversive conditioning by delayed after-effect of concentrated maltodextrin, unpublished manuscript.

GIBSON, J.J. (1979) *The ecological approach to visual perception*, Boston: Houghton-Mifflin.

GILMORE, M.M. and MURPHY, C. (1989) Aging is associated with increased Weber ratios for caffeine, but not for sucrose, *Perception and Psychophysics*, **46**, 555–9.

GLYMOUR, C., SCHEINES, R., SPIRTES, P. and KELLY, K. (1987) *Discovering causal structure. Artificial intelligence, philosophy of science and statistical modeling*. Orlando: Academic Press.

GOLDBLATT, P.B., MOORE, M.E. and STUNKARD, A.J. (1965) Social factors in obesity, *Journal of the American Medical Association*, **192**, 1039–44.

GRAFF, H. and STELLAR, E. (1962) Hyperphagia, obesity and finickiness, *Journal of Comparative and Physiological Psychology*, **55**, 418–24.

GREENLEAF, J.E., CONVERTINO, V.A., STREMEL, R.W., *et al.* (1977) Plasma [Na$^+$], [Ca^{2+}], and volume shifts and thermoregulation during exercise in man, *Journal of Applied Physiology*, **43**, 1026–32.

GREGORY, J., FOSTER, K., TYLER, H. and WISEMAN, M. (1990) *The dietary and nutritional survey of British adults*, London: Her Majesty's Stationery Office.

GROSSMAN, S.P. (1960) Eating or drinking elicited by direct adrenergic or cholinergic stimulation of hypothalamus, *Science*, **132**, 301–2.

HALMI, K.A. and SUNDAY, S. (1992) Macronutrient effects on eating behavior in anorexia and bulimia nervosa, *Appetite*, **19**, 185.

HAMLYN, D.W. (1956) *Perception*, London: Routledge, Kegan & Paul.

HAMLYN, D.W. (1991) *In and out of the black box*, Oxford: Blackwells.

HARRIS, G. and BOOTH, D.A. (1987) Infants' preference for salt in food: its dependence upon recent dietary experience, *Journal of Reproductive and Infant Psychology*, **5**, 97–104.

HARRIS, G., THOMAS, A. and BOOTH, D.A. (1991) Development of salt taste preference in infancy, *Developmental Psychology*, **26**, 534–38.

HEATHERTON, T.F., HERMAN, C.P., POLIVY, J., KING, G.A. and McGREE, S.T. (1988) The (mis)measurement of restraint: an analysis of conceptual and psychometric issues, *Journal of Abnormal Psychology*, **97**, 19–28.

HERMAN, C.P. (1978) Restrained eating, *Psychiatric Clinics of North America*, **1**, 593–607.

HERMAN, C.P. and MACK, D. (1975) Restrained and unrestrained eating, *Journal of Personality*, **43**, 647–60.

HERMAN, C.P. and POLIVY, J. (1980) Restrained eating, in STUNKARD, A.J. (Ed.), *Obesity*, Philadelphia: Saunders, pp. 208–25.

HETHERINGTON, M. (1993) Chocolate craving, *Appetite*, in press.

HILL, A.J., MAGSON, L.D. and BLUNDELL, J.E. (1986) Hunger and palatability: tracking ratings of subjective experience before, during and after consumption of preferred and less preferred food, *Appetite*, **5**, 361–71.

HILL, A.J., ROGERS, P.J. and BLUNDELL, J.E. (1989) Dietary restraint in young adolescent girls – a functional analysis, *British Journal of Clinical Psychology*, **28**, 165–76.

HILL, A.J., WEAVER, C.F.L. and BLUNDELL, J.E. (1991) Food craving, dietary restraint and mood, *Appetite*, **17**, 187–97.

HOEBEL, B.G. and TEITELBAUM, P. (1962) Hypothalamic control of feeding and self-stimulation, *Science*, **135**, 375–77.

HOLLAND, P.C. (1991) Learning, thirst and drinking, in RAMSAY, D.J. and BOOTH, D.A. (Eds), *Thirst: physiological and psychological aspects*, London: Springer-Verlag, pp. 279–95.

HSAIO, S.S., JOHNSON, K.O. and TWOMBLY, I.A. (1993) Roughness coding in the somatosensory system, *Acta Psychologica*, **84**, 53–67.

HUDSON, J.I. and POPE, H.G. (1990) Affective spectrum disorder: does antidepressant response identify a family of disorders with a common psychophysiology?, *American Journal of Psychiatry*, **147**, 552–64.

HUGGINS, R.L., DI NICOLANTONIO, R. and MORGAN, T.O. (1992) Preferred salt levels and salt taste acuity in human subjects after ingestion of untasted salt, *Appetite*, **18**, 111–19.

HUNT, J.N. and KNOX, M.T. (1968) Regulation of gastric emptying, in CODE, C.F. and HIEDEL, W. (Eds), *Handbook of physiology: alimentary canal* Vol. 4: Motility, Washington, DC: American Physiological Society, pp. 1917–35.

HUNT, J.N. and STUBBS, D.F. (1975) The volume and energy content of meals as determinants of gastric emptying, *Journal of Physiology*, **245**, 209–25.

JAHODA, G. (1992) *Crossroads between culture and mind*, Hassocks: Harvester Wheatsheaf.

JOHANSSON, R.S. and WESTLING, G. (1987) Signals in tactile afferents from the fingers eliciting adaptive motor responses during precision grip, *Experimental Brain Research*, **66**, 141–54.

JOHNSON, K.O. and HSAIO, S.S. (1992) Neural mechanisms of tactual form and texture perception, *Annual Review of Neuroscience*, **15**, 227–50.

JOHNSON, S.L., MCPHEE, L. and BIRCH, L.L. (1991) Conditioned preferences: young children prefer flavors associated with high dietary fat, *Physiology and Behavior*, **50**, 1245–51.

KATZ, S.H. (1981) Food, behavior and biocultural evolution, in BARKER, L.M. (Ed.), *Psychobiology of human food selection*, Westport, CT: AVI, pp. 171–88.

KAPLAN, H.I. and KAPLAN, H.S. (1957) The psychosomatic concept of obesity, *Journal of Nervous and Mental Disease*, **125**, 181–201.

KAYMAN, S., BRUVOLD, W. and STERN, J.S. (1990) Maintenance and relapse after weight loss in women: behavioral aspects, *American Journal of Clinical Nutrition*, **52**, 800–7.

KENNEDY, G.C. (1952) The role of depot fat in the hypothalamic control of food intake in the rat, *Proceedings of Royal Society (London) B*, **140**, 578–92.

KERN, D.L., MCPHEE, L., FISHER, J., JOHNSON, S. and BIRCH, L.L. (1993) The postingestive consequences of fat condition preferences for flavours associated with high dietary fat, *Physiology and Behavior*, **54**, 71–76.

KISSILEFF, H.R., THORNTON, J. and BECKER, E. (1982) A quadratic equation adequately describes the cumulative food intake curve in man, *Appetite*, **3**, 255–72.

KLINE, P. (1972) *Fact and fantasy in Freudian theory*, London: Methuen.

KNIGHT, I. (1984) *The heights and weights of adults in Great Britain*, London: Her Majesty's Stationery Office.

KOKINI, J. (1985) Fluid and semi-solid food texture and texture-taste interactions, *Food Technology*, **39**(11), 86–94.

KOKINI, J. (1987) The physical basis of liquid food texture and texture-taste interactions, *Journal of Food Engineering*, **6**, 51–8.

KRALY, F.S. (1990) Drinking elicited by eating, in EPSTEIN, A.N. and MORRISON, A. (Eds), *Progress in psychobiology and physiological psychology*, Vol. 14, New York: Academic Press, pp. 67–133.

KRAMER, F.M., ROCK, K. and ENGELL, D. (1992) Effects of time of day and appropriateness on food intake and hedonic ratings at morning and midday, *Appetite*, **18**, 1–13.

KROEZE, J.H.A. (1990) The perception of complex taste stimuli, in MCBRIDE, R.L. and MACFIE, H.J.H. (Eds), *Psychological bases of sensory evaluation*, London: Elsevier, pp. 41–68.

KUHN, T.S. (1962) *The structure of scientific revolutions*, Chicago: Chicago University Press.

LAKATOS, I. and MUSGRAVE, A. (Eds) (1975) *Criticism and the growth of knowledge*, Cambridge: Cambridge University Press.

LAMING, D. (1986) *Sensory analysis*, New York: Academic Press.

LA MOTTE, R.H. and SRINIVASAN, M.A. (1993) Responses of cutaneous mechanoreceptors to the shape of objects applied to the primate fingerpad, *Acta Psychologica*, **84**, 41–51.

LANGHANS, W., WEISENREITER, F. and SCHARRER, E. (1983) Different effects of subcutaneous D,L-3-hydroxybutyrate and acetoacetate injections on food intake in rats, *Physiology and Behavior*, **31**, 483–86.

LEA, S.E.G., TARPY, R.M. and WEBLEY, P. (1987) *The individual in the economy*, Cambridge: Cambridge University Press.

LEIBOWITZ, S.F. (1982) Hypothalamic catecholamine systems in relation to control of eating behavior and mechanisms of reward, in HOEBEL, B.G. and NOVIN, D. (Eds), *The neural basis of feeding and reward*, Brunswick, ME: Haer Institute, pp. 241–74.

LEIBOWITZ, S.F. and ROSSAKIS, C. (1979) Pharmacological characterization of perifornical hypothalamic dopamine receptors mediating feeding inhibition in the rat, *Brain Research*, **172**, 115–30.

LE MAGNEN, J. (1956) Effets sur la prise alimentaire du rat blanc des administrations postprandiales d'insuline et le mécanisme des appétits caloriques, *Journal de Physiologie*, **48**, 789–802.

LE MAGNEN, J. (1969) Peripheral and systemic actions of food in the caloric regulation of intake, *Annals of New York Academy of Sciences*, **157**, 1126–56.

LE MAGNEN, J., DEVOS, M., GAUDILLIÈRE, J.P., LOUIS-SYLVESTRE, J. and TALLON, S. (1973) Role of a lipostatic mechanism in regulation by feeding of energy balance in rats *Journal of Comparative and Physiological Psychology*, **84**, 1–23.

LEWIS, V.J. and BOOTH, D.A. (1986) Causal influences within an individual's dieting thoughts, feelings and behaviour, in DIEHL, J.M. and LEITZMANN, C. (Eds), *Measurement and determinants of food habits and food preferences (Euro-Nut Report 7)*, Wageningen: Department of Human Nutrition, Agricultural University, pp. 187–208.

LEWIS, V.J., BLAIR, A.J. and BOOTH, D.A. (1992) Outcome of group therapy for body-image emotionality and weight-control self-efficacy, *Behavioural Psychotherapy*, **20**, 155–66.

LIEBERMAN, H.R., Wurtman, R.J., GARFIELD, G.S., ROBERTS, C.H. and COVIELLA, I.L. (1987) The effects of low doses of caffeine on human performance and mood, *Psychopharmacology*, **92**, 308–12.

LISSNER, L., LEVITSKY, D.A., STRUPP, B.J. *et al.* (1987) Dietary fat and the regulation of energy intake in human subjects, *American Journal of Clinical Nutrition*, **46**, 886–92.

LOCKWOOD, G.R. (1992) Psychophysical scaling: judgments of attributes or objects?, *Brain and Behavioral Sciences*, **15**, 567–83.

LOWE, M.J. (1993) Effects of dieting on eating behavior: a three-factor model, *Psychological Bulletin*, **114**, 100–21.

LYMAN, B. (1989) *A psychology of food, more than a matter of taste*, New York: Van Nostrand Reinhold.

LYONS, W. (1988) *The disappearance of introspection*, Cambridge, MA: MIT Press.

MACMILLAN, N.A. and CREELMAN, C.D. (1991) *Detection theory: a user's guide*, Cambridge: Cambridge University Press.

MADDISON, S., WOOD, R.J., ROLLS, E.T. *et al.* (1980) Drinking in the rhesus monkey: peripheral factors, *Journal of Comparative and Physiological Psychology*, **94**, 365–74.

MAHONEY, M.J. (1974) Self-reward and self-monitoring techniques for weight control, *Behavior Therapy*, **5**, 100–4.

MARCEL, A.J. (1983) Conscious and unconscious perception: an approach to the relations between phenomenal experience and perceptual processes, *Cognitive Psychology*, **15**, 238–300.

MARIE, S. (1986) Unpublished Ph.D. Thesis, University of Birmingham (UK).

MARR, D. (1982) *Vision*. San Francisco: W.H. Freeman.

MASLOW, A.H. (1970) *Motivation and personality*, 2nd Edn, New York, Harper & Row.

MATTES, R. (1987) Assessing salt taste preference and its relationship with dietary sodium intake in humans, in SOLMS, J., BOOTH, D.A., PANGBORN, R.M. and RAUNHARDT, O. (Eds), *Food acceptance and nutrition*, London: Academic Press, pp. 129–42.

MATTHEWS, J., GIBSON, E.L. and BOOTH, D.A. (1985) Norepinephrine-facilitated eating: reduction in saccharin preference and conditioned flavor preferences with increase in quinine aversion, *Pharmacology Biochemistry and Behavior*, **22**, 1045–52.

MAYER, J. (1955) Regulation of energy intake and the body weight. The glucostatic theory and the lipostatic hypothesis, *Annals of the New York Academy of Sciences*, **63**, 15–43.

McBRIDE, R.L. and FINLAY, D.C. (1990) Perceptual integration of tertiary taste mixtures, *Perception and Psychophysics*, **48**, 326–30.

McCLEARY, R.A. (1953) Taste and post-ingestion factors in specific-hunger behavior, *Journal of Comparative and Physiological Psychology*, **46**, 411–21.

McGRATH, S.A. and GIBNEY, M.J. (1993) The effects of altered food frequency consumption on plasma lipids in free living healthy volunteers, *Proceedings of the Nutrition Society* (89A), in press.

MEHIEL, R. and BOLLES, R.C. (1984) Learned flavor preferences based on caloric outcome, *Animal Learning and Behavior*, **12**, 421–27.

MEÏ, N. (1985) Intestinal chemosensitivity, *Physiological Reviews*, **65**, 211–37.

MELA, D. (1988) Sensory assessment of fat content in fluid dairy products, *Appetite*, **10**, 37–44.

MOOK, D.G. and WAGNER, S. (1989) Orosensory suppression of saccharin drinking in rat: the response, not the taste, *Appetite*, **13**, 1–13.

MORAN, T.H. and McHUGH, P.R. (1982) Cholecystokinin suppresses food intake by inhibiting gastric emptying, *American Journal of Physiology*, **242**, R491–R497.

MORGANE, P.J. (1961) Medial forebrain bundle and 'feeding centers' of the hypothalamus, *Journal of Comparative Neurology*, **117**, 1–26.

MOSKOWITZ, H.R. (1983) *Product testing and sensory evaluation of foods. Marketing and R&D approaches*, Westport, CT: Food & Nutrition Press.

MRC (1976) *Report on Obesity*, London: Medical Research Council.

NEWMAN, J.C. and BOOTH, D.A. (1981) Gastrointestinal and metabolic consequences of a rat's meal on maintenance diet ad libitum, *Physiology and Behavior*, **27**, 929–39.

NICOLAÏDIS, S. (1974) Short-term and long-term regulation of energy balance, *Proceedings of XXVIth International Congress of Physiological Sciences*, New Delhi, pp. 122–3.

NICOLAIDÏS, S. and EVEN, P. (1984) Mesure de métabolisme de fond en relation avec la prise alimentaire: hypothèse ischymétrique, *Compte Rendu Académie de Sciences (Paris)*, **298**, 295–300.

NISBETT, R.E. (1972) Hunger, obesity and the ventromedial hypothalamus, *Psychological Review*, **79**, 433–53.

NORGREN, R. (1991) Sensory detection of water, in RAMSAY, D.J. and BOOTH, D.A. (Eds), *Thirst*, London: Springer-Verlag, pp. 221–331.

Norwich, K.H. (1990) Informational analysis, in Lawless, H.T. and Klein, B.P. (Eds), *Sensory science theory and applications in foods.* New York: Marcel Dekker.

Orbach, S. (1986) *Hunger strike*, London: Faber.

Panksepp, J. (1971) Effects of fats, proteins and carbohydrates on food intake in rats, *Psychonomic Monograph Supplement,* **4**, 85–95.

Peters, R.S. (1954) *The concept of motivation*, London: Routledge, Kegan & Paul.

Phillips, P.A., Rolls, B.J., Ledingham, J.G.G. and Morton, J.J. (1984) Body fluid changes, thirst and drinking in man during free access to water, *Physiology and Behavior,* **33**, 357–63.

Phillips, P.A., Rolls, B.J., Ledingham, J.G.G., Forsling, M.L. and Morton, J.J. (1985) Osmotic thirst and vasopressin release in man: a double-blind cross-over study, *American Journal of Physiology,* **248**, R645–50.

Pliner, P. and Pelchat, M.L. (1989) Family environment, not heredity, accounts for family resemblances in food preferences and attitudes: a twin study, *Appetite,* **8**, 125–34.

Polivy, J. and Herman, C.P. (1985) Dieting and binging: a causal analysis, *American Psychologist,* **40**, 193–201.

Popper, K.R. (1959) *The logic of scientific discovery*, London: Hutchinson.

Porikos, K.P. and Van Itallie, T.B. (1984) Efficacy of low-calorie sweeteners in reducing food intake: studies with aspartame, in Stegink, L.D. and Filer, L.J. (Eds), *Aspartame*, New York, Marcel Dekker, pp. 273–286.

Powley, T.L. (1977) The ventromedial hypothalamic syndrome, satiety, and a cephalic phase hypothesis, *Psychological Review,* **84**, 89–126.

Rabin, B.M. (1972) Ventromedial hypothalamic control of food intake and satiety – a reappraisal, *Brain Research,* **43**, 317–23.

Ramsay, D.J. and Thrasher, T.N. (1986) Satiety and the effects of water intake on vasopressin secretion, in de Caro, G., Epstein, A.N. and Massi, M. (Eds), *The physiology of thirst and sodium appetite*, New York: Plenum Press, pp. 301–7.

Read, N.W. (1992) Control of hunger and satiety by stimulation of gastrointestinal receptors in man, *Proceedings of the Nutrition Society,* **51**, 7–11.

Reingold, E.M. and Merikle, P.M. (1988) Using direct and indirect measures to study perception without awareness, *Perception and Psychophysics,* **44**, 563–75.

Revusky, S.H. (1968) Effects of thirst level during consumption of flavored water on subsequent preferences, *Journal of Comparative and Physiological Psychology,* **66**, 777–9.

Reynolds, T.J. and Gutman, J. (1991) Means-end laddering theory, method, analysis and interpretation, in Reynolds, T.J. (Ed.), *Understanding consumer motivation*, New York: Wiley.

Richardson, N.J. and Booth, D.A. (1993) Multiple physical patterns in judgements of the creamy texture of milks and creams, *Acta Psychologica,* **84**, 93–101.

Richardson, N.J., Booth, D.A. and Stanley, N.L. (1993) Effect of homogenization and fat content on oral perception of low and high viscosity model creams, *Journal of Sensory Studies,* **8**, 133–43.

Ritson, C., Gofton, L. and McKenzie, J. (1986) *The food consumer*, Chichester: Wiley.

Ritter, R.C. and Epstein, A.N. (1975) Control of meal size by central noradrenergic action, *Proceedings of National Academy of Sciences (USA),* **75**, 3740–53.

Robbins, T.W., Watson, B.A., Gaskin, M. and Ennis, C. (1983) Contrasting interactions of pipradol, *d*-amphetamine, cocaine, cocaine analogues, apomorphine and other drugs with conditioned reinforcement, *Psychopharmacology,* **80**, 113–19.

ROBERTSON, G.L. (1991) Disorders of thirst in man, in RAMSAY, D.J. and BOOTH, D.A. (Eds), *Thirst. Physiological and psychological aspects*, London: Springer-Verlag, pp. 453–77.

RODIN, J. (1980) The externality theory today, in STUNKARD, A.J. (Ed.), *Obesity*, Philadelphia: Saunders, pp. 226–39.

RODIN, J. (1981) The current status of the internal-external obesity hypothesis: what went wrong?, *American Psychologist*, **36**, 361–72.

RODIN, J. (1991) Effects of pure sugar vs. mixed starch fructose loads on food intake, *Appetite*, **17**, 213–9.

RODIN, J. and SLOCHOWER, J. (1976) Externality in the nonobese: the effects of environmental responsiveness on weight, *Journal of Personality and Social Psychology*, **29**, 557–65.

ROGERS, E.M. (1962) *Diffusion of innovations*, 3rd Edn, 1983, New York: Free Press.

ROLLS, B.J. (1991) Physiological determinants of fluid intake in humans, in RAMSAY, D.J. and BOOTH, D.A. (Eds), *Thirst. Physiological and psychological aspects*, London: Springer-Verlag, pp. 391–9.

ROLLS, B.J., WOOD, R.J. and ROLLS, E.T. (1980) Thirst: the initiation, maintenance and termination of drinking, in SPRAGUE, J.M. and EPSTEIN, A.N. (Eds), *Progress in psychobiology and physiological psychology*, Vol. 9, New York: Academic Press, pp. 262–321.

ROLLS, B.J., ROWE, E.A., ROLLS, E.T., KINGSTON, B., MEGSON, A. and GUNARY, R. (1981) Variety in a meal enhances food intake in man, *Physiology and Behavior*, **26**, 215–21.

ROLLS, B.J., HETHERINGTON, M. and BURLEY, V.J. (1988) The specificity of satiety: the influence of foods of different macronutrient content on the development of satiety, *Physiology and Behavior*, **43**, 145–54.

ROLLS, E.T. (1976) The neurophysiological basis of brain-stimulation reward, in WAUQUIER, A. and ROLLS, E.T. (Eds), *Brain-stimulation reward*, Amsterdam: North-Holland, pp. 65–87.

ROLLS, E.T. (1989) Information processing in the taste system of primates, *Journal of Experimental Biology*, **146**, 141–64.

ROLLS, E.T. (1993) The neural control of feeding in primates, in BOOTH, D.A. (Ed.), *Neurophysiology of ingestion*, Oxford: Pergamon, pp. 137–69.

RÖSSNER, S. (1993) Dietary fibre – no panacea, *Journal of Internal Medicine*, **233**, 433–4.

ROZIN, E. (1983) *Ethnic cuisine: the flavor principle cookbook*, Brattleboro, VT: Stephen Greene.

ROZIN, P. and FALLON, A.E. (1985) A perspective on disgust, *Psychological Review*, **94**, 23–41.

ROZIN, P., LEVINE, E. and STOESS, C. (1991) Chocolate craving and liking, *Appetite*, **17**, 199–212.

RUDERMAN, A.J. (1983) The restraint scale: a psychometric investigation, *Behavioural Research and Therapy*, **21**, pp. 253–258.

RUGG-GUNN, A.J., HACKETT, A.F., APPLETON, D.R., JENKINS, G.N. and EASTOE, J.E. (1984) Relationship between dietary habits and caries increment assessed over two years in 405 English adolescent school children, *Archives of Oral Biology*, **29**, 983–92.

RUSSEK, M. (1963) An hypothesis on the participation of hepatic glucoreceptors in the control of food intake, *Nature*, **197**, 79–80.

RUSSEK, M. (1981) Current status of the hepatostatic theory of food intake control, *Appetite*, **2**, 137–43.

RYLE, G. (1949) *The concept of mind*, London: Hutchinson.

SAINTE-ANNE DARGASSIES, S. (1977) *Neurological examination of the infant*, London: Heinemann.

SALMOIRAGHI, G.C. and BURNS, B.D. (1960) Localization and patterns of discharge of respiratory neurons in brain-stem of cat, *Journal of Neurophysiology*, **23**, 2–13.

SANGHERA, M.K., ROLLS, E.T. and ROPER-HALL, A. (1979) Visual responses of neurons in the dorsolateral amygdala of the alert monkey, *Experimental Neurology*, **63**, 610–26.

SCHACHTER, S. (1968) Obesity and eating, *Science*, **161**, 751–6.

SCHACHTER, S. (1971) *Emotion, obesity and crime*, New York: Academic Press.

SCHACHTER, S. and RODIN, J. (1974) *Obese humans and rats*, Washington, DC: Erlbaum/Halstead.

SCHUTZ, H.G. (1991) One small step at a time: healthier and just as nice, *Appetite*, **17**, 157.

SCLAFANI, A. (1990) Nutritionally based learned flavor preferences in rats, in CAPALDI, E.D. and POWLEY, T.L. (Eds), *Taste, experience, and feeding*, Washington, DC: American Psychological Association, pp. 139–56.

SCOTT, T.R. and GIZA, B.K. (1993) Gustatory control of ingestion, in BOOTH, D.A. (Ed.), *Neurophysiology of ingestion*, Oxford: Pergamon, pp. 99–117.

SECKL, J.R., WILLIAMS, T.D.M. and LIGHTMAN, S.L. (1986) Oral hypertonic saline causes transient fall of vasopressin in humans, *American Journal of Physiology*, **251**, R214–R217.

SHEPARD, R.N. (1957) Stimulus and response generalization: a stochastic model relating generalization to distance in psychological space, *Psychometrika*, **22**, 325–45.

SHEPARD, R.N. (1987) Towards a universal law of generalization for psychological science, *Science*, **237**, 1317–23.

SHEPHERD, R. and FARLEIGH, C.A. (1989) Sensory assessment of foods and the role of sensory attributes in determining food choice, in SHEPHERD, R. (Ed.), *Handbook of the psychophysiology of human eating*, Chichester: Wiley, pp. 25–56.

SHEPHERD, R., FARLEIGH, C.A. and WHARF, S.G. (1987) Preferences for salt in different foods and their relationship to availability of sodium, *Human Nutrition: Food Sciences and Nutrition*, **41F**, 173–81.

SHERMAN, J.E., HICKIS, C.F., RICE, A.G., RUSINIAK, K.W. and GARCIA, J. (1983) Preferences and aversions for stimuli paired with ethanol, *Animal Learning and Behavior*, **11**, 101–6.

SIMON, Y., BELLISLE, F., MONNEUSE, M.O., SAMUELLA-JEUNESSE, B. and DREWNOWSKI, A. (1993) Taste responsiveness in anorexia nervosa, *British Journal of Psychiatry*, **162**, 244–6.

SMITH, A.P., MABEN, A. and BRICKMAN, P. (1993) The effects of caffeine and evening meal on sleep and performance and mood the following day, *Journal of Psychopharmacology*, **7**, 203–6.

SMITH, F., HOFFMAN, C. and CAMPFIELD, L.A. (1993) Fall in blood glucose precedes food seeking behavior in fasted rats, *Appetite*, **21**, 208.

SOBAL, J. and CASSIDY, C.M. (1987) Dieting foods: conceptualisations and explanations, *Ecology of Food and Nutrition*, **20**, 89–96.

SPITZER, L. and RODIN, J. (1981) Human eating behavior: a critical review of studies in normal weight and overweight individuals, *Appetite*, **2**, 293–329.

SPITZER, L. and RODIN, J. (1987) Differential effects of fructose and glucose on food intake, *Appetite*, **8**, 135–45.

SPITZER, L., MARCUS, J. and RODIN, J. (1980) Arousal-induced eating: a response to Robbins and Fray, *Appetite*, **1**, 343–8.

Staats, A.W. (1975) *Social behaviorism*, Homewood, IL: Dorsey Press.

Steiner, J.E. (1973) The gustofacial response: observations on normal and anencephalic newborn infants, in Bosma, J.F. (Ed.), *4th Symposium on Oral Sensation and Perception*, Bethesda, MD: National Institutes of Health, pp. 254–310.

Stellar, E. (1954) The physiology of motivation, *Psychological Review*, **61**, 5–22.

Striegel-Moore, R.H., Silberstein, L.R. and Rodin, J. (1986) Toward an understanding of risk factors for bulimia, *American Psychologist*, **41**, 246–63.

Stunkard, A.J. (1975) Satiety is a conditioned reflex, *Psychosomatic Medicine*, **37**, 383–7.

Stunkard, A.J. and Messick, S. (1985) Three-factor eating questionnaire to measure dietary restraint, disinhibition and hunger, *Journal of Psychosomatic Research*, **29**, pp. 71–83.

Sunkin, S. and Garrow, J.S. (1982) The satiety value of protein, *Human Nutrition: Applied Nutrition* 336A, 197–201.

Tanner, W.P. and Swets, J.A. (1954) A decision-making theory of visual detection, *Psychological Review*, **61**, 401–9.

Thompson, D.A., Campbell, R.G., Lilivivat, V., Welle, S.L. and Robertson, G.L. (1981) Increased thirst and plasma arginine vasopressin levels during 2-deoxy-D-glucose induced glucoprivation in humans, *Journal of Clinical Investigation*, **60**, 1083–93.

Thompson, D.A., Moskowitz, H.R. and Campbell, R.G. (1976) Effects of body weight and food intake on pleasantness ratings of a sweet stimulus, *Journal of Applied Physiology*, **41**, 77–82.

Thomson, R. (1982) Side effects and placebo amplification, *British Journal of Psychiatry*, **140**, 64–8.

Thorpe, S.J., Rolls, E.T. and Maddison, S. (1983) Neuronal activity in the orbitofrontal cortex of the behaving monkey, *Experimental Brain Research*, **49**, 93–115.

Thrasher, T.N., Nistal-Herrara, J.F., Keil, L.C. and Ramsay, D.J. (1981) Satiety and inhibition of vasopressin secretion after drinking in dehydrated dogs, *American Journal of Physiology*, **240**, E394–E401.

Thurstone, L.L. (1927a) Psychophysical analysis, *American Journal of Psychology*, **38**, 369–89.

Thurstone, L.L. (1927b) A law of comparative judgment, *Psychological Review*, **34**, 273–86.

Toates, F.M. and Booth, D.A. (1974) Control of food intake by energy supply, *Nature*, **251**, 710–11.

Tordoff, M.G. and Friedman, M.I. (1988) Hepatic control of feeding: effect of glucose, fructose and mannitol infusion, *American Journal of Physiology*, **254**, R969–76.

Tuschl, R.J., Laessle, R.G., Platte, P. and Pirke, K.M. (1990) Differences in food choice frequencies between restrained and unrestrained eaters, *Appetite*, **14**, 9–13.

Ungerstedt, U. (1971) Adipsia and aphagia after 6-hydroxydopamine induced degeneration of the nigro-striatal dopamine system, *Acta Physiologica Scandinavica*, **367**, Supplement, 95–122.

Vague, J. (1953) *La différenciation sexuelle humaine. Ses incidences en pathologie*. Paris: Masson.

Vague, J. (1991) *Obesities*, London: John Libbey.

van Strien, T., Frijters, J.E.R., Bergers, G.P.A. and Defares, P.B. (1986) The Dutch Eating Behaviour Questionnaire (DEBQ) for assessment of restrained, emotional and external eating behavior, *International Journal of Eating Disorders*, **2**, 295–315.

WEINGARTEN, H.G. (1985) Stimulus control of eating: implications for a two-factor theory of hunger, *Appetite*, **6**, 387–401.

WELCH, I.M., SEPPLE, C.P. and READ, N.W. (1988) Comparisons of the effects on satiety and eating behaviour of infusion of lipid into different regions of the small intestine, *Gut*, **29**, 306–11.

WITTGENSTEIN, L. (1953) *Philosophical investigations*, Oxford: Blackwell.

WOLF, A.V. (1958) *Thirst. Physiology of the urge to drink and problems of water lack*, Springfield, IL: C.C. Thomas.

WOLFF, P.H. (1987) *Development of behavioral states and expression of emotion in early infancy*, Chicago: University of Chicago Press.

WOOLEY, S.C. (1971) Physiologic versus cognitive factors in short term food regulation in the obese and non-obese, *Psychomatic Medicine*, **34**, 62–8.

WOOLEY, O.W., WOOLEY, S.C. and DUNHAM, R.B. (1972) Calories and sweet taste: effects on sucrose preference in the obese and non-obese, *Physiology and Behavior*, **9**, 765–8.

WURTMAN, J.J., WURTMAN, R.J., MARK, S., TSAY, R., GILBERT, W. and GROWDON, J. (1985) d-Fenfluramine selectively suppresses carbohydrate snacking among obese carbohydrate craving subjects, *International Journal of Eating Disorders*, **4**, 89–99.

YEOMANS, M.R. and WRIGHT, P. (1991) Lower pleasantness of palatable foods in nalmefene-treated human volunteers, *Appetite*, **16**, 249–59.

ZELLNER, D.A. and KAUTZ, M.A. (1990) Color affects perceived odor intensity, *Journal of Experimental Psychology: Human Perception and Performance*, **16**, 391–7.

Subject Index